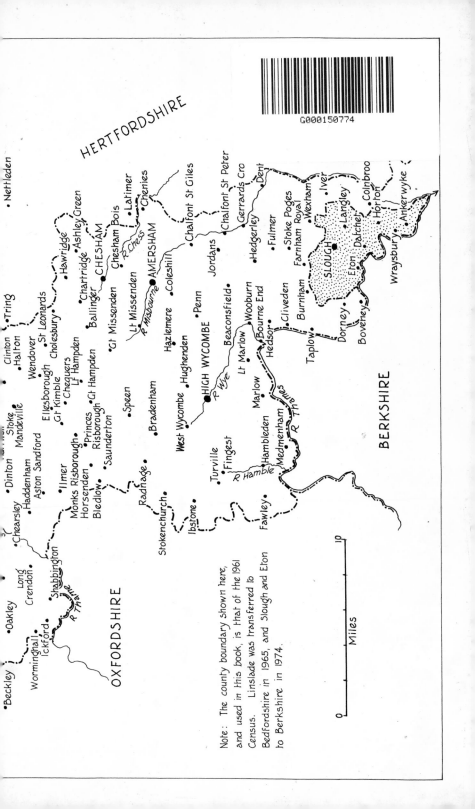

HERTFORDSHIRE

• Nettleden

• Tring
Clinton •
Halton •

OXFORDSHIRE

• Beckley
• Oakley
Long Crendon •
• Chearsley
• Dinton
• Haddenham
Aston Sandford •
Shabbington •
Worminghall •
Ickford •
R. Thame

Wendover
St Leonards
Cholesbury
Hawridge
Ashley Green
Chartridge
CHESHAM
Chesham Bois
Latimer
Chenies
Ballinger
R. Chess
Cholesbury
Ellesborough
Gt Kimble
Lt Hampden
Chequers
Gt Hampden
Princes Risborough
Gt Missenden
Lt Missenden
AMERSHAM
R. Misbourne
Coleshill
Chalfont St Giles
Chalfont St Peter
Gerrards Cross
Dent
Monks Risborough
Horsenden
Bledlow
Saunderton
Spean
Bradenham
Hazlemere
Hughenden
Penn
Jordans
Hedgerley
Fulmer
Stoke Poges
Farnham Royal
Wexham
Iver
Colnbrook
Horton
Langley
Datchet
SLOUGH
Eton
Wraysbury
Ankerwyke
HIGH WYCOMBE
R. Wye
Beaconsfield
Wooburn
Bourne End
Cliveden
Burnham
Taplow
Dorney
Boveney
West Wycombe
Lt Marlow
Hedsor
Marlow
Radnage
Turville
Fingest
Hambleden
Medmenham
R. Thames
R. Hamble
Fawley
Ibstone •
Stokenchurch

BERKSHIRE

Note: The county boundary shown here,
and used in this book, is that of the 1961
Census. Linslade was transferred to
Bedfordshire in 1965, and Slough and Eton
to Berkshire in 1974.

Miles

0   10

THE MAKING OF THE ENGLISH
LANDSCAPE

THE BUCKINGHAMSHIRE LANDSCAPE

THE MAKING OF THE ENGLISH LANDSCAPE
Edited by W. G. Hoskins and Roy Millward

The Making of the English Landscape, W. G. Hoskins
West Riding of Yorkshire, Arthur Raistrick
Dorset, Christopher Taylor
The Northumberland Landscape, Robert Newton
The Shropshire Landscape, Trevor Rowley
The Suffolk Landscape, Norman Scarfe
The Cambridgeshire Landscape, Christopher Taylor
The Oxfordshire Landscape, Frank Emery
The Northamptonshire Landscape, John Steane
The Sussex Landscape, Peter Brandon
The Gloucestershire Landscape, H. P. R. Finberg
The Staffordshire Landscape, David Palliser
The East Riding of Yorkshire Landscape, K. J. Allison
The Hertfordshire Landscape, Lionel Munby
The Bedfordshire and Huntingdonshire Landscape, Peter Bigmore

THE MAKING OF THE WELSH LANDSCAPE

The South Wales Landscape, Moelwyn Williams

THE MAKING OF THE ENGLISH LANDSCAPE

The Buckinghamshire Landscape

by

MICHAEL REED

HODDER AND STOUGHTON

LONDON   SYDNEY   AUCKLAND   TORONTO

British Library Cataloguing in Publication Data

Reed, Michael
  The Buckinghamshire landscape. – (The
making of the English landscape).
  1. Buckinghamshire, Eng. – Historical geography
  I. Title   II. Series
  911'.425'9   DA670.B9

  ISBN 0-340-19044-2

TO GWYNNETH

Preface

I HAVE SPENT five very happy years writing this book, during the course of which I have made many new friends, and renewed an old love, with the county itself. Recollections of childhood days spent on the Wendover Hills have become blended with more recent memories of the translucent green of Chiltern beech woods, the deep silence of the footpath through the Black Hedge, and of picking strawberries on a farm near Beachampton.

A book of this kind must of necessity depend heavily upon the kindness, generosity and forebearance of others. To mention them here seems an entirely inadequate recompense for all that they have done for me. My thanks are due first of all to Professor Hoskins for his kindness and encouragement when I was his student and for starting me off on this book in the first place. I owe a real debt of gratitude to Dr Clifford Butler, who made possible my visit to the Huntington Library in California, to Miss Mary Robertson for help in finding my way through the Stowe Papers when I was there, and to Professor Havard-Williams for encouragement and support whilst this book has been in preparation. Professor Alan Everitt and Charles Phythian-Adams have readily and cheerfully discussed the Buckinghamshire landscape with me when they had better things to do, and allowed me to try out some of my material on their students in a seminar in the Department of English Local History at Leicester University.

Mr E. J. Davies and his successor as Buckinghamshire County Archivist, Mr H. Hanley, did much to make my visits to the County Record Office so enjoyable and so profitable, whilst Miss Rosalind Stark produced with inexhaustible patience a seemingly endless stream of documents. Miss Hailey and Miss Watts gave me every assistance in finding my way through the materials in their care in the Buckinghamshire Collection in the County Library. Mrs Elvey was kind enough to allow documents in her care in the Buckinghamshire Archaeological Society's muniment room to be transferred to the County Record Office. Mr M. Farley very kindly read my first two chapters, saved me from numerous errors and gave me almost open access to the invaluable archive relating to every aspect of the archaeology of the county that he has built up in the County Museum. Mr Hatherly provided me with much valuable information on the south of the county, as did Mr Baines on the Anglo-Saxon charters, and Professor L. M. Cantor on the medieval deer parks. The Secretary of the Natural History Section of the Buckinghamshire Archaeological Society made available to me the results of the survey of the Black Hedge, and I have enjoyed the benefit of several conversations with Mr Croft and Mr Petchey of the Bradwell Abbey Field Centre.

Mrs Margaret Gelling answered with imperturbable good humour a barrage of questions relating to the place-names of the county, whilst Mr George Clarke shared with me his unrivalled knowledge of the history of the house and gardens at Stowe and made my visit there so memorable. Professor M. W. Beresford, Professor G. R. J. Jones, Professor A. C. Chibnall and Professor Kenneth Jackson have all contributed something to the making of this book for which I am very grateful. Mrs Ewins made available for me the records of the Medieval Village Research Group, and Mrs Drummond those of the Archaeology Section of the Royal Commission on Historical Monuments, whilst the Librarian of Magdalen College Oxford was kind enough to allow me access to the splendid collection of documents and maps relating to Thornborough that is in his care.

The editor of this series, Roy Millward, by his kindness, care and skill, has improved beyond recognition successive drafts of this book. For all the errors that still remain in spite of so much advice and learning so readily given I alone can be held responsible. When others have concluded Prefaces by writing that their books would never have been finished but for the help and support of their wives, I thought that they were being merely platitudinous. Now I know the truth of the matter.

MICHAEL REED

8

Acknowledgements

I am grateful to the following for permission to use their unpublished researches: Dr J. P. F. Broad, Mr C. Cheshire, Miss J. Chibnall, Professor J. T. Coppock, Miss M. Courtman, Dr M. E. Turner.

The Warden and Fellows of All Souls College Oxford have been kind enough to allow me to base Fig. 17 upon a map in their possession. The President and Fellows of Magdalen College Oxford have similarly been kind enough to allow me to base Fig. 8 upon a map in their collections. Figs. 3 and 13 are based upon maps made available to me by Mr M. Farley, Field Archaeologist to the Buckinghamshire County Museum. Fig. 15 is based upon a map in the Oxfordshire County Record Office and Figs. 18 and 19 upon maps in the muniment room of the Buckinghamshire Archaeological Society. Fig. 27 is based upon plans kindly supplied by the Milton Keynes Development Corporation, and Fig. 29 upon information given by Buckinghamshire County Council and by the Berkshire, Buckinghamshire and Oxfordshire Naturalists' Trust.

Plates 1, 2, 3, 4, 18 and 19 are published by kind permission of Professor J. K. St Joseph and the Committee for Aerial Photography, Cambridge University. Plates 11, 21, 29, 30, are published with the permission of the National Monuments Record, and Plates 39 and 40 with the permission of the British Library. Plate 25 is published by courtesy of the Trustees of the Chequers Estates, and Plates 26 and 27 by courtesy of the Buckinghamshire County Record Office.

Plates 6, 9, 13, 16, 23, 50 and 55 were taken by H. G. Vaughan. The remaining Plates were taken by the author. I am grateful to the Headmaster of Stowe School for permission to take Plates 38 and 41, and to the National Trust for permission to take Plates 15, 42, 43 and 51.

Contents

Contents

List of plates

List of maps and plans

List of abbreviations

B.A.S. Buckinghamshire Archæological Society, County
Museum, Aylesbury
B.R.O. Buckinghamshire County Record Office, Aylesbury
H.H.L. Henry Huntington Library, San Marino,
California, U.S.A.
P.R.O. Public Record Office, Chancery Lane, London
V.C.H. Bucks *The Victoria History of the County of Buckingham*
4 vols. (1905–1927, 1969 reprint).

Editor's Introduction

THIS SERIES OF books on The Making of the English Landscape originated in 1955 with my own pioneer book under that title. A few county volumes were published under the same format (Cornwall, Leicestershire, Gloucestershire, and Lancashire), but a new and better format was worked out from 1970 onwards, beginning with Arthur Raistrick's *West Riding of Yorkshire* and Christopher Taylor's *Dorset*. Since then there has been a steady flow of such county studies, aiming at covering the whole country eventually. Already there have been volumes as far apart as Northumberland and Sussex; and books are in preparation ranging from Kent in the east to a revised edition of Cornwall in the far west.

Purists might object that the geographical county has no particular unity except for administrative purposes, that the 'region' would be more appropriate. Apart from the fact that few would agree about what constituted a 'region', the primary fact is that the geographical county is a unity so far as the documentary material is concerned; but, more than that, it evokes local patriotism, and again each English county (one ought to say 'British' in view of the fact that Wales has been brought within the orbit of the series) contains a wide variety of landscapes each interesting and appealing in its own right. Every county presents a multitude of problems of Landscape History and their very contrast is illuminating. Even little Rutland has such contrasts, though naturally on a more limited scale; and a large county like Devon has almost every kind of landscape. One other point: when the reorganisation of local government took place a few years ago, and some entirely new names appeared on the administration map of England, such as Avon and Cleveland, I had to consider whether we should stick to the old counties as we have always known them or adopt the new set-up. As the series was by then so far advanced under the old and well-loved names, we decided to retain them and go on as before. There were other good reasons, besides the sentimental one, for sticking to the original plan.

It is a well-worn truism that England is a very small country with an almost infinite variety of rocks, soils, topography, and watercourses by the tens of thousands: all these things create what one might call micro-landscapes at the risk of importing a little professional jargon into something which is meant to be enjoyed and explained in plain English. One look at the coloured map of the geology of England and Wales and above all the way in which the colours change every few miles, is enough to excite the visual imagination. This is especially true when one crosses the grain of a piece of country, instead of travelling along it. There is for example the major grain, so to speak, which runs from the south-west coast in Dorset north-eastwards to the Yorkshire coast round Whitby. If you cut *across* this geological grain, going from south-east to north-west the landscapes change every few miles. On a smaller scale but nearly as complicated, the south-eastern corner of England, running from say Newhaven northwards to the Thames estuary, presents rapid and very contrasted changes of land-scape – in soils, building stones (and hence buildings themselves), in vernacular building – the architectural equivalent of the once-rich variety of local dialects in this country – in land-forms, in farming, in almost everything that is visible.

Most of us enjoy some widespread view from a hilltop or on some grand coast: we enjoy it as 'scenery' but this is really a superficial enjoyment. What I prefer to call 'landscape' as distinct from 'scenery' is that a landscape to me asks questions: why is something like this at all, why does it differ from another view a few miles away? It is the difference perhaps between what an amateur portrait painter sees and puts on paper and what a skilled surgeon sees when he contemplates and reflects over a human body. He sees things, even on a superficial examination, because of his training and his long experience, that the layman never sees. So it is with *landscape*. To see it thus, seeing beneath the surface and the obvious, is to increase one's enjoyment of the English countryside enormously.

The great English painter John Constable makes this point in one simple sentence in one of his *Discourses on Landscape*, a sentence I shall never tire of quoting: *"We see nothing till we truly understand it."* Constable's *Discourses* were an attempt to justify landscape-painting as an end in itself. If we take his great dictum as our text, Landscape History becomes an end in itself, transmuting the textbook facts of rocks and soils, landforms, economic history, industrial archaeology — words calculated to deter all but the most determined reader — into a different way of looking at perhaps commonplace things, into a different language. The art is to use these academic disciplines in a concealed way, never to let them obtrude or, if so, to some essential purpose so that the visual is always paramount.

When I wrote my own book, now more than twenty years ago, I did not answer all the possible questions by a long way, though it still stands as a good introduction to a new field of history. Landscape History is now, I think, a well-accepted and respectable discipline, taught in some universities and in schools, and the subject of theses. I did not answer all the questions for the simple reason that I did not then know what they all were. And even now, after so many books and articles and theses have been written, there is so much that remains unknown, and no doubt questions that I, and others, have still not perceived. This, to me, is one of the great values of these landscape books, treated county by county. Local studies in depth, to use a fashionable phrase, but for once a useful one, will not only enlarge our generalisations about the major changes in the landscape, but also because of their detail bring new lights into the picture. Ideally, as editor of this series, I would like each writer on a particular county to pick out an even smaller area for special examination under the microscope, having in mind such revealing studies as Professor Harry Thorpe's masterly essay on Wormleighton in Warwickshire (*The Lord and the Landscape*, published in 1965) and Dr Jack Ravensdale's *Liable to Floods* (1974) which deals with three Fen-Edge villages in Cambridgeshire. Not only are the topographical settings of these two studies so completely different, but one is concerned with 'peasant villages' and the landscapes they created. So social structure also enters into the many hidden creators of a particular bit of England and the vision it presents.

Some major problems remain virtually unsolved. I myself in my first book fell into the trap, or rather accepted the current doctrine, that until the Old English Conquest most of this country was uncleared woodland or undrained marsh or in many parts primaeval moorland. To a large extent I was deceived by the overwhelming evidence of the number of Old English place-names on the map, or, if not these, then the powerful Scandinavian element in the eastern parts of England. I am no longer deceived, or perhaps I should say that I have become much more sceptical about the ultimate value of this treacherous evidence. Thanks to archaeological advances in the past twenty years (and partly thanks to the opportunities offered by the odious onwards march of the motorways — their only value in my eyes) we know very much more about the density of settlement and of population in prehistoric times right back to the Mesolithic of seven or eight thousand years ago. There is evidence for forest clearance and to some extent for settled farming as early as this, and to an even greater extent by Neolithic times when one thinks of the axe-factories two thousand or more feet up on the wildest mountains of Lakeland. Forest clearance was going on at this height, and axes were being exported as far south as the coast of Hampshire. We now need a completely fresh study of the distribution of woodland by, say, Romano-British times. Not only woodland clearance, but the river gravels which have been exploited by modern man for his new roads have changed our whole concept of prehistoric settlement. The gravels of the Welland valley, almost in the heart of the Midlands, have been particularly intensively studied and have changed our entire thinking in these parts.

That is one aspect of the English landscape which I greatly under-estimated when I first wrote and I welcome every fresh piece of evidence that proves me misguided. Yet all the same the outlines of the main picture remain unchanged, and I stand by that first book subject to such changes of emphasis as I have mentioned.

There are other problems waiting to be worked out, some special to particular bits of England, others of a more general nature. Of the special problems I think of the number of isolated parish churches in the beautiful county of Norfolk: why are they there, stuck out all alone in the fields? Somebody could write a wonderful book on Churches in the Landscape. And there are other special aspects of the landscape wherever one walks in this most beloved of all countries: so much to do, so little done. These closer studies of England county by county will add enormously to our knowledge. Already the study of Landscape History has attracted a growing literature of its own, a great deal of it scattered in local journals and periodicals. Soon, perhaps in ten years' time, we shall need a Bibliography of the subject. This makes it sound dull and academic, but in the end I look upon it as an enlargement of consciousness, a new way of looking at familiar scenes which adds to the enjoyment of life. For those who have eyes to see, the face of Britain will never look the same again.

Exeter, 1976   W. G. HOSKINS

1. The earliest landscapes

The natural setting. Prehistoric landscapes. Roman Bucking-hamshire

BUCKINGHAMSHIRE BEFORE THE local government bound-ary reorganisation of 1974 was one of the smaller English counties. At the census of 1961 it had a population of 486,183, and an area of 749 square miles. It was larger than Bedfordshire, almost exactly the same size as Oxfordshire, but smaller than Northamptonshire. The largest town in 1961 was Slough, with a population of 80,503, followed by High Wycombe, with 50,301. It lacks those mineral deposits which in the nineteenth century were the essential bases of large-scale industrial development and so it remains free from those disfiguring scars which the first stages of industrialisa-tion inflicted on the landscapes of Staffordshire and the West Riding of Yorkshire. Before 1914 Buckinghamshire was essentially an agricultural county. It was the rapid changes induced by the coming of the railway and then the motor car, the development of electricity as an alternative source of power to coal, and finally the quite phenomenal rise of service industries, which transformed the Buckinghamshire land-scape, threatening at one stage to engulf entirely the whole of the south of the county under bricks and mortar. The marked distinction between the north and south, a distinction which has always been present throughout the history of the county, took an entirely new direction. Although on the face of it there are still no very large towns in the county, in fact in the south-east the distinction between town and country has become blurred, and the landscape has come to share with the adjacent parts of Hertfordshire all the characteristics of *urbs in rure*. Only the emergence of the Metropolitan Green Belt and the designation of the Chilterns as an Area of Outstanding Natural Beauty has saved south Buckinghamshire from self-destruction. Pressures in the south have to some extent been relieved by the development of Aylesbury and Bletchley in the north and by the establishment of an entirely new city at Milton Keynes, designed to accommodate eventually a quarter of a million people. Nevertheless the threats to the landscape engendered by one of the most rapid rates of population growth in any county in Great Britain are still very real.

Buckinghamshire is not one of the better known of English counties. There are no obvious tourist attractions. Its best known area of natural beauty, the Chiltern Hills, is for the walker in search of quiet vistas, tamed, man-made landscapes, blackbirds and bluebells, not for the climber in search of rocky crags, ling and curlew. The county lies astride some of the most important communication routes in the country. Watling Street, the Grand Junction Canal, the London to Birmingham and the London to Bristol railways, the M1 and the M4 motorways were each designed in their turn to hurry the traveller across the county as quickly as possible, and there is certainly little along any of them to detain him. But away from them is a landscape of both strong contrasts and of subtle variety. The most obvious contrast is that between the northern and the southern halves of the county. The north is a region of clay vales, gently undulating hills, frequent streams, villages of thatched cottages, pasture, sheep and cattle. The south is a region of steep, chalk hills, woods, arable farming, scattered farms and hamlets, and much suburban residential building. Generalisations like these, however, are both super-ficial and misleading. They serve only to conceal what is in reality an intricate, almost fugal, pattern in which subtle differences reveal themselves only very slowly, to old friends rather than to mere acquaintances. The county where Hooker, Milton, Burke, Gray, Cowper and G. K. Chesterton lived, where Joseph Haydn came to visit Sir William Herschel in his observatory, where 'Rule Britannia' was first heard, and which has given Aylesbury duckling and Cox's Orange Pippin to the world, has much to offer to the discerning traveller.

The natural setting

Although Buckinghamshire is a comparatively small county, stretching no more than fifty-two miles from north to south and only twenty miles across at its widest point, it includes within its boundaries a very wide variety of landscape. This is due to the fact that its main axis, running from north to south, cuts at right angles across the strike of the geological strata of the country as a whole. Nowhere does it encompass a geological formation which it does not share with its neighbours.

The underlying geological structure upon which ultimately the landscapes of the county are based is fundamentally simple,[1] although there is much local variation. A series of strata lie from south-west to north-east, dipping gently to the south-east so that the oldest formations, the Great Oolite limestones, lie in the extreme north of the county. These are then overlain by a succession of later strata, with the youngest, Reading Beds and London Clays, both masked to a large extent by drift deposits and by gravel terraces laid down by the river Thames, in the south of the county.

In the north the Oolite and Cornbrash deposits are exposed only in the Ouse valley, where erosion has stripped away the burden of Boulder Clay which is spread extensively over much of northern Buckinghamshire. Layers of limestone, sometimes suitable for building purposes, are interspersed with clay, sand, marl and rubble. The whole is confused by alluvium from the Ouse itself and by deposits of glacial drift, so that there is often wide variety of soils. Surface drainage in the valley itself is often very poor.

Next in succession come the Oxford and Kimmeridge Clays. The Oxford Clay is widely overlain with patches of glacial drift and Boulder Clay, in their turn often covered with thin deposits of wind-borne silts, producing an undulating landscape of low, rounded hills and broad vales. The Kimmeridge Clays form the basis of the Vale of Aylesbury. They

[1] see R. L. Sherlock, *British Regional Geology. London and the Thames Valley* (3rd ed. 1960), and H. B. Woodward, 'Geology', in *V.C.H. Bucks* I (1905), pp. 1–24.

are just as heavy as the Oxford ones, but considerably softer and so when exposed at the surface they form a low-lying, level landscape. They also are overlain with later deposits. The most important of these are the Portland Beds, which form higher hills and steeper slopes than are to be found on the Oxford Clays. These are often in their turn capped by Purbeck Beds and by Lower Greensands. Portland Beds are found at Long Crendon, Brill, Ashendon and the Winchendons, capped by Purbeck strata at Oving and Whitchurch, whilst Lower Greensands are found at Bishopstone, Bierton, Hartwell, Stone and Brill, and again in the vicinity of the Brickhills, where they form a landscape of very steep hills with light, dry and sandy soils.

Between the Kimmeridge Clays and the Chalk lies the Gault, a stiff, generally calcareous clay, modified locally by scattered patches of glacial drift, the remnants of a very thin bed of Upper Greensand directly under the Chalk, and by downwash from the neighbouring Purbeck and Greensand hills. It occurs at Wing, Cublington and Mentmore and then forms the southern-most portion of the Vale of Aylesbury.

Chalk forms the main foundation of the southern part of the county. The scarp, running from south-west to north-east, rises boldly and dramatically out of the Vale of Aylesbury, reaching heights above sea-level of 799 feet at Bledlow Cop (Plate 1), 756 at Ivinghoe Beacon (Plate 2), and nearly 900 feet in Wendover Woods. The scarp is not continuous, there being major gaps at Princes Risborough and Wendover. Nor is it straight, but rather sinuous and curving, marked by a series of promontories, such as Coombe Hill, and bays, as at Dancers End. The scarp face and crest are in some places, Bledlow Great Wood and Wendover Woods for example, thickly wooded, with the beech tree dominant, although not exclusively so. At other spots, Coombe Hill and Ivinghoe Beacon for example, the hills are clothed in a fine springy turf, a joy to walk on, and the product of centuries of grazing by sheep and rabbits.

More than a third of the Chalk is covered with Plateau Drift and with Clay-with-Flints, of uncertain origin, but probably the product of frost and water action under peri-glacial conditions, and showing considerable variation in structure. There is a tendency for the Clay-with-Flints to be a stony clay near the edges of the plateaux it covers and to be a loamy brick-earth towards their centres. Subsequent erosion has cut deeply into both the Chalk and the Drift, producing a series of steep-sided valleys with the Chalk exposed at their sides and in their bottoms, where it is often overlain with downwash. The narrow ridges separating one valley from the next point, finger-like, towards the Thames. Most of the valleys are asymmetric, their west-facing slopes steeper than those facing east. The valley sides are often very steep, and gradients of one in five are not unknown on the scarp face. In only four of the valleys are there rivers, the Hamble, the Wye, the Misbourne and the Chess. The Chilterns, unlike the northern vales, are almost devoid of running water.

The Chalk dips away south-east, to be masked in the southern part of the county by Reading Beds and London Clays. These have been inextricably mixed with glacial and river gravels, so that true Reading Beds occur as outliers only at Turville Heath, Lane End and Coleshill, and London Clay appears at the surface only between Iver and Farnham Royal. The result is a very wide range of soils, gravels, sands and brickearths and a corresponding diversity of landscape. The Burnham Plateau, for example, is a low plateau cut into by several small streams, with open, very dry, infertile soils which are strongly acid, whilst south of the Bath Road are a series of largely level flood plain gravels, yielding fertile, easily worked soils.

This then is the geological structure of Buckinghamshire. It provides the essential raw material upon which the natural regions of the county are based (Fig. 1). These regions owe their origin to differences of soil, of slope and of drainage, differences which in their turn have influenced vegetation, agricultural practice, the distribution of villages, the materials of traditional building and the network of roads, canals and railways. These regions may be natural in their origin, but their landscapes have been moulded for long ages by the

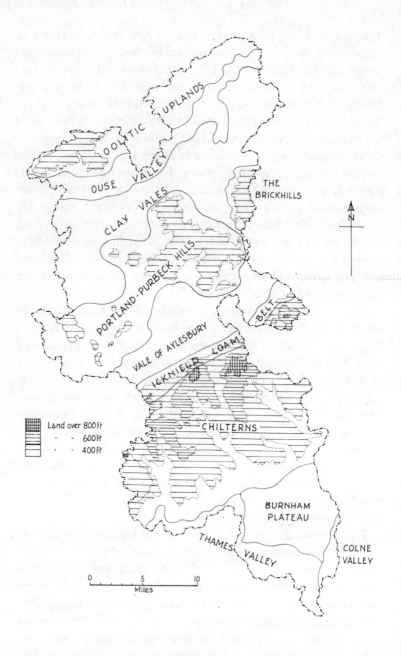

Fig. 1. The regions of Buckinghamshire

activities of man. For example it is very likely that the sterile soils of the Chiltern heathlands and the considerable deposits of downwash in many of the valleys are in fact man-made. Similarly, the traditional view of the north of the county is of a poorly drained region covered with dense forest first cleared by Anglo-Saxon settlers, who alone possessed the equipment with which to turn the heavy, intractable soils. But deciduous temperate forest encourages the development of friable, brown-earth soils, maintains their structure and accelerates drainage.[2] If left alone, then deciduous woodland is self-perpetuating. Only after the forest layer has been removed does soil degradation and subsequent waterlogging set in, and once begun it can prove immensely difficult to reverse. The heavy clay soils of the north are the result of at least four thousand years of human interference with the environment. The present landscape is the product of a very much longer period of its exploitation by man than hitherto we have suspected. This is why any account of the making of the Buckinghamshire landscape must begin with a description of its underlying structure, and start so far back in the past.

Prehistoric landscapes

Palaeolithic men certainly occupied what is now Buckinghamshire. Their flint tools have been found in the gravels of the Thames valley about Iver, Burnham and Chalfont St Peter, as well as in the north of the county in the valley of the Ouse. But the timespan involved is so immense, and the topography has been so profoundly modified by erosion and the effects of successive periods of intense cold and glaciation that we may safely ignore any influence they may have had upon the landscape and begin with the last retreat of the ice-sheets from Britain.

This retreat was due to a rapid, although erratic, rise in temperature from about 12000 B.C. As the ice-sheets melted so a tundra vegetation of dwarf birch, willow and mountain

---

[2] J. G. Evans, *The Environment of Early Man in the British Isles* (1975), pp. 95, 134–142.

avens appeared, to be followed, as climatic conditions continued to improve, by birch and pine forests, and then by hazel, oak, elm, alder and eventually lime and beech. This climatic amelioration and the forest cover it encouraged brought erosion by wind and frost almost to a halt, and soils began to stabilise and mature. At the same time it returned to the sea the vast quantities of water which had been locked up in the ice-sheets. The level of the sea began to rise, and by about 8,000 years ago Britain and Ireland had become separated and both were cut off from the mainland of Europe. Before this took place however, new techniques of working in flint make their appearance in the archaeological record, and a number of these Mesolithic sites has been found in Buckinghamshire. In the valley of the Colne, then a complex system of marsh, fen, interconnecting streams and islands of firmer ground, several groups of Mesolithic hunters and fishermen appear to have settled. But Mesolithic sites are by no means confined to low-lying river valleys. Implements have been found at Ley Hill, a site well over a mile from the valley of the Chess. Other flint-working and occupational sites have been uncovered at Kimble Farm, Turville and at Bolter End, Fingest. Both sites are in the heart of the Chiltern hills, miles from any river valley. In the north of the county assemblages of Mesolithic flints have been found at Stacey Bushes in the Loughton Brook valley, and at Bow Brickhill.

These Mesolithic people have traditionally been represented as small bands of wandering huntsmen, whose impact upon their environment could only have been minimal. But the contributions of science to archaeology, particularly the development of radio-carbon dating and pollen analysis, have forced a reappraisal of the evidence. Mesolithic stone axes were probably capable of felling full-grown trees,[3] whilst those which proved to be too stubborn could have been ring-barked and then allowed to die before being burnt, since men had long known how to control fire. There is in addition some evidence to show that they were now moving on from being

[3] see J. G. D. Clark, *Excavations at Star Carr* (1954, 1971 reprint), pp. 2, 177.

merely predatory upon wild animals and were making the first tentative steps towards domestication.[4] These three factors, tools, fire and control, however slight, over grazing animals, give power over the environment out of all proportion to the actual numbers of men involved, and in the long term they can bring about permanent change in the vegetational cover and its associated soil structure.

There is but a handful of Mesolithic sites known in Buckinghamshire. It is likely that more will come to light in the future, but anything approaching a complete settlement pattern can never be recovered. The evidence is too fragile, its recovery too unsystematic, the time-scale too immense, and in any case it seems likely that Mesolithic men were at least semi-nomadic, using different camp-sites at different seasons of the year. Nevertheless it is becoming increasingly apparent that we must be prepared to accept a much greater density of inhabitation and a much greater power to modify the environ-ment in a much more remote period of time than we have done hitherto. We must even be prepared to accept territorialisation. There are no true wanderers. Even the most foot-loose of nomads move over a known range, however vaguely its bound-aries may be defined. The moulding of the Buckinghamshire landscape under the influence of man's activities began probably ten thousand years ago. It is only fitting that we should give a little more than a passing nod to those who were the first to set their hands to the task.

The first true farmers make their appearance in Britain probably nearer the beginning of the fourth millenium B.C. than the end.[5] The impact of these Neolithic people upon the landscape was to be profound, wide-ranging and permanent. They would have had to come by sea from the European main-land, bringing with them their livestock and seed-corn. They could have arrived only in comparatively small parties, and over a long period of time. Nor could they suddenly have displaced the existing inhabitants, and so a long period of overlap between

[4] see M. R. Jarman, 'European deer economies and the advent of the Neolithic', in E. S. Higgs, ed., *Papers in Economic Prehistory* (1972), pp. 125–148.

[5] C. Renfrew, ed., *British Prehistory* (1974), p. xi.

Mesolithic and Neolithic technologies must be assumed.

The newcomers were farmers. They cultivated the ground, using a hoe or an ard, growing crops of wheat and barley. They kept cattle, sheep and pigs, and had domesticated the dog, as indeed had their Mesolithic predecessors. They were skilled carpenters. They made dug-out canoes. They mined flints.

The cultivation of crops implies the laying out of fields. Some may have been carved from the high forest by felling and burning trees and planting seed in the layers of wood-ash. Once the fertility of this ash had been exhausted, which may happen in as little as two years, then the community would move on to a new site and begin the whole process over again, allowing the old site to revert to forest. But once the forest cover has been removed then its regeneration can be a very slow and uncertain process, easily reversed or prevented altogether, and grazing animals provide one of the severest checks upon this regenerative process. The cultivation of crops implies a measure of semi-permanent settlement if what has been sown is to be harvested. Settlement further implies that the effects of clearing for cultivation and of grazing will be cumulative, and probably permanent. It seems most likely that considerable areas of the chalklands of southern England were cleared as a result of the activities of Neolithic farmers.

A number of Neolithic sites are known in Buckinghamshire: at Gerrards Cross, at Iver, Marlow, Saunderton and at Stacey Bushes, Wolverton, whilst flint mines which are probably Neolithic have been identified on Pitstone Hill. More such sites are likely to be uncovered in the future. Sites of this kind yield flint tools, pottery, animal bones and ashes. Indirectly they can tell us a great deal about the contemporary environment. Thus from the late Neolithic site at Stacey Bushes charcoal from fairly large timbers has been recovered, and an analysis of the species of land snails whose shells have been found indicates open woodland rather than closed high forest.[6]

---

[6] H. S. Green, 'The Excavation of a late Neolithic Settlement at Stacey Bushes, Milton Keynes and its Significance', in C. Burgess and R. Miket, eds., *Settlement and Economy in the Third and Second Millenia B.C.* British Archaeological Reports No. 33 (1976), p. 11.

It would seem not unreasonable to suggest that the clearing of the forest from this part of north Buckinghamshire was already under way.

The influence of these Neolithic farmers on the landscape was certainly very important and long-lasting, but nowhere in the county can we point with assurance to a field and say that this was first cleared and cultivated by Neolithic men. Instead the most conspicuous monuments left behind by these people and still visible today are their burial mounds, or long barrows. They are very numerous in Dorset and Wiltshire, but there is only a small and isolated group in the Chilterns, and only one of these, Whiteleaf Barrow, is in Buckinghamshire. It is situated on a spur overlooking Monks Risborough on the Icknield Way, which was probably already in use as a trackway by the time this barrow was built. Here was buried the remains of a man aged about thirty-five. Land snail shells indicate a damp woodland environment in which the beech tree was present but by no means dominant. It is possible that a barrow of this kind was the focal point for a territorially based community, although we can only speculate as to its size and extent. It must however have included some arable fields since pottery fragments found in the barrow have impressions of two types of wheat-grain, *Triticum decoccum* and *Triticum compactum*. Such impressions would have been left by individual grains, perhaps the debris from the preparation for a meal, scattered at random over the working surface upon which the pottery was made.

By the middle of the third millenium B.C. it is clear that a series of important changes was taking place in many communities throughout much of Britain. First of all the working of metal, both copper and bronze, becomes established. The bronze-smiths themselves may have come to form separate groups of nomadic craftsmen. Four of their hoards of used and broken tools and scrap metal have been found in Buckinghamshire, one at Slough, a very late one of perhaps 650 B.C. at Aylesbury, another at Burnham and a fourth at Waddesdon.

Secondly there are changes in the way in which the dead are interred. The building of long barrows as places of burial peters out, although individual inhumation under round barrows seems to have continued. Eventually, however, by the first half of the second millenium B.C. inhumation is largely replaced by cremation, the ashes then being buried in cinerary urns, sometimes in extensive cemeteries. Considerable uncertainty still surrounds the evolution of these sepulchral conventions. Their chronology is by no means firmly established and in any case there seems to have been much overlapping.

The introduction of metal-working and the changes in burial traditions were until recently confidently ascribed to new immigrants from the continent known, from the pottery considered characteristic of them, as the Beaker People. But there is now sufficient evidence of metal-working and of cremation cemeteries before the appearance of Beakers to cast serious doubts upon this traditional account. Indeed it has been suggested that Beakers as such may have been part of a cult or ceremony that could have been transmitted without any extensive population movement at all.[7] Whatever the truth of the matter may be, these changes have left their mark upon the Buckinghamshire landscape. An urnfield was found at Stokenchurch in 1738, although it is now covered by approach roads to the M40. Such a cemetery may imply a settlement of a more or less permanent nature. Other Bronze Age urns have been found at Stoke Poges, at Barrow Croft, overlooking Wycombe Marsh, and at Taplow.

Round barrows are much more common in Buckinghamshire than are long barrows. They are quite frequent on hill sites along the crest of the Chiltern scarp, overlooking the Icknield Way. Thus there are eight at Saunderton, including two on Lodge Hill, grassy, windswept mounds lying close together on the northern slope of the hill. There are others on Beacon Hill, Ellesborough, on the Cop at Bledlow, on Ivinghoe Beacon (Plate 2), and elsewhere along the Chiltern crest. They are however by no means confined either to the Chiltern scarp or to hilltop sites. Unfortunately, when con-

[7] C. Burgess and S. Shennan, 'The Beaker Phenomenon', in C. Burgess and R. Miket, eds., op. cit., p. 309 et seq.

structed on more level ground, they have proved much more vulnerable to erosion and to ploughing, so that very often all surface remains have long disappeared. They have been re-discovered by aerial photography, which has revealed large numbers of the circular crop marks produced by the long-filled surrounding ditches (Plate 3). Over thirty are known in the north Buckinghamshire part of the valley of the Ouse. If these barrows can be accepted as dynastic graves, serving as the foci for a number of communities, each perhaps with its own territory, then the upper Ouse valley must have been closely settled by the second millenium B.C.[8]

A number of the Ouse valley ring-ditches have been excavated – at Milton Keynes, at Warren Farm and Little Pond Ground, Wolverton, and at Cotton Valley, Willen. These communities appear to have been essentially pastoral, and at Warren Farm there is good evidence of permanent settlement. Analysis of the land snails from these sites reveals an open grassland environment, an environment created and maintained by grazing herds and flocks. Further evidence of the extent of the impact of Bronze Age man upon his environment comes from Pitstone, where a study of downwash soils suggests woodland clearance and subsequent soil erosion before the end of the third millenium B.C.[9]

Aerial photography has also revealed a large number of crop marks along the Buckinghamshire side of the valley of the Thames. These need careful investigation before we can be sure of their origin and purpose, but there are ring-ditches and other crop marks at Datchet and at Marlow which are almost certainly Bronze Age.

Before the end of the first half of the first millenium B.C. the transition to the Iron Age had begun. By this time it is

[8] H. Stephen Green, 'Early Bronze Age Burial, Territory and Population in Milton Keynes, Buckinghamshire and the Great Ouse Valley', *Archaeological Journal* 131, (1974), p. 75.

[9] J. G. Evans, 'Late Glacial and Post-Glacial Subaerial Deposits at Pitstone, Bucks.', *Proceedings of the Geologists' Association* 77, (1966–67), pp. 347–364, and K. W. G. Valentine and J. B. Dalrymple, 'The Identification of a Buried Paleosol Developed in Place at Pitstone, Buckinghamshire', *Journal of Soil Science* 27, (1976), pp. 541–553.

most likely that considerable areas of north Buckinghamshire had been cleared of forest, particularly, although by no means exclusively, in the Ouse valley. There had been sufficient clearance in the Chilterns for soil erosion to have begun, and it is very likely that downwash from other sites in addition to that at Pitstone will prove to be anthropogenic in origin. Bronze Age men were also present in the south of the county, along the valley of the Thames. The extent of clearance, the pattern of settlement, the density of population are still all too vague and uncertain, but we should not under-estimate them.

There is one further intriguing possibility of survival from the Bronze Age. The name of the Chiltern hills, *Chiltern* itself, appears not to be English in origin, and there is no Celtic etymology for it. Could it not therefore be pre-Celtic?

One of the earliest monuments in Buckinghamshire to this period of change from the Bronze Age to the Iron Age is the hill-fort on Ivinghoe Beacon, a bleak, windswept spot 760 feet high (Plate 2). Here an area of just under five and a half acres is surrounded with a single bank and ditch, with a single entrance facing the ridge at the eastern end. There is a large round-barrow at the summit, within the fortifications, and two more, much eroded, just outside. Excavation has revealed a number of late Bronze Age implements, and some ingot metal, suggesting metal-working on the site. The fortifications were a simple box-frame type, the rampart being made of two rows of vertical timbers tied together with horizontals, infilled with the chalk rubble excavated from the ditch. The rampart was poorly built, irregular in its layout, and in some parts probably not finished. A large number of post-holes was uncovered, but it proved almost impossible to discern any building plans, save perhaps that there were some which were rectangular rather than round. The inhabitants practised spinning and weaving, since their spindle-whorls and loom weights were found. They appear to have been essentially a pastoral people: the pollen record reveals no trace of cereals. Occupation seems to have persisted for only a comparatively short time, probably during the eighth century B.C., and then the site was abandoned for ever.[10] The evidence from this excavation of older traditions in metal-working together with innovations in the construction of defensive earthworks makes the dating of this site particularly controversial but it does seem clear that here on Ivinghoe Beacon there is one of the earliest hill-forts to be found anywhere in Britain.

Ivinghoe Beacon is not however the only hill-fort in Buckinghamshire, although it is the one where excavation has proved the most rewarding. There are Iron Age hill-forts at Desborough Castle, at Keep Hill, and at Church Hill, all prominent hilltop sites overlooking the valley of the Wye. The largest in Buckinghamshire is Bulstrode Camp, Gerrards Cross, where a double rampart and ditch enclose an area of twenty-two acres. There is another of fifteen acres at Cholesbury. Neither of these can be conclusively dated, but it would appear that Bulstrode Camp is older than Cholesbury, which may be second century B.C., and neither seems to have been occupied for very long. On Boddington Hill, overlooking Halton, there is a univallate hill-fort of seventeen acres which has yielded early Iron Age potsherds, whilst there is a smaller one, of about four acres, on Pulpit Hill, Kimble, an isolated hill over 800 feet high. Here there is a double rampart on the east side, whilst on the steeper, west side there is only one. There are two at Medmenham, where Danesfield Camp occupies a cliff-like site, a hundred feet high, overlooking the Thames, and the univallate hill-fort known as Bolebec Castle occupies a sixteen acre site north-east of the church. There are several other, smaller, ones in the Chilterns, and at Taplow a ditch and bank under the old church may also be the remains of a fortified Iron Age site. In the north of the county there is an Iron Age hill-fort in Wavendon Wood, where Danesborough Camp is probably early Iron Age, although here care is needed not to confuse its earthworks with those of the medieval deer park in Bow Brickhill. The spread remains, partially destroyed when the canal was built, of an Iron Age defended enclosure have been recognised at Maids Moreton.

[10] M. A. Cotton and S. S. Frere, 'Ivinghoe Beacon Excavations 1963–1965', *Records of Buckinghamshire* XVIII Part 3, (1968), pp. 187–260.

But hill-forts are only isolated phenomena in the Iron Age landscape. Settlements on lowland sites, whether surrounded with banks and ditches or not, are much more common. These settlements may have consisted of a single isolated farm, or of an agglomeration of farms for which the word village may be too grand a label. They may have a complex pattern of banks and ditches, storage pits, trackways and rectangular plots associated with them, as at Ravenstone and Stoke Goldington, Dorney and Marlow, and a dozen other sites up and down the county. Other settlements may have been simpler in layout. Thus there are three Iron Age hut circles at Woughton-on-the-Green, and another hut site at Bradwell, storage pits at Ellesborough, and evidence of occupation at Bledlow, Burnham and Lodge Hill, Saunderton.

One of the chief purposes of the pits which have been found at a number of Iron Age sites in Buckinghamshire was the storage of grain. Corn growing implies fields. A number of the rectangular plots which have been recognised at Pitstone may well be Iron Age fields, marked off by banks and ditches. The possibility that some fields may have been continuously cultivated since Bronze Age times cannot be ruled out, but growing population pressure during the Iron Age must have compelled the laying out of new ones, to be carved out of the woodland. At the same time iron working and smelting would have meant increased demands for fuel, which could have been obtained only from the forest. Together, Iron Age farming and metal-working would have meant yet further reductions in the areas of virgin wilderness in the county, and indeed future archaeological discoveries may yet reveal that by the end of the Iron Age, if not before, the first pioneering frontier had been closed.

At intervals across the dip-slope of the Chilterns, some distance to the south of the crest of the scarp, lies a series of linear earthworks. They are generally assumed to be of Iron Age date. Known collectively as Grim's Ditch they are straight and, when changing direction, angular rather than curving or sinuous, implying open country, since straight ditches of this kind could only be built if their sighting lines were clear of trees. They consist of a simple bank and ditch and appear to face south down the dip-slope. It seems likely that they can be no more than boundary ditches, perhaps for cattle-herding, rather than fortifications. Nor must we assume that, because they bear a common name today, they were built as one overall system. Grim's Ditch or Dike is a term applied indiscriminately to linear earthworks in several parts of the country. There is for example one in south Oxfordshire, and a field in Boarstall was known as Grim's Ditch as late as 1707.

Nowhere in Buckinghamshire do these linear earthworks serve as parish boundaries. This poses the difficult question of why the estates which were the forerunners of our parishes neglected to use so obvious a landmark. In Wiltshire it has been suggested that Wansdyke, which is also not used to mark parish boundaries, is a later intrusion into a landscape already laid out into estates. In contrast, the Grim's Dike, in south Wiltshire, is followed for almost the whole of its length by parish boundaries. It is unlikely that Wansdyke was built much after A.D. 600, whereas the Wiltshire Grim's Dike is of late Iron Age date, the inference being that parish/estate boundaries crystallised at some time after the latter earthwork was built, but at some time before the former.[11] If we may argue from these Wiltshire examples, then either the boundaries of the Chiltern scarp parishes are very much older than we have hitherto been prepared to admit or the Buckinghamshire Grim's Ditches are very much more recent than we have believed until now. Perhaps, on the other hand, there were economic, political and social factors at work when the boundaries were drawn which were sufficiently powerful to over-ride any advantages there may have been in using these earthworks. Only extensive excavation can provide satisfactory solutions to these problems, but we cannot reject out of hand the possibility of an ordered, regulated landscape in the heart of the Chilterns before the end of the Iron Age.

[11] D. Bonney, 'Early Boundaries in Wessex', in P. J. Fowler, ed., *Archaeology and the Landscape* (1972), pp. 168–186.

Roman Buckinghamshire

Caesar's two expeditions to Britain in 55 and 54 B.C. bring to an end the long period of prehistory in which, for the historian, millenia slip past as easily as centuries in the Christian era. From now on we begin to find that we no longer have to rely exclusively upon the archaeological record, since it can be supplemented by written records, scrappily at first, but in due course the scraps become a feast. Archaeology in the sense that it is concerned with material remains can never be dispensed with, but increasingly the written record becomes fuller, more comprehensive and more informative.

Within four years of their landing in A.D. 43 to begin the permanent conquest of Britain the Romans had occupied the area south and east of a line from Devonshire to Lincoln, marked off approximately by the Fosse Way. But of the passage of the legions through Buckinghamshire there is now no trace. The county contains no great Roman fortifications or military camps. Nor are there those silent reminders, such as are still to be seen at Wroxeter or Leicester, of that city life so characteristic of Roman civilisation. Nevertheless archaeological discoveries of recent years have made it clear that the county was densely settled in Roman times, and that the pattern of settlement which eventually evolved was linked by an elaborate network of roads (Fig. 2). In order fully to appreciate the importance of these roads it is necessary to look well beyond the county boundaries, which were of course drawn many centuries after the end of Roman rule, to the whole of the region lying north and west of London and the Thames.

Watling Street was one of the great trunk roads of Roman Britain (Plate 4). It runs in a north-westerly direction from London to Verulamium, and then crosses the north-east corner of what is now Buckinghamshire on its way to Towcester and eventually Wroxeter. It is used today as the A5, but building and rebuilding over the centuries have destroyed almost everything of the original Roman road except its alignment. Nowhere does it mark the county boundary, but for much of

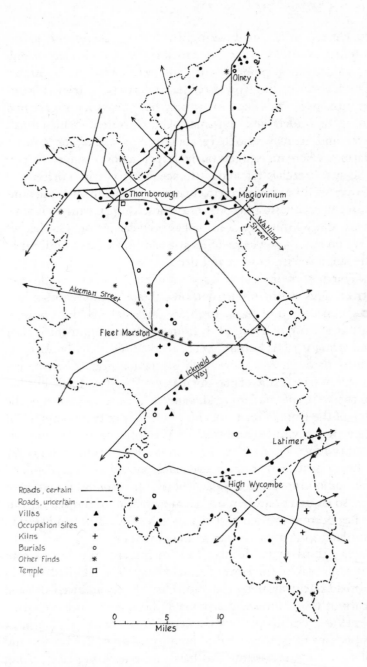

Roads, certain ——————
Roads, uncertain -----------
Villas ▲
Occupation sites ●
Kilns +
Burials ○
Other finds *
Temple □

0   5   10
Miles

Fig. 2. Roman Buckinghamshire

its eleven miles in Buckinghamshire it serves for parish boundaries. Just where it crosses the Ousel near Fenny Stratford, at a point about half way between Dunstable (Durocobrivae) and Towcester (Lactodorum), a town, Magiovinium, grew up (Plate 4). It may have owed its origins to a group of traders and craftsmen who clustered about a small fort, and it may also have contained a *mansio*, or posting station, where messengers of the Imperial post changed horses. The site stretches for some distance along Watling Street and it may well be the largest Roman settlement in Buckinghamshire. It is certainly the only one whose Roman name is known to us. Only limited excavation has been carried out, so that we have no exact knowledge of its size and layout, its buildings or the stages of its growth and decay.

The next main road of Roman Buckinghamshire is Akeman Street. This was an important thoroughfare linking Verulamium to Cirencester and Bath. It enters Buckinghamshire from the east at the top of Tring Hill, from where its alignment is clear and straight to Aylesbury, being marked today by the A41. Its course through Aylesbury itself is now lost, but it re-emerges on the western side of the town as the Bicester Road. Further to the west the modern road wanders away to the north of the line of the Roman road, touching it briefly at two points, until they meet again to the west of Westcott before leaving the county together. At Fleet Marston is a Roman site, marked by a heavy scatter of broken tiles and pottery in the ploughed field adjoining the roadside. The site has not been excavated and so its exact nature must remain a matter of conjecture, but it has been suggested that it may have been a posting station similar in function to that at Magiovinium.

The third major Roman road in Buckinghamshire is that known today as the Lower Icknield Way. The Icknield Way as a broad trackway along the comparatively dry and well-drained scarp of the Chilterns has probably been used since Neolithic times as the principal link between Wessex and East Anglia. It is perhaps to be visualised in prehistoric times as a broad band of open country, as much as half a mile wide in places, along which travellers would make their way from one landmark to another, rather than a pathway confined within narrowly defined margins. It seems likely that some parts of this broad trackway may have been metalled by the Romans. Certainly the line of the B4009 and the A4010, at least from Chinnor in Oxfordshire as far as Terrick, has in its alignment every appearance of being Roman in its origin, although its line beyond Terrick as far as its junction with Akeman Street is less certain.

Another important Roman road marks part of the north-western boundary of the county with Oxfordshire. This road comes north from Silchester and Dorchester-on-Thames, through Alchester and on to join Watling Street near Towcester. The Buckinghamshire boundary meets the road just to the south-west of Finmere, where it forms the modern A421. Between Finmere and Water Stratford the road itself is lost, being marked now only by the county boundary. Once over the Ouse at Water Stratford, the road heads in a north-easterly direction through Stowe Park on its way to Towcester.

These four roads have long been known to archaeologists but research in the years since 1945[12] has revealed that these four were only part of a dense network of roads serving to articulate the pattern of farmsteads and villas which has also been recovered. Thus three more roads converge on Fleet Marston in addition to Akeman Street. Both banks of the Ouse were lined by roads linking together the numerous settlements of every kind to be found in this region of the county. Another road links the important focal point at Thornborough to Magiovinium. Three other roads head in a north-easterly direction out of the county. One has not yet been traced further north than Stoke Goldington, but two converge near Olney and continue to Irchester. Another connects Verulamium with Silchester, running at right angles to the valleys of the Chiltern dip-slope. It clearly provided an important line of communication to the settlements further up each of these valleys.

The marks left upon the landscape by this network of roads

[12] see I. D. Margary, *Roman Roads in Britain* (3rd ed. 1973), and The Viatores, *Roman Roads in the South-East Midlands* (1964).

vary enormously. Watling Street even today strides unerringly across the north-east of the county, whereas that road already mentioned as petering out near Stoke Goldington emerges from the northern edge of Gayhurst Wood as an unmetalled cart track with a deep ditch on its western side. The road from Fleet Marston to Thornborough is a lane to the south-west of Pitchcott, this time made up and with a deep ditch on its western side. It continues as a footpath, then a hedgerow and finally a parish boundary.

All archaeological distribution maps are interim statements, and Fig. 2 is no exception. Future research will undoubtedly add many more miles to the network of Roman roads in Buckinghamshire. Documentary sources can often provide the first clues to set fieldworkers off in the right direction. The Old English word *straet*, which gives us our modern 'street', was almost always applied to Roman roads, and field and furlong names, even from the sixteenth and seventeenth centuries, embodying this word, may sometimes indicate the whereabouts of Roman roads. Thus the Overstreet and Nether-street Fields in Aston Clinton refer to Akeman Street (Fig. 9). Yet other place-names hint at roads waiting to be discovered. *Helewistrete* is mentioned in Wotton Underwood, and there was a *Stretforlang* in Ickford, whilst we know that the southern boundary of Linslade parish is marked by a Roman road because an Anglo-Saxon charter mentions a *straet* here. Clearly much remains to be done before we can be sure that we have recovered in full the pattern of roads in Roman Buckingham-shire.

The Roman conquest brought no sudden revolution into the long, slow process of the evolution of the Buckinghamshire landscape, but it did bring, for generations together, a peace and stability which enabled the farmsteads and villas to be built and the roads to be laid out that are marked on Fig. 2. This, however, is only a very partial representation of the pattern of settlement in Roman Buckinghamshire since it suffers from two serious defects: first of all new discoveries are being made so rapidly as to make it out of date literally within weeks of its being drawn, and secondly it gives a static rather than a dynamic picture in that it does not show the stages in the growth, development and decline of this pattern. Only a handful of the sites has been in any way adequately explored, and so any suggestions as to the stages of this growth and decay must of necessity be very tentative. Nevertheless evidence is beginning to accumulate from which it is possible to give at least an outline of what these stages were.

One of the earliest Roman settlements in the county must have been that at Yewden Manor, Hambleden.[13] It was occupied by the middle years of the first century A.D. and was not finally abandoned until the end of the fourth. One of the villas at Saunderton was also occupied by the end of the first century A.D. but a second, at Saunderton Lee, is known only from an aerial photograph. The villa at Little Kimble may also date from this time, and perhaps the other known but unexplored sites along the Chiltern scarp were also first settled by the end of the first century A.D.

Akeman Street and Watling Street both follow pre-Roman trackways and it is likely that they were among the first roads to be properly constructed after A.D. 43. But the occupational sites known to exist along them have not been excavated, and so we have no knowledge of their history and development, and only the most fragile hints as to the course of the Romanisation of northern Buckinghamshire. Some late first century material has been found at Hartwell. At Stanton Low there is evidence of Iron Age occupation before the erection of Romanised buildings by the end of the first century. The sites at Emberton, Bow Brickhill, Newton Longville and Sherwood Drive, Bletchley, were also occupied by this time, and it is likely that several of the roads in the Ouse valley had been built and a number of farmsteads rebuilt and laid out in the Roman fashion by the end of the first century. This brings to an end the first stage in the development of Roman Buckinghamshire. By A.D. 100 several main roads had been built and a number of farmsteads developed. Some may have been the result of the rebuilding of an Iron Age house. Others were

[13] A. H. Cocks, 'A Romano-British Homestead in the Hambleden Valley, Bucks.', *Archaeologia* LXXI, (1921), pp. 141–198.

erected on virgin sites. All at first were comparatively simple in plan, but show clearly the characteristics that mark them off from their Iron Age predecessors – several rectangular rooms united into one building. At Saunderton there is the possibility of a mosaic floor even at this early date.[14]

The second stage begins with the first decades of the second century A.D., when farmsteads with Roman characteristics begin to appear in the Chiltern valleys, and so regularly are they spaced in the Chess valley, at just under two miles apart, that they have every appearance of the deliberate allocation of estates of approximately the same size. The villa at High Wycombe was erected in about A.D. 150–170, although it does not seem to have replaced an Iron Age farmstead.[15] At Latimer the villa was erected on an Iron Age site at about the same time as that at High Wycombe, but with a gap of perhaps as much as forty years between its two occupations. Extensive additions were made at Hambleden, there was an almost complete rebuilding at Saunderton, and sites at Little Brickhill and Princes Risborough have yielded evidence to suggest that buildings were erected there in the second century A.D.

The years of the second and third centuries were clearly ones of peace and prosperity in what is now Buckinghamshire. Most of the sites marked on Fig. 2 were by this time laid out, and much of the road mileage must have been built. Several small-scale pottery kilns had also been established, at Hedgerley, Gerrards Cross, Stone and perhaps at Taplow. Very little is known about the economy of individual Buckinghamshire villas, but it is clear that they were based upon mixed farming. Cattle and sheep were kept, perhaps in large numbers. Corn-drying ovens have been found at Hambleden, Saunderton and at Bletchley, suggesting that the cultivation of grain was widespread and may have been on a large scale in some areas. Traces of a stone quay have been found at Hill

[14] K. Branigan, 'The Romano-British Villa at Saunderton Reconsidered', *Records of Buckinghamshire* XVIII Part 4, (1969), pp. 261–276.

[15] B. R. Hartley, 'A Romano-British Villa at High Wycombe', *Records of Buckinghamshire* XVI Part 4, (1959), pp. 227–257.

Farm, Haversham, and there is the possibility of a wooden one at Thornton. It is likely that the Ouse as well as the Thames could have been navigated by barges laden with grain, making their way into the network of Fenland canals built by the Romans and so to the military garrison at York.

The extent of the penetration of Roman influences by this time may be judged from two burials, both cremations, which have been excavated, one at Thornborough and the other at Weston Turville. At Thornborough, close to the modern B4034, stand two grass-covered Roman burial mounds (Fig. 8 and Plate 5). Both were opened on behalf of the Duke of Buckingham in 1839. One yielded nothing which was considered of interest at the time. Finds from the other, including a square jug of greenish glass, a bronze lamp and bronze jugs, are of outstanding interest and quality. They are now in the Cambridge Museum of Ethnology and Archaeology. The other burial, at Weston Turville, was discovered in the rectory gardens in 1855. The finds here, now on display in the County Museum, Aylesbury, included glass bottles, samian vessels and fragments of a mirror. Both burials are to be dated from before the end of the second century A.D. and both reveal a thoroughly Romanised background to the lives of the dead.[16]

This second stage closes, in the second half of the third century, with years of turbulence, political unrest, barbarian invasions in the north of Britain, and the appearance of Saxon pirates off the east coast. The effects upon the economic foundations of Roman Buckinghamshire were clearly profound. Signs of decay and decline are to be found almost everywhere, and both Latimer and Saunderton villas may have been abandoned for a time.

The third and final stage in the history of Roman Buckinghamshire opens with the return of more stable conditions after the accession of Constantine in A.D. 306. There is evidence of large-scale rebuilding at many of the Buckinghamshire sites.

---

[16] J. Liversidge, 'The Thornborough Barrow', *Records of Buckinghamshire* XVI Part 1, (1953–1954), pp. 29–32. H. Waugh, 'The Romano-British Burial at Weston Turville', *Records of Buckinghamshire* XVII Part 2, (1962), pp. 107–114.

The farmstead at Hambleden was re-orientated. There was a major reconstruction at Latimer, when the baths were extended. At High Wycombe the bath-house was altered and enlarged. A fourth-century hypocaust has been found at Ravenstone, and the site at Windmill Hill, Bletchley may belong to this period.

But this revival was to prove the Indian summer of Roman Buckinghamshire. Nor did it penetrate everywhere. The site at Sherwood Drive, Bletchley seems to have remained unrepaired. Political disturbances in the middle of the fourth century were followed by widespread and concerted attacks by bands of barbarians in A.D. 367. The villa at High Wycombe was abandoned, and about half of the building at Latimer was blocked off and allowed to fall into ruin. By the end of the fourth century political uncertainty and economic dislocation had forced almost all of their owners to abandon their villas to the ravages of wind, frost and squatters.

These, in outline, were the stages in the growth and decline of Roman Buckinghamshire. The picture must of necessity be so vague because so few of the sites marked on Fig. 2 have been properly explored, and many more undoubtedly remain to be discovered. Extensive field-walking, organised from the County Museum, has revealed scatters of occupational debris in almost every parish in the north of the county and it is rapidly becoming obvious that much of northern Buckinghamshire, even the heavy claylands, was as densely settled in Roman times as any part of south-eastern England. Nor should we think solely in terms of villas and farmsteads. The sites at Haversham and Olney for example have both yielded very large numbers of coins, and a statue of Mercury has been found at Olney, suggesting that both may have been the centres for markets and were perhaps large enough to be called towns. Thornborough, too, was a focal point of importance. Five roads met here. Two large burial mounds were sufficiently richly furnished to suggest connection with a local native aristocracy. A temple with associated buildings, probably erected in about A.D. 265, lies nearby, and several cremation burials have been found. The full significance of this site still remains to be established and it may well prove to be more important than has hitherto been assumed.[17]

What was the contribution of Rome to the making of the Buckinghamshire landscape? There is first of all the network of roads. Very few parts of the county are more than about four miles from a known Roman road, and undoubtedly much remains to be discovered. There are the two burial mounds at Thornborough, far more evocative of old, forgotten, far-off things than the unceasing roar of the traffic along Watling Street.

But the third contribution is perhaps the most important. No villa in the county seems to have been built on the scale of Woodchester or Bignor, and almost all of the surface evidence has long disappeared, leaving little more than a few crop marks visible only from the air or a scatter of broken tiles in a ploughed field. But those which have been explored were provided with baths, centrally heated rooms, decorated walls, glass windows and a wide range of domestic pottery, all of which, together with an absence of weapons and defensive works, indicate standards of comfort, amenity and civilised life that would not be seen again for many centuries. The life-style these objects represent could not have been supported in scattered, self-sufficient farms existing at subsistence level in a landscape of thick, untamed woodland. Instead they imply a landscape from which wide tracts of forest had been cleared, to be replaced with fields from which corn could be harvested in peace and with pastures where cattle and sheep might safely graze. The contribution of Rome to the making of the Buckinghamshire landscape was very much greater than its surviving memorials visible today would lead us to believe.

SELECT BIBLIOGRAPHY

Avery, B. W., *The Soils and Land Use of the District around Aylesbury and Hemel Hempstead* (1964).

[17] C. W. Green, 'A Romano-Celtic Temple at Bourton Grounds, Buckingham', *Records of Buckinghamshire* XVII Part 5, (1965), pp. 356–366. A. E. Johnson, Excavations at Bourton Grounds, Thornborough', *Records of Buckinghamshire* XX Part 1, (1975), pp. 3–56.

Branigan, K., 'Romano-British Rural Settlement in the Western Chilterns', *Archaeological Journal* 124, (1967), pp. 129–159.

Branigan, K., 'Pavements and Poverty in the Chiltern Villas', *Britannia* 2, (1971), pp. 109–116.

Branigan, K., *Town and Country: the Archaeology of Verulamium and the Roman Chilterns* (1973).

Dyer, J., 'Barrows of the Chilterns', *Archaeological Journal* 116, (1959), pp. 1–24.

Evans, J. G., and Valentine, K. W. G., 'Ecological Changes Induced by Prehistoric Man at Pitstone, Buckinghamshire', *Journal of Archaeological Science* 1, (1974), pp. 343–351.

Fryer, D. W., *The Land of Britain. Part 54. Buckinghamshire* (1942).

Gates, T., *The Middle Thames Valley. An Archaeological Survey of the River Gravels* (1975).

Green, M. J., *The Bradwell Roman Villa*. 1st Interim Report, Milton Keynes Development Corporation, Occasional Papers in Archaeology, No. 1 (1975).

Saunders, C., 'The Pre-Belgic Iron Age in the Central and Western Chilterns', *Archaeological Journal* 128, (1971), pp. 1–30.

Temple, M. S. *A Survey of the Soils of Buckinghamshire*. University of Reading, Faculty of Agriculture and Horticulture, Bulletin No. 38 (1929).

Willats, E. C., *The Land of Britain. Part 79. Middlesex and the London Region* (1937).

2. The English settlement

The coming of the English. Churches and estates. The creation of Buckinghamshire. Domesday Book

The coming of the English

HISTORIANS WERE AGREED until quite recently that the English could not have arrived in what is now Buckingham-shire much before the last part of the sixth century A.D. Their coming, it was thought, was marked by destruction and violence, and the scattered remnant of the Romano-British population either fled before them or was taken into slavery. The English then established new villages, avoiding Roman roads and Roman sites, and began all over again the process of clearing and colonisation of the land. However, the accumulation of research since 1945 in archaeology, place-name studies and landscape archaeology has compelled a reappraisal of this rather simplistic interpretation that is little short of revolutionary.

Germanic soldiers were being deliberately settled in Britain by the Roman authorities quite by the middle years of the fourth century, and there is considerable archaeological evidence of the presence of such settlers along the southern banks of the Thames as far up river as Dorchester-on-Thames and beyond before the end of the fourth century. They were given land to cultivate in return for military service against Irish, Pictish and in due course other Germanic pirates, whose raids were becoming too frequent and too far-ranging for the existing military establishment to cope with. The last effective Roman military force left Britain in A.D. 407, together with many of the personnel of the central civil administration. Thus

53

it was to the towns rather than to the governors that Honorius addressed his letter of A.D. 410 telling them that they must look to their own defences. The vacuum created by the Roman withdrawal was filled by the emergence of British kings bearing British titles, and as the machinery of Roman civilisation began to run down, money ceased to be used as a medium of exchange, the pottery factories stopped producing their wares, and villas were abandoned. There was nevertheless a period of comparative peace and prosperity in the first decades of the fifth century. However the numbers of the Germanic settlers began to grow, both by natural increase and by regular immigration from across the North Sea, but now as allies rather than as bondsmen. They moved further and further away from their original settlements, filling, almost always without violence, niches created in the existing patterns of occupation by the gradual disintegration of Romano-British rural society. An increasingly precarious balance between Romano-British and Germans was suddenly and violently upset when the Germans, whom we may now call English, rebelled. A long period of fighting ended with the British victory at Mons Badonicus, the site of which is unknown, towards the end of the fifth century, and the English military advance was halted. It resumed again in the second half of the sixth century, and Aylesbury was captured by the English in 571. By the end of the sixth century politically independent British were confined to Wales, to the south-west peninsula and to the border regions with Scotland.

The final establishment of English political authority had been preceded by a long period of peaceful intercourse between the two people in which there was certainly intermarriage at royal and aristocratic level, and probably lower down the social scale as well, together with some measure of bilingualism. There was no wholesale slaughter of the British by the English. Instead it is possible that the fusion of the two peoples had gone far before the erosion of British political power became apparent.

Thus the older view that the coming of the English marked a complete break in the evolution of the landscape would appear now to be untenable, and it seems that we must look instead for continuity rather than catastrophe.

Nevertheless we must be careful how we define continuity, since much that is basic to our understanding of many features of the landscape will depend upon what we mean by it. Continuity may mean first of all continuity of a settlement site, which does not mean either continuity of population or uninterrupted settlement. Secondly it may mean continuity of population in a small unit of settlement, for example within the boundaries of an estate or a parish, but this does not necessarily imply continuity of occupation of the actual habitation sites themselves. Finally it may mean continuity of occupation of a place, which does not necessarily mean that the population itself remained ethnically unchanged.[1] Thus to establish any kind of continuity between Roman Buckinghamshire and Anglo-Saxon Buckinghamshire is clearly a task of considerable complexity to which, in the present state of our knowledge, it would be premature to suggest any definitive answers. Nevertheless the problem is one of such importance, perhaps the most important of all before the spread of industrialisation in the nineteenth century, that we are justified in spending some time in searching for answers, however tentative.

To help us in our search we have two kinds of evidence, that provided by archaeology and that to be derived from the study of place-names. Such documentary records as survive from Anglo-Saxon Buckinghamshire make very little contribution towards a solution of the problem.

The archaeological evidence to which hitherto the most importance has been attached is that from the discovery and excavation of the graves in which the first English settlers buried the remains of their dead, either by direct inhumation or else after cremation, together with weapons, personal ornaments and domestic utensils. These grave goods can often be dated within broad limits, but with the conversion to Christianity, probably not completed in Buckinghamshire, even at a superficial level, much before about A.D. 700, the

[1] see W. Janssen, 'Some Major Aspects of Frankish and Medieval Settlement in the Rhineland', in P. H. Sawyer, ed., *Medieval Settlement* (1976), p. 41.

pagan practices of cremation and burial of grave goods come to an end, and with them one of the most important and significant threads in the archaeological evidence.

The great majority of known pagan English cemeteries in the county are grouped about the headwaters of the Thame and along the foothills of the Chiltern scarp (Fig. 3). Almost all were discovered and excavated long before archaeology had developed reliable techniques, with the result that they are nearly all badly recorded and a great deal of irreplaceable historical evidence has undoubtedly been lost. The largest cemetery seems to have been that at Cursley Hill, Bishopstone, where discoveries were made in 1866 and again in 1875. All the burials were inhumations, and altogether about fifty graves were discovered. This means that in comparison with the great pagan English cemeteries in other parts of the country, such as that cremation cemetery at Caistor-by-Norwich, those in Buckinghamshire are very small and could have served only small groups of people for a comparatively short period of time. On the other hand the single inhumation burial at Taplow, excavated in 1883, was, until the finding of the Sutton Hoo ship-burial, the richest and most splendid English pagan burial in the country. This was the grave of no ordinary warrior but of some powerful chieftain, almost certainly buried in the first quarter of the seventh century, and sufficiently renowned for his followers to perpetuate the memory of his name. Taeppa's *hlaw*, or burial mound, has become Taplow.

To the known pagan cemeteries must be added the undiscovered ones. Other place-names in addition to Taplow are composed of a personal name and the element *hlaw*, including Bledlow, Cottesloe, Calley farm in Hartwell, and Winslow. Pagan burials are known from Bledlow and Hartwell, but not from Cottesloe or Winslow. In addition there are the burial mounds mentioned in the boundary clauses to tenth-century charters. The description of the Linslade boundary refers to seven burial mounds at one point, to a middle-most burial mound at another and to a separate single burial mound at a third. That for Olney of 979 mentions *Hildes hlaw*. That for Monks Risborough of 903 mentions heathen burials, as does

Plate 1 An aerial view of the Cop, Bledlow, looking east, showing the heavily wooded nature of this part of the Chilterns and the way in which the lower slopes are being invaded by scrub.

Plate 2 The early Iron Age hill-fort on Ivinghoe Beacon. The burial mounds, both inside and outside the ramparts, are just visible. The Chilterns here are almost treeless, in contrast to Bledlow Cop (plate 1).

Plate 3 Crop marks, visible only from the air, of what are probably ploughed-out Bronze Age burial mounds near Bledlow Ridge.

Plate 4 Watling Street, looking north-west. The Roman town of Magiovinium lies somewhere in the fields in the right foreground, with Fenny Stratford in the middle distance. Bletchley is in the left middle distance.

Plate 5   The Roman burial mounds at Thornborough.

Plate 6   The church at Wing, showing the tenth-century blind arcading to the polygonal apse. The rest of the external stonework is medieval.

the perambulation of the Forest of Bernwood (Fig. 7). Those for Chetwode and Winchendon both list a rough hill or *hlaw* in their boundaries and these may also have been burial mounds. None of these burial mounds can now be identified on the ground but they certainly once existed, and these references to them serve to emphasise just how patchy is our knowledge.

With the whereabouts of pagan English cemeteries once established, the next step in looking for threads of continuity between the Romano-British and the English has usually taken the form of remarks upon the close proximity of these pagan cemeteries to known Roman occupation sites. But our knowledge of the density of Roman settlement has changed beyond recognition in recent years, making such remarks supererogatory. The pagan English could not avoid burying their dead within about a mile of a Roman occupation site even if they had wanted to (see Fig. 2).

The evidence from the pagan cemeteries is however, being increasingly supplemented by that from Anglo-Saxon occupation sites, making it clear that pagan cemeteries can no longer be regarded as the only reliable guides to the areas where the English first settled. Five house sites, with sunken or partially sunken floors, have been excavated recently at Walton near Aylesbury, yielding evidence to suggest occupation from the fifth to the seventh century.[2] Grass-tempered, handmade pottery, 'one of the hallmarks of early Anglo-Saxon domestic pottery',[3] was found, and similar pottery has been found at Waddesdon, Oving, Bierton and Haddenham. Sites at Caldecotte in Bow Brickhill, at Bierton and at Stantonbury have yielded evidence of Romano-British occupation as well as early English materials, but no conclusive evidence of unbroken continuity of occupation. Taken together these fragments of evidence may be sufficient to indicate the presence of groups of English settlers in Buckinghamshire before the end

[2] M. Farley, 'Saxon and Medieval Walton, Aylesbury. Excavations 1973–4', *Records of Buckinghamshire* XX Part 2, (1976), pp. 153–290.

[3] J. G. Hurst, 'The Pottery', in D. M. Wilson, ed., *The Archaeology of Anglo-Saxon England* (1976), p. 294.

Fig. 3. Anglo-Saxon pagan cemeteries

Winslow

Cottesloe

• Known pagan cemeteries
o hlaw in place-names
+ hlaw in charters
△ Heathen burials in
   charters & boundaries

Calley Farm

Bledlow

Taplow

Weston
Underwood

Chicheley

Lt Linford □ △ Broughton

△ Bradwell   • Brickhill

□ Foxcote

• Chetwode

Winslow △

□ Grendon
  Underwood

• Crafton

Panshill •

• Brill

Wendover • St Leonards
            □
            Cholesbury △

• Romano-British place-names
  Churches dedicated to
△ St Lawrence
□ St Leonard

Pressmore

Chesham Bois □

Crendon Lane
• (Penn?)

West △
Wycombe

Chalfont

Upton
△

(Datchet?) •

Fig. 4. The Romano-British survival

of the fifth century. There is not, however, conclusive evidence of continuity of site occupation, and continuity of this kind must remain for the present not proven. Nevertheless this is not the only kind of continuity, and other lines of approach may not be quite so negative.

The second kind of evidence which may be used to trace the development of English settlement in Buckinghamshire is that of place-names. But this evidence is particularly difficult to interpret and recent research has cast serious doubt upon many of the old certainties. It is first of all becoming increasingly apparent that many of what we may regard as habitation site names, that is the names of places where people live, were in fact the names of estates, within which there could be several habitation sites, and that such sites could, and did, move to new locations quite frequently. One of the most important threads running through the landscape archaeology of the Anglo-Saxon centuries is the break-up of such large estates,[4] and it may be only on the occasion of this break-up that a habitation site acquired a name, or perhaps a new one. Secondly it is clear that the names of habitation sites and of estates could and did change, and that all too often the only name that we have today is a comparatively late one. We cannot assume from this alone that the settlement itself was established late. Thus the names Winslow, Taplow and Bledlow are probably late, from the last part of the seventh century at the earliest. As we have seen, all three contain a personal name together with the old English word *hlaw*, meaning a burial mound. There is every likelihood that there was already a settlement in the vicinity at the time of the burial, that the personal name in fact commemorates the person interred in the burial mound, and that his fame and status were sufficient to cause the place-name to be changed. The name of Whitchurch is probably of similar origin. It is very unlikely that there was no settlement at all there when the stone church implied in the name was built, and this cannot

[4] P. H. Sawyer, 'Anglo-Saxon Settlement, the Documentary Evidence', in T. R. Rowley, ed., *Anglo-Saxon Settlement and Landscape* British Archaeological Reports No. 6 (1974), p. 108.

have been much before about 700, and may have been very much later. Instead it is much more likely that such a church was sufficiently prominent and unusual a landmark to have given a new name to the settlement. This renaming process continued into the late middle ages. Langley was once called *Laverkestoke*, and Ankerwyke was once *Basing*. It was only the association of the Cheyne family from the thirteenth century with *Isenhamstede* that led eventually to it being called Chenies, a change-over that was still incomplete in 1535.

This has far-reaching implications for our understanding of the history of settlement in the Chilterns. Many settlements in the Chilterns have medieval names – Wardrobes in Princes Risborough for example, or Chequers in Ellesborough. That Chequers takes its name from the Scaccario family and first appears in the documents in the last quarter of the twelfth century tells us almost nothing about the age of the settlement itself. With the example of *Isenhamstede* before us we cannot say that Chequers was established only when the site came into the hands of the Scaccario family. We simply do not know how old it was when it came into their possession. Settlement in the Chilterns is very much older than has been generally conceded. The deserts of Chiltern are a myth. The phrase, in the form *de desertis Ciltine*, occurs in a text of the early eighth century.[5] It does not imply that the Chilterns were uninhabited, merely that there were wastes surrounding settlements, and we cannot in any case be sure that it refers to the Chilterns at all, since there is no way in which *Ciltine* could have become Chiltern. There is every likelihood that the Chilterns were settled much earlier and much more densely by the English than has hitherto been allowed.

The search through place-name evidence for the earliest settlements is an *ignis fatuus*. Both habitation sites and place-names have changed too much for this to be at all successful. It is probably better to arrange the place-name evidence itself into broad chronological bands, early, middle and late, bearing in mind always that this refers to the age of

[5] B. Colgrove, ed., *The Life of Bishop Wilfrid by Eddius Stephanus* (1927), pp. 84–85.

the *name*, not to the age of the settlement, and that it makes no statement about the length or continuity of occupation. When the evidence is arranged in this way then it may yield us important information.

The English transformed place-names in a way which neither the Romans nor the Normans were able to do.[6] This transformation was almost universal, affecting fields and natural features as well as towns and villages, and could have been carried out only by the settlement of large numbers of peasant farmers. Such a mass movement of comparatively humble people followed neither the Roman nor the Norman conquest. Latin never became the mother tongue of the great bulk of the population of Roman Britain, and of the 350 or so place-names known from the period fewer than twenty-five are Latin. The remainder are British. The number of French based place-names introduced by the Normans is similarly small.

In spite of this transformation, however, sufficient place-name evidence survives to indicate a period of peaceful intercourse between the Romano-British population and incoming English settlers (Fig. 4). Chalfont, meaning 'calf spring', contains the element *funta* which, it has been suggested, was taken into Old English direct from the Latin *fontana*, learnt from Latin speakers before the collapse of Roman administration. Crafton and Crendon Lane both contain *croh*, from the Latin *crocus*, perhaps passed on by Romano-British people familiar with the name of a conspicuous flower.[7] Wendover preserves the dative plural of a British word to be translated as 'white waters'. The other place-names on Fig. 4 are hybrid in their formation, that is they combine British and English elements. Brickhill and Brill contain British and English words for hill, Chetwode is made up of two words for wood, whilst Panshill probably preserves the actual British name for an area of woodland together with the English element *healh*, or nook. Pressmore contains the British word for brushwood

[6] M. Gelling, 'The Evidence of Place-names', in P. H. Sawyer, ed., *Medieval Settlement* (1976), pp. 200–201.

[7] M. Gelling, 'Latin loan words in Old English place-names', in P. Clemoes ed., *Anglo-Saxon England* 6, (1977), pp. 1–14. M. Gelling, *Signposts to the Past* (1978), pp. 83–84, 80–82.

and the English word *mor*, a waste land. Even in hybrid form such names could have been transmitted from one people to the other only in a period of relative peace. It is uncertain whether or not the names of Datchet and Penn are of British origin.

Yet further fragile threads of continuity may perhaps be detected in certain church dedications.[8] In Germany at any rate those churches dedicated to St Lawrence can be shown to be of Roman origin. Those with this dedication in Buckinghamshire are grouped about known areas of Roman settlement, with no less than four in the north-east of the county in the valley of the Ouse where, as we have seen in chapter 1, the pattern of Roman settlement was particularly dense. Those at Cholesbury and West Wycombe are situated within the ramparts of Iron Age hill-forts, perhaps implying a continuity of political and religious significance for a very long period of time indeed, whilst Winslow is about two miles from the Roman sites at Horwood, which may well prove to be more than simple farmsteads. Winslow is in any case in that area of central Buckinghamshire where field-walking in recent years has dramatically revised our view of the density of Roman settlement on these heavy claylands.

Dedications to St Leonard may be of similar significance. St Leonard is said to have possessed some of the attributes of the Celtic hunter god, Cernunnos. The chapels of St Leonards in Aston Clinton and in Chesham, the latter becoming the separate parish of Chesham Bois by the end of the fifteenth century, are in what was probably a heavily wooded district, but within a mile or two of known Roman occupation sites. That at Foxcote is near a villa, and also on the edge of what later became Whittlewood Forest. Little Linford is in the valley of the Ouse, where Roman settlement was dense, and yet also on the edge of a wooded area, later the Forest of Salcey. Grendon Underwood was also in a wooded area, later the purlieus of Bernwood Forest, and just under a mile from Akeman Street.

[8] S. Applebaum, 'Roman Britain', in H. P. R. Finberg, ed., *The Agrarian History of England and Wales* I, ii, (1971), p. 260, n.

Taken in isolation such crumbs of evidence are ludicrously fragile, but when all the pieces are put together then the claim for a measure of continuity becomes very much stronger. It is likely that these place-names were the names of estates rather than of actual habitation sites, and it may not be impossible to detect very ancient estates centred on Brickhill, Chetwode, Brill, Chalfont, Wendover and Wycombe, estates which, as we shall see when we come to look more closely at one of them, Brill, may well be of Roman origins or perhaps even earlier. At the same time the case for the existence of a Romano-British population holding out in the Chilterns surrounded by hostile English tribes loses much of its strength since there is as much evidence of Romano-British continuity in the north of the county as there is in the south with, as we shall see, place-name evidence for the presence of British people in the neighbourhood of Brill.

These British survivals represent the oldest stratum of place-names to be found today in the Buckinghamshire landscape. There may well be others, since the British element in Buckinghamshire place-names has been only sketchily studied, and further research may well reveal more. There may also be place-names where the English disguise of a British word has so far proved to be impenetrable.

On Fig. 5 are marked what would appear to be the oldest surviving place-names which are English in origin. All, with the exception of Weedon, are likely to have been in existence by A.D. 650. Those containing the element *-inge* must certainly be among the oldest, since they incorporate a linguistic element probably obsolete by that date.[9] Those composed of a topographical element together with -*hām* have been shown in other counties in south-eastern England to be closely associated with Roman roads and settlements,[10] and, as Fig. 2 reveals, this can scarcely fail to be true for Buckingham-

[9] J. McN. Dodgson, 'The English Arrival in Cheshire', *Transactions of the Historic Society of Lancashire and Cheshire* 119, (1967), pp. 1–37.

[10] J. McN. Dodgson, 'Place-names from *hām* distinguished from *hamm* names, in relation to the settlement of Kent, Surrey and Sussex', in P. Clemoes ed., *Anglo-Saxon England* 2, (1973), pp. 1–50.

shire. There is every possibility of their having come into existence when such an association was still significant, perhaps during the fifth century. Those ending in *-hāmstede* and *-hāmtun* may be a little later, and perhaps at first referred to buildings on a large estate, a further pointer to the longevity of such entities.

The last group of place-names on Fig. 5 and probably the most recent in date is that incorporating *-ingas* or *-inga-*. These indicate the names of communities of people, names which in due course were extended to the territory in which they lived. They also contain a personal name, and it is generally thought that this may be the name of the real, or mythical, founder or leader of the community. Place-names of this kind are the only ones incorporating a personal name which are undoubtedly early, but even so they are unlikely to belong to the first phase of settlement.[11] As far as other place-names containing a personal name element are concerned, there is always the possibility that this is the name of some lord into whose hands the estate came, perhaps as late as the tenth century and with some implication of incipient manorialism, and long after the settlement itself had been established. This is particularly true for *-tun* place-names, but it may well apply to others. This possibility cannot apply to place-names composed entirely of topographical elements.

The remaining, and probably the most recent, name marked on Fig. 5 is that of Weedon, a name meaning a hill where a pagan temple or idol was to be found. This is probably not an early name, but may instead indicate an area in which paganism continued to be practised after its neighbours had been converted to Christianity. Whitchurch is about two miles away to the north. Could its stone church, so conspicuous and unusual that it gave the name to the village, have been built deliberately as a counterpoise to an isolated outpost of paganism?

From the fog of uncertainty surrounding the place-name

[11] J. McN. Dodgson, 'The Significance of the distribution of the English place-names in *-ingas, -inga-*, in south-east England', *Medieval Archaeology* 10, (1966), pp. 1–29.

Fig. 5. The earliest surviving English place-names

evidence and its interpretation certain broad generalisations emerge which are of the first importance, however difficult it may be to apply them in individual cases. Fig. 4 reveals a thin but widespread scatter of place-names indicating communication between British and English peoples, a social and linguistic continuity between the two which is beyond the reach of archaeology. Fig. 5 reveals a similar scatter of place-names which could have been formed only in the earliest period of the English settlement, and these are only the names which have survived unchanged. These two sets of names are almost certainly among the oldest to have survived into the twentieth century, but they are equally certainly not the only ones to have been formed by the middle years of the seventh century. There are well over thirty major place-names in the county which are composed entirely of topographical elements and which are just as likely to be as old. They include Stone, the various Stratfords, Linford, Horwood, Swanbourne, Hawridge, Claydon, Missenden, Twyford, Boveney, Dorney and Thorney, as well as the Rye in High Wycombe.

The Anglo-Saxon Chronicle gives A.D. 571 as the date for the capture of Aylesbury by the English. There is no reason to doubt the substantial accuracy of this if it is seen as a military and political event, something far removed from the peaceful penetration of existing settlement patterns by peasant-farmers, for whose presence in Buckinghamshire well before 571 there is now substantial evidence. We might go on to ask what exactly it was that the English captured at Aylesbury, and what it was called before they took it, but at present there are no answers to these questions.

Churches and estates

Within a generation of the establishment of English political authority over what was to become Buckinghamshire St Augustine had landed in Kent to begin the conversion of the English to Christianity. But progress was slow, and in 635 another missionary, St Birinus, came to work among the heathen in England. He established his see at Dorchester-on-

Thames and from here for the next fifteen years until his death in 650 he carried on his missionary work. According to legend Bapsey Pond in Taplow was one of the places where he baptised some of his converts. Bede records that Birinus built and consecrated churches but as far as we know no remains of these churches survive. Apart from these tantalisingly brief notices, there is no record of the spread of Christianity over what was to become Buckinghamshire. The see of Dorchester-on-Thames had a chequered history until eventually at some period after 1070 William the Conqueror transferred it to Lincoln.

The coming of Christianity did not lead to any rapid building of parish churches. Indeed the very concept of a village served by a priest from a parish church developed only very slowly and was not fully established on a country-wide scale until well after the Norman Conquest. Before this parochial organisation became established large areas of the country were served by a group of clergy living together communally and attached to a minster church. The word minster is derived from the Latin *monasterium*, but it is clear that in the eighth and ninth centuries it was a term applied to communities which were not strictly monasteries in the sense of being bound by a monastic rule. Domesday Book mentions quite casually the presence of a minster at North Crawley and there is some evidence to show that the church at Aylesbury, actually mentioned in Domesday Book, was also a minster.

A Christian community could practise its faith for a long period without a church and even when it acquired one it was not necessarily at first built of stone. Stone churches were however being built by the end of the seventh century, although only a handful of Buckinghamshire ones still retain any evidence of pre-Conquest work.[12] The nave and chancel at Hardwick are probably Anglo-Saxon on the evidence of the double-splayed round-headed window over the north door. The walls of the nave at Iver are also probably Anglo-Saxon. The lower part of the west tower at Lavendon, together with

[12] see H. M. and J. Taylor, *Anglo-Saxon Architecture* Vols 1 and 2, (1965), Vol. 3 (1978).

the main walls of the nave, are also late Anglo-Saxon, perhaps tenth-century. Important and interesting though these are they are far surpassed by the church at Wing[13] (Plate 6). Here is a stone-built church of basilican plan which may date from the end of the seventh century. It has a crypt, which had entrances from the nave. The crypt at first was a plain polygonal chamber with three recesses in its interior walls. It may have been a burial chamber, for whom we can only guess, perhaps for whoever it was who endowed the church, the recesses being used for his, or her, relics. Aelfgifu, a kins-woman of king Edgar, gave her estate here at Wing to him in her will at some date before 975. This royal association with Wing may have been a very long one and may well have been the reason for the building of the church and its crypt in the first place, since it is clear that no peasant-farmer would have been buried in so costly and imposing a tomb. Perhaps here at Wing is one of the earliest Christian equivalents of the princely pagan burial at Taplow, then less than a century old. At some time in the tenth century the crypt was vaulted over in stone, its central chamber was built, the apse walls were re-aligned and given their exterior decoration. Again we can only guess at the purpose of this rebuilding. We have only just begun to probe the history of one of the most fascinating buildings in the Buckinghamshire landscape. Excavation may yet tell us a great deal more about how and when it was built, but the almost total absence of documents means that we can never know why.

The gradual development of a network of parishes, each with a church and attendant priest, depended upon the building and endowment of individual churches on their estates by kings and lay noblemen. This was a very protracted affair. It was by no means completed by the time of the Norman Conquest, and it was but one facet of that fragmentation of great estates which was going on throughout the Anglo-Saxon centuries. This becomes clear from a study of those Anglo-

[13] E. D. C. Jackson and E. G. M. Fletcher, 'The Apse and Nave at Wing, Bucks.', *Journal of the British Archaeological Association* 3rd Series 25, (1962), pp. 1–20.

Saxon charters for Buckinghamshire which contain perambulation clauses describing the bounds of the estate being transferred. There are six of these, for Chetwode, Linslade, Olney, Monks Risborough, Upper Winchendon and Wotton Underwood.[14] The boundaries described correspond quite closely to ancient parish boundaries, but in only one case, that of Upper Winchendon, does the document we have record a grant made for pious purposes, and then the estate went to the monastery of St Frideswide in Oxford, and not to a parish church.

Some estates could be yet further sub-divided. That described in the Chetwode charter in fact comprised the parishes of Chetwode, Hillesden and Preston Bissett. Parish boundaries and names as they existed before the changes of the nineteenth century show that this process of subdivision must have been quite common. Thus the three Brickhills and the three Claydons in all probability each once formed one large estate, and the two Kimbles, Missendens, Linfords, Horwoods, Marlows, Wycombes and Chalfonts must also once have been one, whilst the parish boundaries of Lee and Bradenham give every appearance of having once been carved out of Wendover and West Wycombe respectively. That sub-division of an estate could take place by means of a charter which has subsequently been lost is hinted at in the place-name Buckland, which contains the Anglo-Saxon word for a charter, *boc*. It must have been the subject of a grant of some significance for the document to have given its name to the estate. This subdivision led to the creation of one of those very long, narrow estates, later parishes, which seem to be so marked a feature of the landscape of chalk scarp country in many parts of England. This shape has been traditionally ascribed to the need for each settlement along the spring-line at the foot of the scarp to have access to arable land in the vale, and pasture and woodland on the scarp and the dip-slope. This may well have been so, but not all of the Buckinghamshire scarp parishes are shaped like this. Neither Wendover nor Ellesborough could be

[14] M. Reed, 'Buckinghamshire Charter Boundaries', in M. Gelling, ed., *Early Charters of the Thames Valley* (forthcoming).

called long and narrow, whilst we know that the two Risboroughs once were one, giving a combined shape much less noticeably elongated than they appear to be when separate. We are only just beginning to appreciate the subtlety and complexity of the factors influencing settlement patterns, and such an explanation, by emphasising only one factor at the expense of others, is probably over-simple.[15] In any case such an explanation may be looking to the wrong reasons altogether, since the subdivision of an estate which is implied in the place-name itself could have been carried through with almost no reference to settlement patterns at all. We must look to a very much wider range of explanations, including political, personal and legal as well as economic, for the subdivision which created these extraordinary shapes.[16]

The perambulations in which the boundaries of these estates are described give us a great deal of incidental information about the Anglo-Saxon landscape. The references to headlands, where the plough was turned, to open land and to woods imply a variegated landscape, whilst the two sloughs and the reed-clearing mentioned at Chetwode hint at reclamation work still remaining to be done. On the other hand the use of what must have been isolated trees as boundary marks must surely imply that the woods had been cleared even from the boundaries at some parts of the estate. The Risborough charter contains the first surviving reference to the Icknield Way, and that for Olney suggests that the water-mill close by the church was already in existence. The boundaries themselves are composed for long sections of hedges and ditches which may have been constructed especially for the purpose. These often still survive, and counts of the species of shrub and tree in these hedgerows testify to their great age. The Black Hedge marks the boundary of Monks Risborough (Plate 7). It has been carefully studied by a group of naturalists and it contains on average 12.44 species in a thirty yard stretch. Such a score

[15] see P. J. Fowler, 'Agriculture and Rural Settlement', in D. M. Wilson, ed., *The Archaeology of Anglo-Saxon England* (1976), p. 34.

[16] cf. T. H. Aston, 'The Origins of the Manor in Britain', *Transactions of the Royal Historical Society* 5th Series VIII, (1958), pp. 59–83.

would suggest that the hedge may have been over two hundred years old when it was first mentioned in the charter of A.D. 903, implying a regulated, ordered landscape in the central Chilterns in the eighth century. The Black Hedge is exceptional in that it has been recorded and surveyed in this way. Its great size and the fact that it runs through a designated Area of Outstanding Natural Beauty would seem to indicate that its future is safe. Those hedges of the other recorded boundaries are not so fortunate, but are equally deserving of study and preservation.

The estates described in these documents are unusual only in that written accounts of their boundaries have survived. We may expect to find similar estates, with similar boundaries, all over Buckinghamshire, but there is no document to describe them for us. There are over twenty other Anglo-Saxon charters referring to places in Buckinghamshire, but none has a boundary clause. A closer look at one of these places, Horwood (Fig. 6), raises questions which are central to our understanding of the evolution of the Anglo-Saxon landscape.

The six known Roman occupation sites, one every 3.5 square kilometres, still have to be explored, but their presence suggests a large but dispersed Romano-British population, and we cannot be sure that there are not others still waiting to be found. These sites noticeably avoid the known Roman roads, but this appears to be characteristic of Roman rural settlement. The tendency of the English also to avoid Roman roads can be exaggerated, but perhaps they were merely fitting, or were fitted, into a recognised scheme of things. We know nothing of the history of these sites but it is likely that they were all deserted by the end of the fifth century.

But desertion must be seen in perspective. It does not necessarily mean the total depopulation of vast tracts of the countryside. It may simply mean that the inhabitants have moved a hundred yards down the road, held to the same locality by the irresistible pull of the arable fields. None of the Romano-British habitation sites in Horwood is more than a thousand yards from a settlement which has survived into more recent times, and some are very much closer. Such close

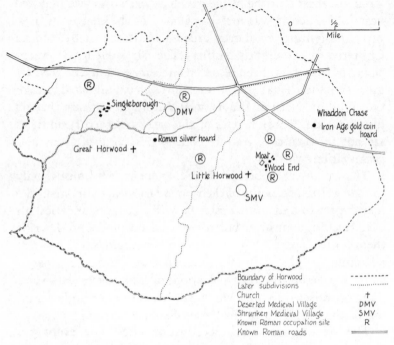

Fig. 6. Horwood

proximity suggests that the first English settled, or were settled, within an existing, known, framework which was only marginally disrupted by their coming, and that they in their turn became caught up in that slow ebb and flow of settlement, with no pattern stable for very long, which is characteristic of the prehistoric and Roman landscape. This ebb and flow of settlement is one of the most profoundly influential factors at work in the evolution of the Buckinghamshire landscape and it is discernible as far back in prehistory as it is possible to penetrate. The rate of change in this settlement pattern fluctuates markedly over time in response to a complex of political, social, economic and geographical factors, any one of which may predominate at any one moment in time and in relation to any one settlement. No single explanation will serve all the time, and to see the location of every village and farmstead solely in terms of soil quality or the availability of water is to be guilty of gross over-simplification. The emergence of written records, especially from Domesday Book, that arch-deceiver, onwards, by transforming territorial and kinship names into place-names, coupled with the seeming permanence of parish churches, has contributed immeasurably, both to the slowing down of this settlement drift and also to our own sense of the immutability of the towns and villages in which we live, but when seen *sub specie aeternitatis* it is ever-present, and the evidence for it is indelibly engraved upon the landscape.

But even if settlement did drift, as Fig. 6 would seem to show, we cannot on the other hand be really sure that any settlement is entirely new, occupying a virgin site. Of the twelve occupation sites in Horwood we know the names of only four. We may speculate a little as to the age of these names, but this tells us nothing of the age of the settlements. Somewhere under the houses and lanes of Great and Little Horwood, Wood End and Singleborough may well lie Roman and Anglo-Saxon occupation sites, undiscovered and undiscoverable.

This slow movement of settlement does not however seem to have been entirely without structure. Occupation sites appear to have circulated within ancient estate boundaries. Some of these boundaries are clearly very old indeed, whilst others represent a subdivision of large estates into smaller ones. It is most likely that Horwood was itself once part of a larger estate, and in due course it was broken into three. Singleborough is mentioned in Domesday Book, implying that it was a separate estate for tax purposes, and it may have had a long history as such, but it never became an ecclesiastical parish. Horwood is also mentioned in Domesday Book but the two are undifferentiated, although they became two separate ecclesiastical parishes. King Offa granted Horwood to the abbey of St. Albans in a document which, as it stands, is spurious but may well embody genuine material. It was Little Horwood that was the estate of the abbey and its boundaries may have been drawn at this time, although they were not described. They follow a Roman road for almost a mile in one part, and in other parts have that 'step' pattern which is consequent upon drawing boundaries around existing furlongs of arable land.

The case for continuity within an ancient estate at Horwood rests upon inference from the flimsiest evidence. There is much better evidence for an ancient multiple estate, bisected when the boundaries of Oxfordshire and Buckinghamshire were drawn at some time during the tenth century, centred on the royal manor of Brill, where there was in due course a prescriptive borough and market (Fig. 7). Several entirely unexplored Roman occupation sites are known. Two hybrid place-names, containing both British and English elements, are to be found here, namely Brill and Panshill. Two minor place-names, now lost, *Walecombe* and *Comberthornweye*, reveal that English settlers knew of the presence of British inhabitants. The name of a stream, *Geht* or *Yhyst*, also now lost, is pre-English. Documents of the fourteenth and fifteenth centuries[17] describe a number of services rendered by surrounding villages to the *caput* of the estate at Brill. Wotton Underwood and Chilton owed suit of oven. Other villages, including Beckley, Long Crendon, Ambrosden, Horton and Blackthorn owed unspecified tolls. Yet other villages paid agistment, a toll for the pasturing of livestock, and others, including Dorton, Arncote and Oakley, owed plough services. Land in Swanbourne paid rent measured in bowls of honey. The ecclesiastical centre of the estate was at Oakley, which had dependent chapels at Brill, Boarstall and Addingrove. Oakley church as late as 1853 was in fact in Brill parish, whilst the inhabitants of Boarstall were expected to contribute to its repair. All the features of this estate are echoes of features of well-recognised multiple estates in Wales and northern England.[18] There is even evidence of its progressive dismemberment, of which the grant in the middle of the ninth century

[17] H. E. Salter, ed., 'The Boarstall Cartulary', *Oxford Historical Society* LXXXVIII, (1930), pp. 194–197, 199–212.

[18] G. R. J. Jones, 'Post-Roman Wales', in H. P. R. Finberg, ed., *The Agrarian History of England and Wales* I, ii, (1972), pp. 281–382, esp. 380. G. R. J. Jones, 'Multiple Estates and Early Settlement', in P. H. Sawyer, ed., *Medieval Settlement* (1976), pp. 15–40.

74

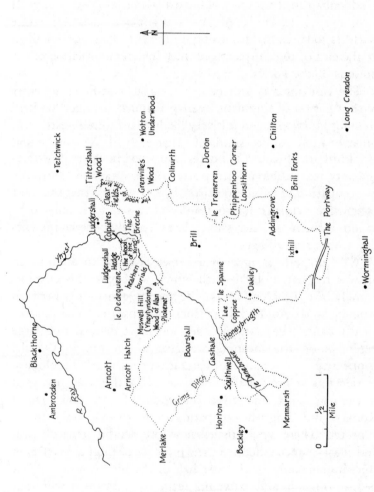

Fig. 7. The Multiple Estate at Brill and the Forest of Bernwood

by which king Berchtwulf gave Wotton Underwood to the thegn Forthred is but the earliest recorded stage. Henry I gave Kingsey to William Bolebec, by which time Radnage and Haddenham had also been alienated. King John and Henry III gave away other lands. All that was left of a once huge estate with its roots embedded deeply in the Iron Age was described at the end of the thirteenth century in a perambulation of the bounds of the Forest of Bernwood.

The case for a degree of institutional continuity together with a period of linguistic overlap is much stronger for Brill than for Horwood, and it is very likely that future research will uncover more estates similar to that at Brill. Wycombe and Brickhill are obvious candidates. Horwood however illustrates the very real problems facing attempts to establish continuity of occupation of habitation sites. It may well be that the most conclusive evidence for continuity of this kind is only to be found in the most inaccessible places, namely beneath present-day towns and villages.

We are perhaps now in a better position to attempt an answer to that problem with which we began this chapter, namely the problem of the degree of continuity between Roman and Anglo-Saxon Buckinghamshire. The answer clearly cannot be a simple one, and must depend to a large extent upon the meaning we give to continuity. On the continuity of occupation of habitation sites the archaeological evidence is at present inconclusive, but within the context of settlement 'drift' and given the extent of our knowledge of Roman and English occupation sites this is only to be expected. There is nevertheless now considerable archaeological and place-name evidence for the presence of English settlers in Buckinghamshire in the first half of the fifth century, if not before. Figs 4 and 5 would seem to indicate a thin but widespread distribution. That there was extended and peaceful contact between British and English there can be no doubt. There is sufficient linguistic, place-name and topographical evidence to suggest a significant measure of social and institutional continuity. Continuity of this kind could easily mask comparatively rapid ethnic change and is something which cannot be detected in the archaeological record. It is real nonetheless.

These conclusions can of necessity be only very tentative at present, but all the indications are that future research is likely to strengthen rather than to demolish them. Their most important implications are already clear. English peasant-farmers were to be found in Buckinghamshire well before A.D. 571. With their presence established we can be sure that there was no apocalyptic break between Romano-British and Anglo-Saxon Buckinghamshire. That the making of the Buckinghamshire landscape began again *ab initio* with the coming of the English can no longer be accepted.

The creation of Buckinghamshire

The Danish invasions and settlements of the ninth century and later, so important for the landscapes of Leicestershire and Lincolnshire, have left comparatively little permanent trace upon the Buckinghamshire landscape, although Danish armies marched through and across the county on a number of occasions, causing much destruction. The extent of their direct influence appears to be confined to a handful of personal and place-names. The personal names behind the place-names of Turville and Owlswick are of Scandinavian origin, and those behind Ravenstone and Turweston are probably so, whilst Fingest and Skirmett owe their modern form to Scandinavian influence. There is also good evidence for the existence of families of Scandinavian descent in Hughenden as late as the twelfth century, and field names containing Scandinavian names are to be found in Fawley, Risborough, Stewkley and elsewhere. The grouping of Scandinavian names in the Chilterns is very intriguing and would probably well repay further investigation.

The extent of their indirect influence is however very much more significant since it was English reaction to their invasions that led to the creation of the county itself. At the beginning of the tenth century king Edward the Elder began the reconquest of the Danelaw and as part of his military operations he built in 914 two fortresses at Buckingham, one on either side of the Ouse. A document called the Burghal Hidage,[19] to be dated to this time, gives details of the way in which fortresses like these were to be repaired and defended. Sixteen men could defend twenty-two yards of wall. The surrounding countryside, which was assessed in terms of hides, was to provide these men at the rate of one man from every hide. Buckingham is assessed at 1,600 hides, implying a mile and a quarter of fortifications. In some towns, such as Cricklade, Southampton and Portchester, the assessment in the Burghal Hidage can be checked against the surviving fortifications, and the two coincide to a quite remarkable degree. At Wareham, Lydford and Lyng the assessments take no account of any defences on a naturally protected side.[20] Unfortunately nothing survives on the ground of the fortifications of Buckingham, and the very limited excavation which has proved possible in the town has failed to locate them. On the other hand the perimeter defended by the Ouse may have been left out of account when making the assessment and so we may well be looking in the wrong place for signs of Buckingham's Saxon fortifications. Saxon Buckingham was probably much altered after the Norman Conquest since the building of the castle would almost certainly have meant the demolition of at least some houses, perhaps erasing that grid pattern of streets found in other Anglo-Saxon towns. The market place has the appearance of a later addition to an already established settlement, but any reconstruction must of necessity be highly conjectural. Only extensive excavation is likely to provide any accurate account of what may be called the first town in Buckinghamshire.

Buckinghamshire is first mentioned as such in 1016, but it is very likely that it was deliberately created as an act of state early in the tenth century to provide the territorial basis for the defence of Buckingham. Whoever drew its boundaries was

[19] D. Hill, 'The Burghal Hidage: the establishment of a text', *Medieval Archaeology* 13, (1969), pp. 84–92.

[20] C. A. Ralegh Radford, 'The Later Pre-Conquest Boroughs and their Defences', *Medieval Archaeology* 14, (1970), pp. 83–103.

over-generous. By the time of Domesday Book the county appears to have contained 2,074 hides, although of course the bases of assessment could have changed in the intervening period.

Buckinghamshire was an entirely artificial creation, and it is very possible that its boundaries cut across older, long-established political groupings. Thus it seems likely that the *Cilternsaetna,* a people mentioned only once, in a document called the Tribal Hidage, which may be dated at any time from the end of the seventh to the end of the eighth century, extended in a north-east to a south-west direction across the vale, the scarp of the Chilterns and much of the dip-slope, into Oxfordshire and Hertfordshire as well as Buckinghamshire. On their south-eastern boundary, drawn somewhere along the southern slopes of the Chilterns, they probably met the Middle Saxons, the ancient boundaries of whose kingdom may well be preserved in that privilege which the men of London claimed in the twelfth century, namely to hunt over the Chilterns, much of Surrey and that part of Kent west of the river Cray. The name *Cilternsaetna* means no more than a group of people who live by Chiltern, it makes no statement about their origins. As we have seen in the previous chapter the word *Chiltern* could well be pre-Celtic. By the time the Tribal Hidage was drawn up the people who lived by Chiltern had acquired some social cohesion, since they were responsible for 4,000 hides of taxation, and, to say the least, it is likely that their ethnic composition was predominantly English, but might there not be just a hint here of a territorial unit a thousand years old when the Tribal Hidage was compiled?

The boundaries of Buckinghamshire as they hardened, differed only very slightly from those of today. In the north Boycott and Lillingstone Lovell were detached parts of Oxfordshire, whilst Caversfield and a tiny parcel of Stratton Audley, both now part of Oxfordshire, were in Buckinghamshire, as was Towersey. In the south-west half of Ibstone and the whole of Stokenchurch were in Oxfordshire, as was Ackhampstead, represented now by a ruined chapel to the south of Lane End. Coleshill was in Hertfordshire, whilst much of Ashridge,

Nettleden, Frithsden and Great and Little Gaddesden, now in Hertfordshire, were in Buckinghamshire, as were four small detached portions of Drayton Beauchamp parish.

With the county and its boundaries now firmly established then the history of the making of the Buckinghamshire landscape may be said truly to begin.

Domesday Book

Within two centuries of the creation of Buckinghamshire as a separate county one of the most important, intriguing and elusive of all historical documents was compiled. Domesday Book has fascinated generations of scholars and historians. Indeed in some ways its very uniqueness as an historical record, the thoroughness and accuracy with which it appears to have been compiled, have tended to obscure appreciation of what it can reveal about eleventh-century England and what it cannot. It has by no means yielded all of its secrets and there is still controversy as to much of its meaning.

An immense amount of material is brought together in Domesday Book, but the clerks who compiled it entered their information in summary fashion and arranged it on the basis of the tenure of property rather than by geographical location. This means that for any one place a number of separate entries have to be brought together in order to give a complete picture. Thus there are six separate entries for Amersham and five for Chesham. Fortunately this preliminary work has been done for Buckinghamshire, and, indeed, for the rest of the country.[21] Nevertheless even when this problem has been overcome considerable difficulties still surround the interpretation of the text. For all its seeming air of precision the reality underlying Domesday Book remains all too often nebulous, intangible, just out of reach.

Domesday Book was compiled as a guide to the yield of estates to their lords and to record what taxes were due to the king. Its compilers were interested only in places through

---

[21] H. C. Darby and E. M. J. Campbell eds., *The Domesday Geography of South-East England* (1962, reprinted 1971), pp. 138–185.

which such payments were made, and ignored all the rest. Thus Domesday Book is quite unreliable as a guide to settlement patterns at the end of the eleventh century and the omission from it of any place is no indication that it did not then exist. Because neither Beaconsfield nor Fingest, Fulmer nor Hedgerley, Boarstall nor Hogshaw, appear, we cannot assume that they were not created until after 1087. All it means is that their taxes and dues were paid through some other place.

At the same time it is becoming increasingly clear that Domesday Book entries under individual places by no means always refer to nucleated villages but instead often aggregate dispersed hamlets and farmsteads. It seems likely that the resources of Anglo-Saxon England were almost as fully exploited in the seventh century as they were in the eleventh, and that the intervening centuries formed a period of shifting but not of expanding settlement. Those nucleated villages, so characteristic of some, but not all, parts of northern Buckinghamshire today, may well be the result of developments after the compilation of Domesday Book rather than before, whilst the pattern of dispersed settlement found in the Chilterns is probably much older than we think and may once have prevailed in the north of the county as well.

However, in spite of all the difficulties, some preliminary generalisations can be made. First of all it would appear from the information given in Domesday Book that Buckinghamshire north of the scarp was more densely populated than the south outside the Thames and Colne valleys. In the north the density was between five and ten persons per square mile, with eleven in the Vale, an area of heavy, poorly drained clays just below the scarp. In the Chilterns on the other hand the density varied between two and five persons per square mile, with eight in the Thames and Colne valleys.

Secondly, it is clear that some areas of the county were very much more thickly wooded than others. Woodland in the Buckinghamshire Domesday Book is measured in terms of the number of swine which it could support. Wendover had woodland for two thousand swine, and several other places,

Hanslope, Lillingstone Dayrell, Chesham, Wycombe and Marlow, could support over a thousand each. On the other hand no woodland at all is recorded for Ashendon, Granborough, Charndon, Chearsley, Haddenham, Hardwick and Mursley, nor for any of the townships in Cottesloe Hundred. These omissions may of course be due to oversight on the part of the clerks who compiled Domesday Book. From the Domesday record it would appear that the extreme north-west of the county, later to become part of Whittlewood Forest, the north-east, in due course to become part of Salcey Forest, Bernwood Forest and its purlieus, together with the Chilterns and the Burnham Plateau, were all substantially wooded. Much of the rest of the county was fairly open. But here a note of caution may not be out of place. If we assume for a moment that the estates described in Domesday Book correspond, even approximately, with ecclesiastical parishes, and if we equate a pig with an acre of woodland, then a rather different picture emerges: Chalfont, Chesham, Marlow and Wycombe would have about eleven to fourteen per cent of their area wooded, Wendover about thirty-four per cent, whilst Akeley would be sixty-two per cent wooded, and Leckhampstead, Tingewick and Grendon Underwood from twenty to thirty-eight per cent. The assumptions upon which these figures rest are open to very serious objections[22] but there may be just sufficiently firm a basis to cast some doubt upon the traditional view of a densely wooded Chilterns in the eleventh century, and to suggest that some parts certainly were as free of woodland as some districts in the north of the county.

Woodland was certainly important in Domesday Buckinghamshire as a source of fuel, building material, timber for every kind of domestic and manufacturing purpose, and of pasturage for livestock, but of greater fundamental importance was the arable. There are however two basic questions relating to the arable in Buckinghamshire in the eleventh century to which there can be no satisfactory answers: how much of it was there, and how was its cultivation organised? The arable in

[22] see H. C. Darby *Domesday England* (1977), pp. 172–3.

Buckinghamshire is measured in terms of ploughlands and ploughteams. The entries are usually comparatively straight-forward and uniform and it would appear that there should be as many ploughteams as ploughlands. Frequently when the number of teams is smaller than the number of ploughlands the deficiency is pointed out. On a few holdings, as at Milton Keynes, there were more teams than ploughlands. The connection between ploughlands and teams and reasons for the discrepancies have caused endless discussion but no very satisfactory explanation. Even more intriguing, and intractable, is the question as to what is meant by ploughlands and teams. It is clear that to a greater or lesser extent many of the measures given in Domesday Book are artificial in that they represent taxation assessments which often bore little relationship to reality. Nevertheless, bearing this reservation in mind, it would appear that in Buckinghamshire at any rate a plough-team could cultivate about 120 acres of arable land. If this is so, then we are presented with an astonishing picture. More of Buckinghamshire was under the plough in the eleventh century than in the twentieth, and this arable was as extensive in the Chilterns as in the north of the county.

How was the arable cultivated? We can see now that the traditional picture of the Anglo-Saxon landscape as one of huts clustered about the church to form a nucleated village and surrounded by great open fields carefully and systematically divided up into furlongs and strips is really a back-projection of the late medieval scene. The development of the mature common-field system of agriculture was a very long process and changes and refinements were being introduced in individual townships up to the eve of final enclosure, in itself a very long process.

Those estate perambulations that we have already discussed in this chapter refer to acre headlands, to a barley croft, a gore and to boundary hedges and ditches, to open ground, pasture and a herdsman's cabin. The presence of arable and pastoral agriculture is incontestible, but there is no hint that the arable was cultivated in common or that there was common of pasture either over the waste or over the stubble. It has been suggested[23] that the oldest element of the mature common-field system was the right of common grazing over waste and pasture. There is evidence of this in Buckinghamshire from before the end of the twelfth century and inter-commoning by several villages over one stretch of waste is not at all unusual. We find it over Lenborough Wild, Horwood Common, Wycombe Common and in Bernwood Forest. Rights of this kind may well go back long before the time of Domesday Book, but we cannot prove it.

Some form of sharing of the cultivation of the arable is known from the end of the seventh century in Wessex, although it is quite possible that only two or three partners were involved rather than a whole community. We cannot assume however from the Domesday Book entries alone that the arable, meadow and pasture of eleventh-century Bucking-hamshire was everywhere ploughed, mown and grazed in common from nucleated villages, even in the north of the county, by the thirteenth century a classic area for the traditional picture of the Midland common-field system. It is the tenth century before charters generally reveal any certain evidence of a common-field system, by which time it appears to be well-established in some parts of Berkshire with, as at Ardington, common share-land in pasture, meadow and arable. In many areas of Buckinghamshire, both in the north and in the Chilterns, the organisation of the arable into fields, furlongs and strips crystallised only during the course of the twelfth century, with further reorganisation of two fields into three during the thirteenth and fourteenth centuries. That the cultivation of some arable was, by the tenth century, shared, and that there was inter-commoning over waste, is fairly certain, but we cannot project these features of the rural landscape any further back into the past. Instead we must expect to find their gradual development in the landscape over a period of at least three centuries, with the compilation of Domesday Book coming in the first part of this period rather than towards its close.

[23] J. Thirsk, 'The Common Fields', *Past and Present* No. 29 (1964), p. 4.

How was the arable cultivated before the evolution of the common-field system was complete? The short answer is that we do not know. Ancient field boundaries, whether of the so-called 'Celtic' type, enclosing small, rectangular fields and perhaps as much as three thousand years old, and a more specifically Roman type, in which the fields are oblong and laid out in a regular pattern, have been recognised at a number of sites in England. Unfortunately however such fields are almost entirely unknown in Buckinghamshire. Several small square fields have been recognised near Iver from aerial photographs, but there is no visible trace on the ground. Others have been seen on aerial photographs of Pitstone Hill, but ploughing has obliterated any real surface evidence. The Chilterns generally, unlike large areas of chalk country in Wiltshire and Hampshire, appear to be remarkably free from traces of ancient cultivation, but this may be due to the fact that much of the chalk in Buckinghamshire is capped with Clay-with-Flints, with two consequences. Clay is much less responsive than other soils to the probing eye of the aerial camera, and the Chilterns are much more heavily wooded than the open downs of Hampshire and Wiltshire. These however are merely physical obstacles. Future research may find ways of overcoming them.

Nevertheless archaeology and field-walking, however meticulous, have their limitations. They cannot provide evidence that fields were cultivated in common, whether by small groups of partners or by a whole community, nor can they provide details of crop rotation and the common grazing of stubble and fallow. Only documents can do this, and they do not begin to survive for Buckinghamshire before the middle years of the twelfth century.

By the end of the eleventh century we can at last begin to talk about the Buckinghamshire landscape. The county boundaries have been established for at least a hundred years, and would remain unchanged until the nineteenth century. Many parish boundaries have been marked out, although here there are many more changes to record in the centuries from Domesday Book to the accession of Queen Victoria than there are for the county boundaries. There were already a number of stone churches in the landscape, although we cannot be sure exactly how many, since the great wave of building and rebuilding of the twelfth and thirteenth centuries and later has left behind so little work from any earlier period. It is very unlikely that any other building in the landscape would have been of stone, however imposing in the eyes of contemporaries. Timber buildings in-filled with a variety of materials except brick, and with thatched roofs, would have been universal, save for the poorest cabins, which might have been entirely of turf.

It is likely that more land was under the plough at the end of the eleventh century than at the end of the twentieth. In contrast however, in spite of the toil of generations, there was then very much more woodland and heath. Rivers were entirely uncontrolled and unimproved, so that extensive flooding in the valleys of the Thames and Colne, the Thame and the Ouse, must have been expected almost every winter. There were wide expanses of marsh in the valley of the Ousel, and the sloughs and reed beds of the Chetwode charter underline the very limited control of men over their environment at this time. On the other hand we must take care not to exaggerate the extent of woodland, especially in the Chilterns. Here it is possible that settlement and clearing had proceeded very much further than traditional accounts would allow. Certainly when the first documents begin to survive from the Chilterns they betray no signs of the hills being an untamed frontier.

It is also very likely that almost all the towns, villages and hamlets of twentieth-century Buckinghamshire had already been established, by the end of the eleventh century, so that the broad outlines of the modern settlement pattern were already laid. But the settlement pattern would have differed from that of today in two important respects. First of all even those places with the largest numbers of recorded inhabitants in Domesday Book, Wing, Waddesdon, Wycombe, Buckingham, Marlow, were very small indeed. Nowhere would there have been as many as five hundred people living together in one place. Secondly, there were then very many more small villages and hamlets than there are today. As we shall see later, many disappeared entirely, the victims of economic change, in the fifteenth and sixteenth centuries, whilst three, Gayhurst, Stowe and Wotton Underwood, were almost totally de-populated at the dictate of aristocratic taste in the eighteenth. As a corollary to this second point, many villages which today appear to be one were in the eleventh century composed of two or more distinct parts which have slowly grown together during the course of the intervening centuries. In spite of the immense changes those centuries have seen, the main lineaments of the landscape of Domesday Buckinghamshire are the oldest to have endured in a coherent pattern and as such they can still be recognised in the landscape today.

SELECT BIBLIOGRAPHY

Barley, M. W. and Hanson, R. P. C., eds. *Christianity in Britain, 300–700* (1968).
Chadwick, N. K., ed., *Studies in Early British History* (1954).
Cox, B., 'The Place-names of the Earliest English Records', *English Place-name Society Journal* 8, (1975–1976), pp. 12–66.
Gelling, M., 'Recent Work in English Place-names', *Local Historian* 11, (1974), pp. 3–7.
Gelling, M., 'Topographical Settlement Names', *Local Historian* 12, (1977), pp. 273–277.
Mawer, A. and Stenton, F. M., 'Place-Names of Buckinghamshire', *English Place-Name Society*, II, (1925, 1969 reprint).
Meaney, A., *A Gazetteer of Early Anglo-Saxon Burial Sites* (1964).
Ralegh Radford, C. A., 'Pre-Conquest Minster Churches', *Archaeological Journal* 130, (1972), pp. 120–140.
Sawyer, P. H., *Anglo-Saxon Charters: An Annotated List and Bibliography* (1968).
Sawyer, P. H., *From Roman Britain to Norman England* (1978).
Stenton, F. M., *Anglo-Saxon England* (3rd ed. 1971).

3. The early medieval landscape, 1150-1350 – I

The rural landscape. The quickening pace of change – Roads and bridges – Markets and fairs – Boroughs and new towns – Industries

FROM THE MIDDLE years of the twelfth century documents begin to survive in increasing numbers. From these it is possible to piece together something of the medieval landscape as it developed in the years up to the coming of the Black Death in 1348. At the same time the traces surviving of man's interaction with his environment during these centuries become both more numerous and more easily discernible in today's landscape than those of preceding ages. But man's mastery over his environment was still very precarious. He was entirely at the mercy of fire, flood, disease and famine. The great majority of men were illiterate, dependent upon ceaseless labour of the harshest kind for their survival. Theirs was a hand-made world, of wattle huts and thatched roofs, the parish church the largest building, and the only stone one, that many would ever see, horse-back the fastest they would ever travel, whilst the irrefrangible, iron cycle of ploughing, sowing and harvest marked off the years of their lives. Society was intensely and overwhelmingly rural, and was to remain so for centuries to come, and so it is to the medieval rural landscape that we must first turn.

The rural landscape

Those topographical differences between the two parts of the county described in chapter 1 make it necessary that we should deal with each part separately.

Documents, principally title deeds to parcels of land, begin to survive for north Buckinghamshire from the middle years of the twelfth century. From a study of these documents two points emerge. First of all it is clear that many features of the common-field system of agriculture were already present in the landscape, and secondly several of them contain sufficient to hint that they survive from a period which may have been critical in the development of this system. This second point is particularly important since, like every other feature in the landscape, the common-field system of agriculture has its own history. We must be careful not to project back into the remote past a vision of common-field villages based upon those marvellous sixteenth-century estate maps we have for Padbury (Fig. 17), Thornborough (Fig. 8), and Maids Moreton.[1] These maps portray a late sixteenth-century landscape, not an early medieval one. The system was neither static, since enclosure was going on throughout the medieval centuries, nor was it uniform, since almost every village and hamlet had some feature of its field system that defies any simple explanation, making generalisation both inaccurate and misleading.

However, after these preliminaries, let us begin our account of the rural landscape by looking at the arable fields. During the twelfth century there were usually only two in the village, so that half of its arable land would be lying fallow at any one time. But if the arable were divided into three then only a third would need to lie fallow, and this would lead to an increase in the amount of grain produced. During the course of the thirteenth and subsequent centuries many villages in the county changed over from two fields to three. Thus Hadden-ham had three by the early seventeenth century, as did Bradwell, Newton Longville, Wolverton, Westbury and Addington, for all of which there is early evidence of only two fields. Other villages clung to their two fields until final enclosure, as did Little Brickhill, Dinton, Steeple Claydon and Hardwick. The date of the change-over in almost all cases can be fixed only within very broad limits, but we are fortunate in having for Buckinghamshire an almost unique document

[1] see M. W. Beresford, *History on the Ground* (1971 ed.), p. 71.

recording such a change. In 1345 the lords of the manors of Mursley and Dunton agreed with their free and customary tenants that, their ancient mode of cultivation having proved unprofitable, they should in future sow two-thirds of their land each year, instead of half,[2] from which it is clear that the third field was to be created from a re-arrangement of the existing two, and was not taken in from the waste. Documents from Thornborough show that the change from two to three fields took place between 1317 and 1331.[3] Many of the furlongs in these fields are named on a map of 1613, from which it has proved possible to construct Fig. 8 showing this process of change.

These great open fields, whether there were two or three, sometimes stretching almost to the horizon, were not featureless plains. First of all they were divided from the waste and woodland, and sometimes from each other, by a hedge, combined with a ditch and bank. These served to keep grazing animals, both wild and domestic, out of the growing crops. Secondly these fields were in turn divided into furlongs, and the furlongs themselves were divided into strips. The strips of an individual villager lay intermingled with those of his neighbours and it is this pattern which some of our earliest documents enable us to see. For example in about 1220 Thomas de Hampton gave to the abbey of Oseney four and a half acres of land in Steeple Claydon. One *virga* lay in a furlong called Great Bancroft, next to the land of Henry de Kaam. Two more lay separately on Little Bancroft, both next to the land of Henry de Kaam. On Great Fiehuhhle lay two separate half acres, both next to the land of Henry de Kaam. In another document he gave land in *Kimmidesland,* in another field lying towards Padbury, and on *Manneslond,* all lying next to the land of Henry de Kaam.[4]

Documents of this kind, and they are very numerous, raise

[2] F. K. Gurney, 'An Agricultural Agreement of the Year 1345 at Mursley and Dunton', *Records of Buckinghamshire* XIV, (1941–1946), pp. 245–264.

[3] G. R. Elvey, ed., 'Luffield Priory Charters', Part 2, *Buckinghamshire Record Society* XVIII, (1975), pp. 343, 352.

[4] H. E. Salter, ed. 'The Cartulary of Oseney Abbey', Vol. 5, *Oxford Historical Society* XCVIII, (1935), pp. 215, 216.

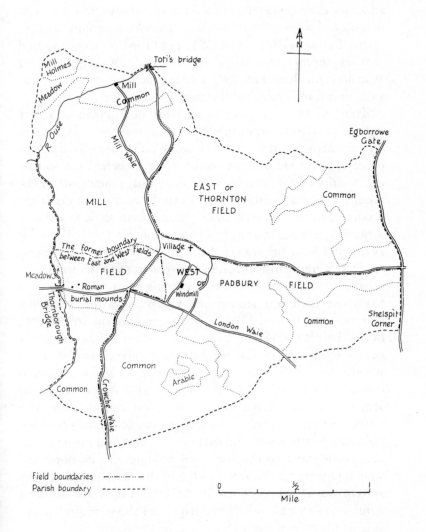

Fig. 8. Thornborough. Mill Field was carved out of East or Thornton Field and West or Padbury Field between 1317 and 1331.

an important question. Was it purely by chance that everywhere in the fields of Steeple Claydon the land of Thomas de
Hampton lay next to the land of Henry de Kaam, or does it
instead betray some regular pattern for the allocation of strips,
an arrangement whereby one man would always have the same
neighbours wherever his land lay? Frederick Seebohm, writing
in his *English Village Community*, published in 1883, noticed
that of seventy-two strips in the fields of Shipton, near
Winslow, no less than sixty-six had the same tenant on one
side, and forty-three had the same on the other.

There is evidence from many parts of England of a very
regular pattern of arrangement of houses in the village street
and of strips in the common fields called sun-division. Its
characteristics are as follows: the village was laid out so that
the widths of the houseplots of individual households in the
village were made proportional to the assessment to tax of the
holding attached to each house. Thus a farm assessed at half a
virgate would be attached to a house on a plot only half as wide
as the plot for a farm assessed at a full virgate. The houseplots,
or tofts, were themselves often arranged in two rows facing one
another across a street, and were considered to be arranged in a
clockwise direction around the village, and this clockwise
direction was followed for the arrangement of the strips in the
fields. This is significant, because the path of the sun across the
sky is clockwise in the northern hemisphere, and it was a
widely held belief that the lucky way to make a circular
motion is clockwise – hence sun-division. Accordingly, the
sequence of the strips in the fields was counted out with
reference to the apparent course of the sun across the sky. Thus
holdings in the south and east of each part of a furlong were
said to lie 'next to the sun', and holdings in the north and
west lay 'towards the shade'. One of the consequences of this
system was that everywhere in the fields a man had the same
neighbours on each side of his strips, and also of course on each
side of his toft in the village.[5]

The examples of Steeple Claydon and Shipton may refer,

[5] S. Goransson, 'Regular Open-Field Pattern in England and Scandinavian
Solskifte', *Geografiska Annaler* 43, (1961), pp. 80–104.

although indirectly, to sun-division. There is however, clear and unequivocal evidence of its presence in Buckinghamshire. At Water Stratford, a little before 1225, half an acre in the field towards Shalstone was said to lie *versus solem*, towards the sun. At East Burnham in 1208, seven plots of land were said to lie either towards the sun or towards the shade, together with one rood of meadow of the meadow of *Buveneia* (Boveney) towards the shade. In 1238 there was mention of land lying towards the sun at Sherington. In 1241 a moiety of thirty acres of land in Chesham was granted as it lay everywhere in the fields towards the shade. The latest example which can be dated is at Littlecote. Here in 1254 a moiety of six acres was granted as they lay towards the shade, and a moiety of another six as they lay towards the sun. Finally, an undated example. At Westbury at some time in the thirteenth century several parcels of land in an assart there lay towards the shade.[6]

These examples are widely scattered over the county, and further research will undoubtedly produce more. They do not seem to be confined to the claylands of the north, since Chesham is in one of the principal valleys of the Chilterns, and East Burnham lies on the southern slopes of the Burnham Plateau, with Boveney right on the Thames' edge. At the same time sun-division appears to have been applied both to assarted land and to meadowland.

Sun-division has been found in villages all over England, suggesting that the whole concept of the assessment of holdings in village and field for fiscal purposes is to be sought in a period well before the Norman Conquest. On the other hand the complete replanning of a village, perhaps on a new site, in order to give concrete representation to such assessment on the ground could take place very much later, perhaps as late as the twelfth or thirteenth centuries. There is now an impressive body of evidence from many parts of the country for the re-planning of villages,[7] although the purpose of this

[6] H. E. Salter, ed. op. cit. p. 421. M. W. Hughes, ed., 'A Calendar of the Feet of Fines for the County of Buckingham', *Bucks Archaeological Society, Records Branch* IV, (1940), pp. 33, 74, 77, 102. British Library, Harleian MS.4714, f. 321.

[7] M. W. Beresford and J. G. Hurst, eds., *Deserted Medieval Villages* (1971), pp. 117–131.

re-planning is in individual cases beyond the reach of archaeology. As part of this reorganisation peasants may have been brought together from scattered farms and hamlets into a regularly laid out village. Strips may have been allocated systematically and existing furlongs grouped into fields. That rearrangement of two into three fields, already discussed, may have been only the final phase of what must have been a protracted affair. Documentary references to sun-division constitute one kind of evidence for replanning, the plans of some villages represent another. A village such as Newton Longville is far too regular in the layout of its house tofts for it to have grown spontaneously. Even its name, new farmstead, estate or village, suggests deliberate creation, and at a date prior to 1086 since it is mentioned in Domesday Book. The original nucleus of the village may have been centred upon the church, with later extensions, marked by very regular tofts, south to Moor End, and to the west along Westbrook End Road. Much very detailed research at microscopic level is necessary before we can hope to know even some of the answers to the questions prompted by the possibility of deliberately replanned villages, but there is now sufficient evidence to suggest that such research may well be very rewarding indeed.

Arable fields and their layout were, literally, of vital importance to the medieval peasant. From them came grain for his bread and drink, and the wherewithall to pay his rents and taxes. Meadow, pasture, wastes and woodland were of almost equal importance since they provided grazing and fodder for livestock, especially the all-important draught oxen without which the arable fields could not be cultivated in the first place. Both meadow and pasture were often scattered in quite small parcels throughout a village. At Ilmer, for example, in 1337 there was one piece of pasture called the Hurst of an acre, and another, called *Chalfegate*, of only half an acre.[8] Frequently meadow and pasture were worth twice or three times the value of arable land. Thus at Little Brickhill in 1307 a hundred acres of demesne arable was worth 2d. the acre, but twelve acres of

---

[8] P.R.O. SC. 11/79.

meadow were worth 18d. the acre.[9] Wastes and commons were often shared for grazing by two or more villages, the inhabitants of which might enjoy yet other rights there as well. The villagers of Great and Little Horwood shared with those of Nash the right to graze horses, cows and sheep over the waste lands lying between the three villages, lands represented today by The Common, a cluster of houses on the road from Great Horwood to Nash, and by Common Farm, on the B4034 road from Buckingham to Bletchley. They also had liberty to mow furze, cut turf and dig mortar, gravel and sand.

Woods were as important as waste and common land, since they provided fuel and timber in addition to feeding grounds for pigs. The inhabitants of Little Linford had the right to cut wood in Little Linford Wood for fuel and to repair their houses, hedges, carts and ploughs. But some villages had no woodland at all. Thornborough, for example, had no recorded woodland at the time of Domesday Book, although of course this may have been merely an oversight on the part of the clerks who compiled the record. Nevertheless, that map of 1613 upon which Fig. 8 is based shows that there was no woodland there at that time either. The scrub which would have covered some parts of the commons may have provided the villagers with some firewood, but the absence of large timber for building purposes may have forced them to turn to other materials. A kiln, perhaps for the making of tiles, and a stone quarry, are both mentioned before the middle of the thirteenth century.

The clearing of the woodland from a village like Thornborough went entirely unrecorded. For other villages there is some documentary evidence of this clearing, although this evidence is fragmentary, recording only some parts of the final episodes in a very long story, and it disappears altogether by the first decades of the fourteenth century. In the extreme north-west of the county the monks of Luffield Priory played a major part in this process of clearing, a process called assarting from a French word meaning to grub up tree roots. Parcels of Lillingstone Wood and of Westbury Wood were granted to them during the

[9] P.R.O. C. 133/128 No. 26.

course of the thirteenth century, and the deeds of gift usually mentioned that they might assart and enclose their new acquisitions. Thus in about 1260 they received from James son of Geoffrey le Sauvage a gift of two acres of his wood of Westbury lying next to the three acres which he had already given them, and extending from the way called the Cowpath as far as the wood which Simon de Sancto Lycio had already given to them. This they could clear and enclose with a bank and ditch. Here we can see the monks adding quite small pieces of woodland to their existing holdings, with the right to clear and enclose. The progress of this assarting was quite fortuitous, depending as it did upon the generosity of the pious, but its long-term effect was a steady, and permanent, reduction in the area of woodland. Examples such as these reveal, quite incidentally, that the woodland to which they refer was not an untamed wilderness but rather an area of specialised land use, carefully divided up into comparatively small plots, its economic value fully realised and fully exploited.

Assarting was also taking place further south, both within the royal Forest of Bernwood itself and in its purlieus, during the thirteenth and fourteenth centuries, but again we can only guess at its extent. The king could allow assarts to be made in the royal Forests whenever he wished, and several licences to enclose and assart are known for this part of Buckinghamshire. In 1305[10] John de Haudlo was given permission to enclose with a ditch and low hedge 401 acres of land in six separate pieces, including one of 20 acres in *Le Wecche* near to Ludgershall, 59.5 acres in Costowe, and another 138.5 acres called *lescleres* of Ludgershall. He could bring the land into cultivation but was to have no rights of common in the Forest. For this he paid a fine of £7 18s. 10½d., and agreed to pay a rent of 29s. 8½d. a year. Clearfields Farm, in the parish of Brill, stands today in fields cleared of trees by the men of John de Haudlo in the early years of the fourteenth century (see Fig. 7).

By the middle of the fourteenth century much of north

[10] *Calendar of Patent Rolls, 1301–1307*, p. 310.

Buckinghamshire was densely inhabited and pressure upon land and resources must have been intense. The common fields and their organisation, characteristic of many north Buckinghamshire villages, were in some respects a response to this pressure. In some areas marginal land was being pressed into cultivation. The ploughing of comparatively steeply sloping hillsides in parallel with the contour has produced terrace-like strip lynchets in a number of parishes, including Chearsley, Upper Winchendon and Cheddington, where they are now overgrown with gorse and scrub. As we shall see in the next chapter only the Forest Laws and the authority of the Crown were able to preserve any really extensive areas of woodland in the face of these pressures, and even here clearing and enclosing for cultivation were going on. We must now look at the rural landscape of south Buckinghamshire before turning to some other features of the early medieval landscape.

The early medieval rural landscape of south Buckinghamshire differed markedly from that of the north of the county. The contrasts are brought out by Figs. 9 and 10, respectively the northern, lowland, part, and the southern, Chiltern, part, of the parish of Aston Clinton. The evolution of both landscapes was influenced by the underlying characteristics of their geologies. The Chilterns are marked by steep-sided valleys between long ridges of hills. This difficult terrain imposed upon its inhabitants a discipline altogether different from that prevailing in the more open, flatter north. However we must be careful not to push geographical determinism too far since we are only just beginning to appreciate something of the complex interplay of physical, social, political and economic factors at work in the making of the Buckinghamshire landscape and much remains to be done before we can be sure that we have a satisfactory explanation of the differences between the north and the south of the county.

There certainly were common arable fields in the Chilterns by the end of the twelfth century, but there were very many more of them and they were much smaller than would be found in a village in the north. Thus there were nine arable fields in Little Hampden and seven at Lee. Much arable was

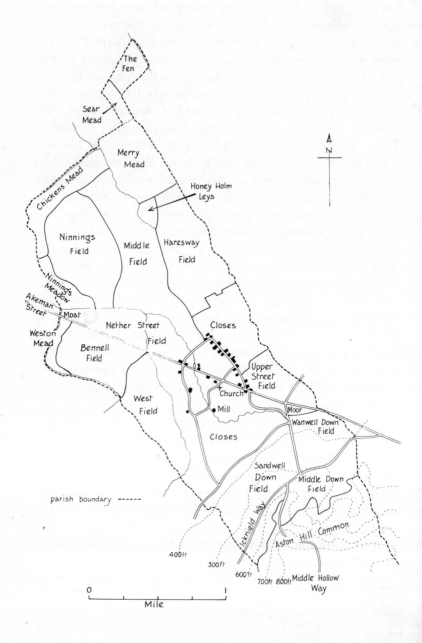

Fig. 9. Northern Aston Clinton

Icknield Way

Aston Hill
Common

Middle
Hollow
Way

Sandwell
Hollow
Way

Sawfield
Wood

Bradninch
Wood

Tatnalls
Wood

Heath

Hen
Grove

Heath

Chivery

St Leonards

Dundridge

N

parish boundary ------

0   1

Mile

Fig. 10. Southern Aston Clinton

also enclosed and held in severalty, particularly demesne lands. In the middle of the thirteenth century the demesne arable of West Wycombe manor lay, enclosed and in severalty, in eight fields. These eight were arranged into three groups for purposes of crop rotation. At Ibstone about half of the cultivated land of the manor was in demesne, and this lay in ten enclosed fields. Two contained at least seventy acres each, two more were over thirty acres each, whilst the remaining six were all smaller than this.[11] Nowhere in the Buckinghamshire Chilterns is there evidence of a simple three-field system extending over the whole of the arable of a parish.

Arable land seems almost always to have been surrounded with hedges. Indeed enclosure may have been a preliminary step to bringing the land into cultivation. Thus during the course of the second half of the twelfth century the monks of Missenden Abbey were granted all the land in Peterley which they had surrounded with hedges and ditches, and which, before they had possession, lay waste and uncultivated. At the same time the subdivision of existing fields was also taking place. At the end of the thirteenth century the abbey of Missenden was given land in two fields, *Denefeld* and *Porinfeld*, in Kingshill, lying next to land already in the abbey's possession in the fields, from which it was divided by a hedge.

In spite of the dominance of arable farming in the rural economy of the Chilterns in the medieval centuries, sheep were important and landowners often had sizeable flocks. But meadow and pasture for livestock generally depend upon a good supply of water for the grass, and so the borders of streams were frequently set aside for this purpose. The foundation endowment of Missenden abbey included meadow along the Misbourne. The absence of running water in the Chilterns away from the main valleys meant that meadow and pasture were often scarce, or of poor quality, or both, and frequently lay in small parcels. Thus at Wendover in 1302 there were 250 acres of arable in demesne, worth 4d. the acre a year, but the twenty acres of meadow were worth 12d. the

[11] D. Roden, 'Field Systems in Ibstone during the Later Middle Ages', *Records of Buckinghamshire* XVIII Part 1, (1966), pp. 43–57.

acre, and the pasture, which was in severalty and lay in scattered parcels which could not be measured, was worth 6s. 8d. a year in all, whilst three and a half acres of meadow in Great Missenden in 1332 were said to be worth 12d. the acre and no more because they were dry and exhausted.

Meadow and pasture, like arable, could be held in common or in severalty. At Chesham in 1330 the seven acres of meadow in demesne were in severalty only between Lady Day and Midsummer, just when the grass would have been at its best. It is clear too that grazing rights were exercised over the arable when it lay fallow. When the abbot of Missenden's third field at Honor End was not sown then, in about 1180, it was agreed that Alexander son of Richard of Culworth and his men should have common of pasture there. Some pasture lay in parks, where the deer despoiled it. At Chesham in 1330 the grazing in the park would have been worth 13s.4d. a year but for the deer, whilst at Penn in 1325 the pasture in the park there was said to be worthless because the deer grazed there.

In spite of centuries of clearing and colonisation the Chiltern hills in medieval times were still characterised by extensive woodlands and heaths. As late as 1576 Wycombe Heath was said to extend over two thousand acres. Assarting was drawing to an end by the beginning of the fourteenth century, since the economic value of woodland and the fact that it was not limitless was becoming increasingly appreciated.

Medieval woodland in the Chilterns was generally much more mixed than it has since become, and much of it was a mixture of fully grown standard trees yielding timber at irregular and infrequent intervals, and coppice or underwood which could be made to yield wood annually if properly managed. The underwood was composed of a wide variety of species of trees, including ash, oak, hazel, maple and elm. These were cut regularly to produce firewood, fencing stakes and poles. Almost all medieval valuations of Chiltern woodland show that any profit came from this underwood rather than from mature timber.[12] The importance of this aspect of

[12] D. Roden, 'Woodland and its Management in the Medieval Chilterns', *Forestry* 41, (1968), pp. 59–71.

woodland management was probably due to comparatively easy access to good markets. Much firewood was sent from Marlow to London along the Thames, and so continued until well into the eighteenth century, whilst cartloads of firewood and charcoal were from time to time sent from Ibstone to Merton College, Oxford, the landlord of that village, and to other College manors in the vale.

The other profit from woodland was pannage, the payment of a sum of money on the part of a farmer in order that he might turn his pigs into the woods to feed, particularly on beech mast. But the beech does not produce mast every year; there is a good fall perhaps every four to seven years, and so yields from pannage dues fluctuate according to the mast. This is made clear in several medieval valuations of Chiltern woodland. At Penn in 1325 the pannage in a hundred acres of wood was worth 4s., when the mast fell. At Great Missenden in 1332 forty-eight acres of woodland yielded 40d. when the mast fell, and at Chenies in 1335 twenty acres were worth 12d., again when the mast fell.

Some woods were private, others common. Private ones were frequently marked off by hedges and ditches, and larger ones were divided up into sections by this method. By the end of the twelfth century there is documentary evidence of an active market in the buying and leasing of plots of woodland in much the same way as arable or meadow, causing both fragmentation and consolidation of holdings, as well as providing an indicator of the value attached to woodland.

In addition to private woods there were also extensive areas of common woods. The right of tenants and villagers to graze their livestock over common woodlands and to cut wood for fires, fences and for house repairs was known in the Chilterns as 'Hillwork' and this, in a corrupted form, has left an indelible mark on the landscape in the place-name Hillock Wood, above Princes Risborough. Rights of common imply indiscriminate felling and uncontrolled grazing, leading eventually to the conversion of even the thickest woodland into scrub and heathland. This is the reason for the zeal with which woods were hedged and ditched. Only by keeping out domestic animals could the woodlands be preserved, and this required enclosure and tenure in severalty. As early as 1183 the common wood called *Raueningus* in Great Missenden was divided up so that the abbey of Missenden could hold its part in perpetuity, and in 1284 Robert Mantell gave up his rights of pasturage in Hydegrove Wood, agreeing to its enclosure by the abbot of Missenden. The more people with rights of common the more difficult it could be to secure agreement to enclose or to stint, and the greater the likelihood of the woodland degenerating into heath and scrub. It was alleged in 1576 that the inhabitants of Penn, Hughenden, Great and Little Missenden and the Foreigns of Wendover and High Wycombe could all pasture all manner of cattle on Wycombe Heath, and take thorns, bushes, holly, hazel and *wrygge* – the local dialect word for willow. There was probably not much else to take.

Chiltern woodland has altered a great deal since early medieval times. The beech woods of today are essentially the creation of the last two hundred years, during which time there has been extensive felling and planting. It is estimated that at least a third of today's woodland occupies land which was once arable.[13] Some woodland is undoubtedly ancient, such as much of Penn Wood, but it is clear first of all that the boundaries of woodland have fluctuated markedly, with some woodland remembered only in place-names such as Prestwood and Nairdwood Farm, both in Great Missenden, and secondly that the nature of the tree cover itself has changed considerably from one in which oak, ash and other trees were just as common as beech, to one in which over considerable areas the beech tree far outnumbers any other species.

Before we turn to other aspects of the landscape of early medieval Buckinghamshire one final point needs to be made. We have looked in turn at fields, woods and meadows, but this was merely for our own convenience. Such an approach can give an impression of a neatly compartmentalised landscape

---

[13] A. Mansfield, The Historical Geography of the Woodlands of the Southern Chilterns, 1600–1947. Unpublished M.Sc. thesis, University of London, (1952), p. 27.

which is entirely false. The maps of Thornborough (Fig. 8) and Padbury (Fig. 17), and Aston Clinton (Figs. 9 and 10) point instead to an untidy, unkempt landscape in which boundaries between arable, meadow, waste and wood were often ill-defined and poorly maintained, overgrown with weeds, brambles and thorn scrub. Roads were broad tracks worn hollow with use in the absence of proper surfacing, unfenced and lacking any signs to guide the traveller. We must not allow recollections of today's trim and ordered landscape to colour our reconstruction of that of these early medieval centuries.

The quickening pace of change

Arable fields, pasture, meadow, wood and waste were but one part of the medieval landscape. Medieval villages were isolated, cut off from their neighbours by a combination of bad roads and a tight-knit social organisation which regarded strangers with hostility and suspicion. But this isolation can be exaggerated. People did travel, and at times they could cover immense distances. We know, for example, that Ivo of Barton Hartshorn could, before the end of the twelfth century, at least contemplate a pilgrimage to Jerusalem, and among the burgesses living in Wendover at the time of Edward I were two from Leicester, one from Berkhamsted and four from Hampden. Such travel, whether near or far, is both the reason for, and made easier by, the development of a network of roads, fords and bridges, for which there is increasing evidence as the thirteenth century wears on. Travellers are not, how-ever, inanimate objects. They carry with them goods and merchandise, new ideas and new skills. Markets and fairs were established, at first spontaneously, but then increasingly as a deliberate political act intended to attract trade, and hence wealth, either to hitherto isolated rural settlements or else to towns newly established. At the same time new industries emerged, old ones developed, and trades and occupations became increasingly specialised. Each of these facets of medieval society has left its own mark upon the landscape.

Each was part of an infinitely varied and complex whole. Each was subject to, and the vehicle of, a slow but quickening process of change, a process that accelerates as we draw nearer to our own time.

Roads and bridges

Some parts of that dense network of Roman roads described in chapter 1 fell into disuse, whilst other parts, to a greater or lesser extent, became the basis for a pattern of roads and lanes clearly of considerable complexity by the beginning of the thirteenth century. Two of the principal Roman roads in the county have continued in use down to the present, and it is by their English names, Akeman Street and Watling Street, that we know them. That from Towcester to Dorchester-on-Thames, crossing the Ouse at Water Stratford, has also continued in use over much of its length, being known in the early thirteenth century as *Buggeldestreet*, the street of goblins.

Two of the four great roads on which, by the end of the eleventh century, travellers enjoyed the king's special peace, crossed Buckinghamshire. They were Watling Street and the Icknield Way, the other two being Ermine Street and the Fosse Way. Gradually the king's peace was extended to all the major roads in the country, and the concept of a national network, based upon London, slowly emerged. Towards the middle of the fourteenth century the course of the majority of these roads was drawn, on the whole with considerable accuracy, upon the Gough Map, now in the Bodleian Library at Oxford. Five main roads are marked, of which three crossed Buckinghamshire. The first was the London to Bristol road, crossing the southern part of the county from Colnbrook to Taplow. The second was the London to Oxford road, running through Denham, Beaconsfield and High Wycombe, this last being one of the three recognised stages on the journey, the other two being Uxbridge and Tetsworth. The third ran from London to Carlisle, passing through Stony Stratford.[14]

[14] F. M. Stenton, 'The Road System of Medieval England', in D. M. Stenton, ed., *Preparatory to Anglo-Saxon England* (1970), pp. 234–252.

It is clear from documentary references from the last half of the twelfth century that the gaps between these main roads were filled with a dense network of roads, lanes and ways. There was a *Woddeway* in Shalstone, represented today by the lane running north to Wood Green and Three Parks Wood, as well as a *Rugeway* and *Huntemilnewey*, this last surviving in Huntsmill Farm. In Thornborough we learn of the Millway before the middle of the thirteenth century. It is clearly marked on the map of 1613 which served as the basis for Fig. 8, and survives today as an unfenced cart-track leading off into the fields in a north-westerly direction from the Thornborough to Leckhampstead road.

These roads, whatever the name and however important they were, constantly needed repair. Roman engineering skill went with the last of the legions and it was to be the end of the eighteenth century before English roads again reached the standards obtaining during Roman rule. The heavy clays of north Buckinghamshire must have been particularly difficult to cross. Roads here, with no adequate foundations and lacking the most elementary drainage, must have been thick with mud in the winter and baked hard in the summer. Conditions are brought vividly to life in the terms of an indulgence of twenty days granted in 1292 by the bishop of Lincoln to all those who would contribute to the repair of the public highway called Walton Street in Aylesbury, and the neighbouring roads, where the mud lies so deep as to prevent travellers passing along, especially in winter.

None of the rivers in Buckinghamshire, not even the Thames, was a serious barrier to travel. All could be crossed either by bridges or fords or ferries, and sometimes by all three. The Romans built bridges at important river crossings. Timber uprights have been found at Thornborough which may be the foundations of a bridge carrying what is now the B4034 over a tributary of the Ouse. But bridges are even more susceptible to decay and neglect than are roads. Winter floods would quickly carry away rotting timbers and cause stone piers to collapse. Two of those Roman roads which the English continued to use must at one time have crossed rivers by means of fords, as the place-names, Water Stratford, Stony Stratford and Fenny Stratford, testify. Perhaps the collapse of a bridge over the Thame compelled early English travellers to find a convenient ford a little to the north, explaining the divergence of Akeman Street away from the line of the Roman road between Haydon Hill and Fleet Marston.

Bridges over rivers were certainly being built by the first half of the thirteenth century, as references in documents testify. Avicebridge in Barton Hartshorn is mentioned as early as 1225, Boycott bridge in the following year, and the warden of Marlow bridge in 1227. Toti's bridge, referred to before 1231, still carries the Leckhampstead to Thornborough road (Fig. 8) although of course it has been many times rebuilt since the eponymous Toti first saw it. A bridge at Stony Stratford is mentioned in a document to be dated between 1200 and 1205, and that at Newport Pagnell is referred to in 1187.

However, of these medieval bridges only one now survives, and that is at Thornborough, on the road to Buckingham. A *Bryggewey* is referred to in Thornborough before 1331, by which time the bridge we see today may well have been built. A new bridge, a little further upstream, has recently been erected, and the road with its heavy motor traffic now bypasses the medieval one, so that its preservation for future generations seems now assured (Plate 8 and Fig. 8).

Markets and fairs

Traffic in goods and merchandise led to the establishment of markets and fairs, in which commerce could be carried on openly, honestly and safely.[15] Markets and fairs differed only in that a market was held weekly, a fair annually. At first both markets and fairs could arise spontaneously, but by the end of the thirteenth century the Crown had firmly established its claim that they could be held only after a grant by a royal charter.

There is no overt reference to a market in the Domesday

[15] M. Reed, 'Markets and Fairs in Medieval Buckinghamshire', *Records of Buckinghamshire* (forthcoming).

Book entries for Buckinghamshire, although the toll in Aylesbury was said to be worth £10. The first clear reference to a market in the county comes in the charter of 1187 by which Gervase de Paganell granted to the monks of Tickford priory, licence to buy and sell their necessities free from toll in the *forum* of Newport Pagnell. Then in 1194 Richard I gave a weekly market to Gilbert Basset at his manor of Strafford, which can be identified with Stony Stratford, and in July of 1200 king John granted a Friday market and a two day fair at Amersham. After this, grants of markets and fairs followed in quick succession, so that by 1348 all but eight of the markets and fairs ever to be created in Buckinghamshire had been established.

Grants of markets and fairs were almost always obtained by the lord of the township. He would be very well aware of the profits he could expect from the rents and tolls he would charge those who attended his market. At the same time, at the height of the main period for the creation of markets, that is to say the years from 1200 to 1348, it is clear that the grant of a market from the Crown became almost fashionable, a mark of political prestige and royal favour. Little attention seems to have been paid to the long-term prospects of the market, and to obtain a royal charter did not necessarily mean that a market actually came into existence or that it lasted for very long. For example Hugh de Vere, Earl of Oxford, was granted a market at Whitchurch in 1245. It is last heard of in 1330, when its tolls were said to be worth 18s. a year. Nevertheless this market has left a permanent mark in the landscape. Market Hill is still to be found in Whitchurch today, partially encroached upon by sixteenth- and seventeenth-century cottages, but still there, outside what is left of the Earl's castle, where he laid it out over seven hundred years ago (Plate 9).

By 1500 only fifteen markets survived in the county, and by the end of the nineteenth century more than half of these had also disappeared, but a number of Buckinghamshire towns and villages still retain evidence of their markets, whether or not the market itself still survives. The open space in front of the

Crown Inn at Great Horwood was where the market granted in 1447 must have been held. It is last mentioned in 1666, when it was said to be long discontinued. The Market Square in the centre of Winslow is now used as a car park. The Market Hall at Amersham, built at the expense of Sir William Drake in 1682, still remains as one of the most attractive buildings in a very attractive town.

Boroughs and new towns

The growth of market towns is closely associated with the development of boroughs and with the planting of new towns, since all boroughs had markets, but not all market towns were boroughs. Boroughs could be prescriptive or they could be the result of grants from the Crown or from an overlord. The features distinguishing boroughs from other towns and villages are complex and vary over time. During the medieval centuries a number of attempts were made to draw up lists of boroughs, since they paid taxes at a different rate from that of rural villages, but no two lists are alike, several towns appearing on one list and not on another. Boroughs also had the privilege of returning members to Parliament, but again there is no consistent list of those with this privilege. What is perhaps the touchstone of a borough is the presence of burgage tenure.[16] Under this form of land-holding the tenant paid only a small annual rent in cash to his lord, was exempt from the often onerous labour dues which villeins in rural manors had to perform, and could sell his property as well as bequeath it by will. The achievement of borough status is marked by the creation of burgage plots. These had a comparatively narrow frontage on to the street, but often were very lengthy, extending back sometimes for as much as two hundred feet. Such plots were often laid out regularly by professional surveyors. The boundaries they created have proved to be one of the most permanent marks in the landscape. Only modern town-planning, with its combination of compulsory purchase and the bulldozer, has been able to erase them.

[16] M. W. Beresford and H. P. R. Finberg, *English Medieval Boroughs* (1973), p. 26.

If we put together all these indicators of borough status, then we find that there were no less than sixteen towns in Buckinghamshire which could claim to be boroughs at some time during the medieval centuries (Fig. 11). Only two, Buckingham and Newport Pagnell, are clearly boroughs at the time of Domesday Book in that they are said to have burgesses living in them. In the others borough status seems to have been acquired after 1086, although for none of them is there evidence that it was acquired by royal charter. Certainly Amersham, Wendover and High Wycombe would in due course be described as prescriptive boroughs. There is not space here to discuss all of these boroughs and in any case much research still remains to be done on their early history. Evidence for the borough at Eton, for example, depends at present upon a single reference to a *burgagium* there in a document dated 1217.[17] In some of the others a study of their plans can tell us something of their past history, revealing that burgage plots were added to an already existing village. At Wendover, for example, the borough was established on a new site about half a mile to the north of the parish church at the very beginning of the thirteenth century. Over a hundred burgesses are recorded there at the end of the thirteenth century, and the borough appears to have been so successful that it pulled to itself any settlement that there might have been about the parish church, leaving the church in a rather isolated position. A borough is recorded at Olney as early as 1237, and the town plan[18] reveals that the burgage plots were laid out according to a regular plan north of the old village, with the market place at the junction of old and new. By 1301 there were fifty-six burgesses, making the borough at Olney little more than half the size of that at Wendover. On the other hand that at Whitchurch was altogether much smaller. In 1264 the rents paid by the burgesses amounted to 40s., indicating that there were perhaps twenty in all.

One of the most interesting, and most obscure, of these burghal additions is to be found at Winslow. References to the

[17] British Library, Cotton MS. Cleopatra C vii f. 86.
[18] see M. W. Beresford, *New Towns of the Middle Ages* (1967), p. 107.

Fig. 11. Medieval boroughs in Buckinghamshire

'new town' on the manor of the abbot of St Albans at Winslow occur frequently through much of the thirteenth and early fourteenth centuries, and in 1279 ten burgesses were recorded, each paying 3s. a year in rent.[19] Little further is known of this attempt to plant a new town in the Buckinghamshire landscape, but the outlines of the burgage plots laid out by the monks and their surveyors in the thirteenth century are still to be seen in the town today. A market was granted at Winslow in 1235, and a market square was laid out to the south of the church. The island of buildings between the churchyard and the market place, and that on its southern side containing the George Hotel, are probably later encroachments. To the west of the market place lay the old village, an agglomeration of lanes and buildings with no recognisable plan. But to the east of the church and the market a series of regular plots was laid out, with narrow fronts on to the street, and with a back lane to give access to the rear. The shops on this front are still fairly symmetrical in breadth, although at least one now takes up two plots, and Greyhound Lane still gives access to the rear (Fig. 12).

Thus by the middle years of the fourteenth century a number of settlements could be distinguished from the great majority of villages in the county, first of all by the legal privileges enjoyed by their inhabitants, and secondly by the distinctive marks upon the landscape these privileges entailed, namely the laying out of a market place and of burgage plots. The two were sometimes combined in a borough, although, as we have seen, there were a number of Buckinghamshire villages with markets but no pretensions to burghal status. No medieval Buckinghamshire borough ever acquired economic, political or social significance beyond its immediate region, and several, including Whitchurch, Denham and Winslow, in due course quietly gave up any claim to be different from their neighbours.

[19] F. Seebohm, *The English Village Community* (1883), p. 22, n. 1. and *Rotuli Hundredorum* ii, p. 338.

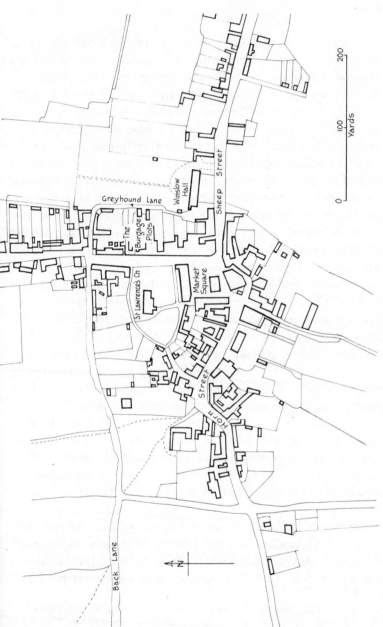

Fig. 12. The Medieval borough at Winslow

Industries

The growth of markets and towns in Buckinghamshire is matched by the development of industries. The seemingly inexhaustible clays of Buckinghamshire were being worked to make tiles and pottery by the early years of the thirteenth century. Sampson le Poter and Walter le Poter are mentioned in Brill by 1220, where in 1254 a number of potters were paying 3d. a year to the Crown for their furnaces and for the right to collect loppings for fuel. The potters of Brill created one of the most important medieval industrial sites to be found in all Buckinghamshire. Here, on the brow of a hill immediately to the north of the town, four medieval kilns have been excavated, whilst others are known to exist. The earliest of those excavated dates from the late thirteenth century, but all had undergone considerable reconstruction. All had two stoke-holes, and one was built of tiles and specially shaped bricks. During the thirteenth and fourteenth centuries the kilns at Brill were operating on a considerable scale, and it has been estimated that a quarter of a million pots were made there in less than a century. Bricks and tiles were also made. Production on this scale was obviously of more than purely local importance and pottery manufactured at Brill has been recognised over a fifty-mile radius from the town.[20]

The manufacture of pottery and tiles continued in Brill until the late nineteenth century. The pits and hollows, mounds and depressions, now often much overgrown, which surround the town of Brill on almost every side, are permanent reminders of a long-established and once flourishing industry (Plate 14).

Brill was probably the most important, but not the only, place where bricks, tiles and pottery were made in Buckinghamshire. A late medieval kiln, making roof tiles, bricks and patterned floor tiles, has been excavated at Little Brickhill.

[20] E. M. Jope, 'Medieval Pottery Kilns at Brill', *Records of Buckinghamshire* XVI Part 1, (1953–1954), pp. 39–42, and E. M. Jope, 'The Regional Cultures of Medieval Britain', in I. LL. Foster and L. Alcock, eds., *Culture and Environment* (1963), pp. 327–350.

Roof tiles from here were used to repair the roof of Wing church in 1527 and in 1530, and its products have been recognised as far afield as Blakesley and Wappenham in Northamptonshire, over twenty miles away.[21] There was a considerable industry for the manufacture of coloured and patterned floor tiles at Penn, where several medieval kilns are known. Roof tiles were made at Hedgerley and the Chalfonts. Medieval kilns are also known at Great Brickhill, and at Olney Hyde a stone-built circular single flue kiln of late medieval construction has been found, together with the associated workshops and clay pits. Brick kilns were in operation at Mursley from about 1580, and eighteenth-century kilns are known from Fingest and Fulmer, the latter being commemorated in Duke's Kiln Road, since its products were used in the building of the Duke of Portland's house at Bulstrode. Finally, brick kilns were working in the neighbourhood of Slough from the middle years of the fifteenth century, their products going to the building of Eton College.

The facets of the early medieval landscape which we have looked at so far were the work of villagers and peasants, burgesses and craftsmen, merchants and tradesmen. They were not the only groups of people who, by going about their everyday affairs, were contributing to the shaping of the early medieval landscape of Buckinghamshire. The nobility and the gentry, the clergy, whether regular or secular, also had their parts to play.

SELECT BIBLIOGRAPHY

Baker, A. R. H. and Butlin, R. A., *Studies of Field Systems in the British Isles* (1973).

Chibnall, A. C., *Sherington. Fiefs and Fields of a Buckinghamshire Village* (1965).

Miller, E. and Hatcher, J., *Medieval England: Rural Society and Economic Change 1086–1348* (1978).

---

[21] D. C. Mynard, 'The Little Brickhill Tile Kilns and their Products', *Journal of the British Archaeological Association* 3rd Series 38, (1975), p. 55.

Roberts, B. K., *Rural Settlement in Britain* (1977).

Roden, D., Studies in Chiltern Field Systems. Unpublished Ph.D. thesis, University of London, (1965).

Roden, D., 'Demesne Farming in the Chiltern Hills', *Agricultural History Review* 17, (1969), pp. 9–23.

Roden, D., 'Enclosure in the Chiltern Hills', *Geografiska Annaler* 51B, (1969), pp. 115–126.

Rowley, T., *Villages in the Landscape* (1978).

Vollans, E. C., 'The Evolution of Farmlands in the Central Chilterns in the Twelfth and Thirteenth Centuries', *Transactions of the Institute of British Geographers* 26, (1959), pp. 197–235.

4. The early medieval landscape, 1150-1350 – II

Castles and manor houses. Moats and fishponds. Forests.
Parks. Watermills and windmills. The Church in the landscape. Conclusion

IN THE LAST CHAPTER we looked at the contributions of
townsmen and villagers to the making of the early medieval
landscape. In this chapter we must turn our attention to the
contributions made by the great men in the land, both lay and
ecclesiastic, in their pursuit of power, safety, prestige,
pleasure or eternal felicity.

Castles and manor houses

Castles are primarily a Norman contribution to the landscape.
A number were certainly built by royal authority in the years
after the Conquest, but some may well have their foundations
in a fortified manor house of pre-Conquest origins. Early
castles consisted of a mound or motte of earth surrounded by a
ditch and bank with a wooden palisade. The space enclosed
was known as the bailey. The motte may have been completely
sheathed in timber, forming the central core to a tower, also of
timber. Some castles were very small and simple. The castle at
Bradwell seems to have occupied no more than half an acre.
Others were more complex, their final shape the result of much
rebuilding. At Castlethorpe there seems to have been both an
inner and an outer bailey, and at Lavendon there were no less
than three rectangular baileys. In due course a minority of
these wooden castles were rebuilt in stone, a much more
elaborate and costly venture. There is no certain evidence that
any of those in Buckinghamshire were rebuilt in this way,

although there is a tradition of a stone keep at Whitchurch, and what would appear to be a masonry wall is mentioned by an eighteenth-century visitor to the site of Lavendon castle.[1]

All the castle sites in Buckinghamshire, both certain and probable, are marked on Fig. 13. The exact site of some, as that at Aylesbury, is uncertain, and the very existence of those at Wendover, Saunderton and Newport Pagnell is problematical. All were in ruin by the late middle ages, and today their sites are marked solely by ditches and grass-covered earthen mounds. The motte at Lavendon was finally destroyed in 1944. That at Buckingham was levelled in about 1670 to make a bowling green, and the parish church was rebuilt on it between 1777 and 1781. Castlethorpe, where the castle was destroyed by Fawkes de Breauté in 1215 and never rebuilt, and Whitchurch (Plate 10), have the best preserved earthworks at the present time, and there are quite substantial remains at Weston Turville, tucked away between the church and the manor house. It is very difficult today to see castles, even wooden ones, on these quiet tree-covered mounds.

Castles were the most obvious fortifications in the early medieval landscape, but the uncertainties and insecurity of the times meant that many houses with no pretensions to being castles were provided with fortifications of some kind or another, usually a wall with a gatehouse, sometimes surrounded with a moat. However, as we shall see later in this chapter, the moats to many houses were either much more utilitarian, being used as fishponds, or else were purely ornamental. Such fortifications required the consent of the Crown, this being given by means of a licence to crenellate, of which there are several for Buckinghamshire. James de la Plaunche received a licence for his house at Haversham in 1334, Sir John Moleyns for his at Stoke Poges in 1331 and John de Haudlo for his at Boarstall in 1312, the peel or tower of Boarstall being mentioned in 1322. These fortified houses have long disappeared, but the gatehouse to that at Boarstall still stands (Plate 11). It was built in the first half of the fourteenth century. It has two big towers with battlements and

[1] *V.C.H. Bucks*, III, p. 443, IV, p. 380.

Fig. 13. Medieval castles in Buckinghamshire

arrow slits on either side of the entrance. The site was once entirely surrounded by a moat and entrance was by means of a drawbridge, but the moat is now partially filled in and a bridge was built in 1735. Such gatehouses must once have been fairly common in Buckinghamshire. Two large gates with dwelling rooms over them are mentioned for the manor house of Stewkley Grange in 1331, and there was a gatehouse with chambers over at Stowe as late as 1624.

Fortified or not, manor houses were very common in the landscape by the fourteenth century. They could vary considerably in size and building materials, and in the range and complexity of their ancillary buildings. The house itself may well have been built of stone. The site of a large thirteenth-century hall with flint footings and a tiled roof is known at Low Farm, Fulmer. More modest buildings of timber and thatch were just as common. Fundamentally these manor houses consisted of one large room, the hall, open to the roof. This hall could be divided, to provide service rooms at one end and a solar, or family retiring room, at the other. Ancillary buildings could include a dove cote, barns, stables, a chapel and even, as at Burnham in 1368, a henhouse. The manorial complex would be completed by a garden, or, as at Cippenham in 1299, two, where there was also fishing in the ditch around the manor. A manorial *curia* of this kind could extend over several acres, six at Whitchurch in 1264, and was occasionally set in its own park, as at Chesham in 1264, and Penn in 1325. One of the largest fourteenth-century manorial complexes in Buckinghamshire must have been that of the Black Prince at Princes Risborough. The site, directly to the south-west of the church, seems today to be largely covered with a car park. Here the walls of an extensive range of buildings were made of flint or chalk, or else of wichert, a compound of mud, chalk and chopped straw. Some of the buildings were thatched, some were tiled, whilst many had floors of paving tiles from the kilns at Penn. Here too was a stud for the breeding of horses. The buildings were probably first erected during the course of the thirteenth century, the custody of the manor passing to the Black Prince in 1344. Excavation has

Plate 7   The Black Hedge, Monks Risborough. This immense hedge is mentioned as an estate boundary in a document of A.D. 903.

Plate 8   Thornborough Bridge, the only medieval bridge remaining in the county.

Plate 9   The market place at Whitchurch. A market was granted in 1245 and is last heard of in 1330, but the open space where it was held still survives in the landscape.

Plate 10   The grass-covered mounds of what was once the castle at Whitchurch.

Plate 11   The fortified gatehouse to the moated manor house at Boarstall. It was built in the first half of the fourteenth century.

Plate 12   The water-filled ditch to the medieval moated site at Marsworth.

Plate 13 The Mill House at the west end of Amersham High Street. Seventeenth-century buildings disguise a site which has been occupied since the time of Domesday Book.

Plate 14 The surviving windmill at Brill, built at the end of the seventeenth century. The disturbed ground on the right is the result of clay-digging for Brill's medieval pottery industry.

revealed signs of occupation down to the seventeenth century.[2]

The buildings on many manorial sites in Buckinghamshire have long been demolished or rebuilt almost beyond recognition. Many other sites have been abandoned altogether. It is probably true to say that there is no surviving secular building in the county which is older than the first part of the fourteenth century, and that only four sites, the gatehouse at Boarstall, the Savoy, or Savehay Farm, at Denham, Creslow manor house and Huntercombe manor house, contain anything still standing which is earlier than 1350. Even these have been much altered, rebuilt and added to as tastes have changed and standards of comfort have risen, while a fifth, the early fourteenth-century house known as the Old Manor or Bell's Farm at Askett, was demolished as recently as 1969. Since so few manor houses have survived from before 1350 we shall look at those which have come down to us in more detail in the next chapter and turn instead to two of the most characteristic, and much more permanent, features of medieval manorial sites, moats and fishponds.

Moats and fishponds

Moats and fishponds together probably form the commonest of medieval earthworks. There are 159 moats at present recorded in the county.[3] The great majority of these are to be found either in the north of the county or else in the far south beyond the Chilterns, although a handful are known actually in the hills themselves.

The origins of these moated sites remain obscure, and only three have been excavated in Buckinghamshire. The great majority appear to have been constructed in the thirteenth century, although both earlier and later ones are known. Their functions are equally uncertain. Many undoubtedly had build-

---

[2] F. H. Pavry and G. M. Knocker, 'The Mount, Princes Risborough, Buckinghamshire', *Records of Buckinghamshire* XVI Part 2, (1955–1956), pp. 131–178.

[3] County Museum Archaeological Group, 'Moated Sites in Buckinghamshire – A List', *Records of Buckinghamshire* XIX Part 3, (1973), pp. 336–339.

ings on the central island, sometimes a substantial manor house and its associated farm buildings. At Grove Farm, Ashley Green, there is an L-shaped medieval building of flint, remains of curtain walling and evidence of a gatehouse. At Bradwell there were four stone buildings and a lime-kiln within the moated area. Of the buildings two were probably dovecotes, the third an aisled barn, whilst the fourth had a floor paved with decorative tiles made at Penn, and associated pottery came from Brill and from the north-west of France. However, several are known from other parts of the country with no trace of buildings and so it is very likely that a number of the Buckinghamshire ones will prove not to have been inhabited. The defensive potential of the sites is often strictly limited. They do not appear to have been excavated in order to improve drainage since low-lying spots with a good water supply to keep the moat filled seem to have been commonly sought. The moat may have had some value for the watering of livestock and the keeping of fish, probably the purposes for which the uninhabited ones were made. The one at Boarstall is actually called a fishpond in a lease of 1633.[4] But no single explanation is entirely satisfactory, and in any case the likelihood of their being built at the dictates of fashion and ostentation cannot be ruled out.

The great majority of homestead moats are rectangular in shape, with a single central island, joined to the mainland by a causeway or a bridge. Such rectangular ones are to be found at, for example, Nash Lee, Ivinghoe Aston, Marsworth (Plate 12) and Tetchwick. There is a semi-circular one at Church Farm, Pitstone, and a very oddly shaped one at East End, North Crawley. Occasionally there were two islands in the moat, as at Apsley and at Edlesborough. Many moats are still to be seen in the landscape today. Some still have water in them, such as that behind the church at Hulcott, whilst others are partially or entirely dry, as at Vatches Farm, Aston Clinton. At least one, Grove Farm, Ashley Green, still has buildings on the central island. Others, at Little Horwood and Boarstall for

4 B.R.O. D/AF/3/19.

example, are deserted and overgrown, a tangle of brambles, nettles, trees and in the moat itself, rushes and water plants. A handful are marked by the proximity of a Moat Farm, as at Wotton Underwood, Little Crawley and Ford.

Many Buckinghamshire moats are to be found in villages, and often very close to the church. The connection between manor house and church has long been intimate and the buildings on these moated sites, if indeed there were any, may well prove on excavation to have had some manorial function. Moats are also to be found in what are now deserted villages, in Hogshaw, Fulbrook and Aston Mullins (see Fig. 16), and others now stand isolated in fields far from villages and hamlets, hinting at the possibility of deserted habitation sites. When the moat at Bradwell was excavated it was discovered that when it was made, perhaps early in the thirteenth century, a timber building occupying the site was destroyed in the process. This may indicate that the moat was constructed as part of a reorganisation of the lay-out of the village, a reorganisation that only the lord of the manor would have been able to push through. Perhaps such reorganisation could contribute to the decline of a settlement as well as to its growth and development. Only much more detailed research and excavation can provide us with some of the answers to these questions. Moats may be fairly common relics from the medieval landscape, but they are also among the more enigmatic.

Fish were important in medieval times as a source of fresh food, particularly during Lent, when the eating of meat was forbidden by the Church. The construction of artificial fishponds could sometimes be very elaborate, involving a series of dams, sluices and channels, leading from one pond into the next, each pond probably being devoted to only one stage of the life-cycle of the fish. Running water could be led in by means of a cut from a stream, and it is not unknown for a stream to be dammed, creating a pond across the floor of a shallow valley. Fishponds as such are recorded early in the county, and from all parts. There was one at Buckingham in 1198, one at Ditton in Stoke Poges in 1205, and a third at

Hillesden in 1207. Two at Wendover in 1302 were worth 6s. 8d.

Almost all of these fishponds are now silted up and grown over, leaving behind a series of banks and hollows, the latter sometimes still sufficiently damp to attract moisture-loving plants which may provide for the observant the first clue as to their purpose and extent. The earthworks of abandoned fishponds are to be found at Denham, Chesham, Langley, Stoke Mandeville, Chetwode, Foxcote, Waddesdon and Gayhurst, to name but a few. Several have been destroyed in the years since 1945. Those at Home Close, Stoke Goldington, for example, have now been filled in. On the other hand several have been carefully surveyed.[5] At Loughton is a complex range of earthworks, including house platforms, moats, fishponds and connecting channels, clearly marking out the old course of the Loughton brook before it was diverted in the 1930s. These are scheduled for preservation by the Milton Keynes Development Corporation, as are those at Great Woolstone. Here there is a moated site and a series of interconnected fishponds, some of them roughly rectangular, all of which probably drew their water supply from the nearby river Ousel. Some fishponds were undoubtedly intended to serve the needs of a particular manor house, but for an intricate web of ponds such as those at Loughton and Great Woolstone the possibility of commercial fish farming cannot be ignored.

There is no comprehensive list of known sites of medieval fishponds in Buckinghamshire, and the whereabouts of a number recorded in medieval documents has been lost since they ceased to fulfil their purpose, something which may not have happened before the middle of the eighteenth century. Here is an area in which research has scarcely begun, whether in documentary sources or on the ground, and where a rich haul of new material may be expected.

---

[5] Milton Keynes Development Corporation, Earthworks Survey, in *Council for British Archaeology*, Group 9 Newsletter No. 6 (1976), pp. 54–57.

Forests

The medieval royal forest was a tract of country set aside for the preservation of beasts of the chase, which the king alone might hunt. It was subject to the Forest Laws, not to the common law, and had its own elaborate administrative machinery. It was not, however, necessarily entirely heavily wooded, and it was quite usual for village communities to be settled in a forest, cultivating their fields and pasturing their livestock within the forest, subject always to the over-riding needs of the beasts of the chase. These were first of all the red and fallow deer, which were always strictly preserved. The roe deer was demoted to a beast of the warren in 1339 because it drove the other deer from their feeding grounds. The wild boar, already rare by the thirteenth century, was also a beast of the chase, but the hare and the wolf were not. The royal forests in England were divided in 1238 into two parts, with the Trent as the boundary. Each part was under the care of a Justice, later called a Keeper. Each forest within the two parts was under the control of a Warden. Thus all the forests in Northamptonshire, Oxfordshire, Huntingdonshire and Buckinghamshire were grouped together under a Warden of the Forests between the bridges of Oxford and Stamford. Under each Warden were Foresters, who were in charge of a particular forest. The office of Forester could become hereditary, as did that of Bernwood from about the middle of the twelfth century.

Five areas of Buckinghamshire were subject to the Forest Laws in the early medieval centuries. In the extreme south parts of the parishes of Datchet, Langley Marish, Upton and Eton lay within the Forest of Windsor. In the far north Lillingstone Lovell, Lillingstone Dayrell and parts of Akeley, Biddlesden and Stowe were in the Forest of Whittlewood. The parishes of Hanslope, Lathbury, Gayhurst and Haversham lay within Salcey Forest. The bulk of these forests however lay within other counties. The largest Forest in Buckinghamshire was Bernwood, already a royal forest by the time of Domesday Book. Indeed as we saw in chapter 2 it may represent the last fragment of a very ancient and much larger estate.

The Forest of Bernwood (see Fig. 7) was at its widest extent during the reign of Richard I, who added the woods of Wotton and Pollicott to those afforested by his father Henry II. Henry had already taken in the woods of Tetchwick, Grendon, Ludgershall, Twyford and Oakley, Lee Wood in Quainton, and woods in Middle Claydon, as well as several woods in Oxfordshire. The Charter of the Forest, issued in 1217 during the minority of Henry III, provided for the immediate disafforestation of those woods taken in by Richard I and John, but those of Henry II were to be given up only where they had injured land-owners and were outside the royal demesne. In the following year it was ordered that the royal forests should be surveyed and their boundaries perambulated, and this was done on several occasions down to 1229. The Charter of the Forest was re-issued in 1297, and further perambulations were made. A perambulation of the Forest of Bernwood was made in 1298,[6] and the boundaries fixed then, enclosing perhaps 8,000 acres, remained those of the Forest until its final disafforestation in the 1630s. They correspond for much of their length with old parish, manor and county boundaries. A large area to the south-west, called the Quarters on a map of 1590,[7] seems to have been included within the Forest in a perambulation made in about 1294 of the western boundary only,[8] but not in that of 1298 of the whole boundary. It may have been disafforested in the years between the two, although areas which have been disafforested are usually called Purlieus.

The Forest was in its turn subdivided into three Walks, Panshill, Ixhill and Frith, each being in the charge of a Keeper and an Underkeeper. Theirs was the responsibility of maintaining the woods and making sure that the Laws of the Forest were observed. The Forest of Bernwood was not a stretch of unbroken woodland. Open spaces, known as *laundes*, existed

[6] V.C.H. Bucks, II, p. 132, H. E. Salter, ed., 'The Boarstall Cartulary', *Oxford Historical Society* LXXXVIII, (1930), pp. 182–184. H.H.L., Stowe Papers. Grenville Cartulary ST 29 f. 163.

[7] E. M. Elvey, ed., *Buckinghamshire Estate Maps* (1964), No. 2.

[8] H. E. Salter, ed., 'The Boarstall Cartulary', *Oxford Historical Society*, LXXXVIII, (1930), p. 181.

within the woodland, where cattle might graze provided the king's deer were not disturbed. Cattle and sheep were generally permitted to graze within the Forest except during the fortnights before and after midsummer, when the deer were supposed to be fawning. Pigs, however, were usually allowed in only during the month from mid-September to mid-November. The inhabitants of Brill, Boarstall and Oakley had common of pasture without stint for all their animals within the Forest except in the Ixhill Walk. The villagers of Dorton, Ludgershall, Merlake, Nash End, Tetchwick and Wotton Underwood, on the other hand, had to pay for the pasturing of their animals, their villages lying within the purlieus of the Forest and not in the Forest itself.

Villagers within the Forest cultivated their land in common fields divided into furlongs and strips, as in other villages in Buckinghamshire north of the Chilterns, although the hedges had to be low and the ditches shallow around any and every kind of enclosure. This was so that the deer could pass easily in and out to graze where they willed. The three fields of Boarstall were called Frith Field, Cowhousefield and Arnegrovefield, whilst the demesne arable lay in another field called the Deerhyde. One of the oldest of all English maps was made for this village in about 1440.[9] It is remarkably accurate, provided it is remembered that it has south at the top.[10] The three common fields can be identified, as well as the approximate location of the demesne arable. The 1440 map also reveals a substantial village lying to the south of the church and the manor house, and a survey of 1586 makes the population 201.[11] The medieval landscape of Boarstall was quite unlike that of today. It was, as we shall see in chapter 6, the disafforestation of the Forest of Bernwood in the 1630s that brought it to an end.

The fifth area in Buckinghamshire of forest in the formal meaning of the word was Whaddon Chase. A chase is strictly an area of forest which has been granted by the Crown to a

[9] E. M. Elvey, op. cit., No. 1.
[10] M. Aston and T. Rowley, *Landscape Archaeology* (1974), p. 67.
[11] British Library, Lansdowne MS 47, No. 3.

subject, and Whaddon was granted to John FitzGeoffrey in 1242, from whom it descended to the Giffard family. The boundaries of the Chase are fairly well-established, although it was claimed in 1494 that neither Tattenhoe Bare nor Nichols Wood were part of it. It extended over about 22,000 acres of woodland, heath and common, including Great Horwood Common, Whaddon Common and Shenley Common. Here, as in Bernwood, it was the deer which were the first consideration. The Chase was much neglected during the sixteenth and seventeenth centuries. Timber was felled recklessly, deer and domestic animals broke into the coppices and destroyed the young trees, and poaching went unchecked for long periods. There was some improvement by the end of the eighteenth century so that when the first edition of the Ordnance Survey map was published it could show extensive coppices divided by long straight drives. The Chase was enclosed by an Act of Parliament passed in 1841. Enclosure was followed by extensive felling and clearing, and the building of new farms, such as Chase Farm and Woodpond Farm, in the newly created fields. Nichols Wood has gone entirely but the footpath from Wood End, Nash, leading in a south-westerly direction to the Six Lords Inn at Singleborough still curves round a hedgerow which once was the southern boundary. Much of College Wood still remains, but all that is left of the Grove is the memory of its name in Grove Farm, with its outline preserved in curving field boundaries and hedgerows.

Whaddon Park was carved out of the Chase early in the thirteenth century, if not before, since it is mentioned quite casually in a document of 1219. It lay, not where Whaddon Park is today, that was once part of Whaddon Common, but to the south of Church Hill. Much of its boundary is still marked by hedgerows, to the west following the parish boundary between Whaddon and Great Horwood, with Parkhill Farm just outside, and on the east following the road from Whaddon south to join the B4034 road past Coddimoor Farm. This farm was itself actually in the Chase, but its fields have long been cultivated, and the boundary ditches, dug when they were enclosed, can still be traced.

Forest and Chase were not however the only areas to be set aside as game reserves during the course of the early medieval centuries. Parks were far more numerous, and, when taken together, probably just as extensive.

Parks

One of the commonest features of the medieval landscape was the deer park.[12] Such a park was part of the demesne lands of the lord of the manor, its chief function to provide an enclosure in which he could hunt deer, both for pleasure and for supplies of venison. They were rarely more than three hundred acres in size and were almost always well-wooded to provide cover for the deer, although it is recorded that the park at Eakley in Stoke Goldington included meadowland, and it was stated in 1272 that the pasture in the park at Newport Pagnell would be worth 35s. a year if the deer were removed. Parks were securely enclosed within an earthen bank, topped with a wooden paling fence, and a ditch on the inside. This presented an insuperable barrier to the deer on the inside. They would have been unable to escape into the open countryside. The bank and ditch were pierced occasionally by gates, and sometimes by a deer-leap. A deer-leap was made by lowering the bank at one particular point, and at the same time widening and deepening the ditch on the inside. This made it possible for the deer from outside the park to get in, but prevented the escape of those already inside. All deer, except those actually inside parks, belonged to the Crown. Thus a deer-leap meant that the stock of royal deer could quickly and easily be diminished, and so the right to have a deer-leap was a privilege to be had only by royal licence, granted with reluctance.

Parks existed in Buckinghamshire at the time of Domesday Book. At Oakley we are told that the woodland would have fed 200 swine were it not in the king's park, and that there was a park for beasts of the chase at Long Crendon. Next, we hear of

[12] L. M. Cantor and J. Hatherly, 'The Medieval Parks of Buckinghamshire', *Records of Buckinghamshire* (forthcoming).

a park at Lavendon in the middle years of the twelfth century as part of the original endowment of Lavendon abbey, and in 1187 Gervase de Paganell gave the tithe of the venison of the park of Newport Pagnell to Tickford priory. From the first years of the thirteenth century references to parks increase steadily, so that by 1230 at least twenty must have been in existence, including those at Haversham, Bow Brickhill and Stowe.

The creation of parks was not confined to a comparatively short period of intense activity such as characterised, for example, the creation of markets, and the Crown continued to grant licences to empark well into the seventeenth century. Thus in 1336 Sir John Moleyns had licence from the Crown to enclose and make a park of his woods of Ilmer and la Sale, together with a hundred acres of pasture in Beaconsfield, Burnham and Cippenham, and in 1339 he was licensed to empark his wood of Ludgershall called *la Breche* (see Fig. 7) and a hundred acres of meadow and pasture adjoining. In 1447 John Hampden was licensed to enclose and empark 500 acres of land and 100 acres of wood at Hampden and to hold them as a park, and in 1616 Robert Lord Dormer was licensed to make a park in Buckland. By this time however parks were becoming increasingly ornamental and had lost their utilitarian purpose.

There are well over sixty recorded medieval deer parks in Buckinghamshire, and it is quite likely that several, such as those at Pollicott in Ashendon and at Wooburn, known from the sixteenth century, will in fact prove to be medieval in origin. Several, such as that at Le Ho, are referred to only once. Others, such as those at Hampden and Hanslope, became the basis for a later, landscaped, park, whilst that at Stowe has been swallowed up in the great gardens there. Yet others have been disparked, their trees grubbed up, their deer sold, the land divided up into fields and turned to arable or pasture. This had happened at Denham before 1680. The park at Fulmer had been divided into three arable fields by 1706, and that at Great Brickhill was divided into eight closes by 1708. Some have been more or less obliterated under twentieth-century housing estates. This has occurred at Aylesbury for example. Nearly all, however, have left at least one place-name in the landscape as a memorial. Le Ho survives as Hoo Wood, to the south-west of Gayhurst, and bisected now by the M1 motorway. There is a Park Farm in Great Brickhill and another in Lavendon. The park at Olney eventually emerged as the separate parish of Olney Park. Many have left more tangible evidence behind.

The curving hedges and field boundaries marking the outline of what was once Whaddon Park have already been described, and a number of other medieval deer parks survive in similar fashion in the landscape of today. A road has been driven through what was once the deer park at Denham, but at least one section of boundary hedge still survives. Curving hedges and ditches between Tickford Lodge Farm and Tickford Park Farm preserve the outline of the park of Gervase de Paganell, and ditches and field boundaries surrounding Seagrave's Farm in Penn, together with the name Park Grove, indicate where was once the deer park mentioned in a document of 1325. At Bow Brickhill much of what was once the park has been planted with conifers but the massive earthworks of its southern boundaries are still visible. At Langley almost the whole of the medieval deer park is now preserved as a Country Park under the auspices of the Countryside Commission. It is probably true to say that the boundaries of the majority of the county's medieval deer parks could be recovered by the careful combination of the study of documents and maps with fieldwork such as that recently carried out for Cippenham Park.[13] This promises to be one of the most fruitful areas of research in landscape archaeology for the future.

Watermills and windmills

A building probably more common than the parish church in the landscape up until the beginning of the twentieth century was the mill, whether water-powered or wind-powered. They

[13] see L. M. Cantor and J. Hatherly, op. cit.

were to be found everywhere. Almost every Buckinghamshire parish had at least one mill, many had two and of both kinds. Only those parishes completely without running water seem to have lacked a watermill, since it took only a very small stream to provide sufficient energy to turn the wheel of a simple undershot mill, and only in a very small number of parishes, including Fawley and Turville, Edgcott and Creslow, does there appear not to have been a mill of any kind, and further research will undoubtedly fill some of the gaps.

Mills, whether wind or water, were an important item in the property of the lord of the manor, since his tenants owed him suit of mill. In other words he could compel them to bring their grain to his mill to be ground, and at the same time he charged them a toll for the privilege. Mills are mentioned frequently in manorial extents and accounts in the medieval centuries. The watermill at Princes Risborough was worth 13s. 4d. in 1243, two at Chesham in 1264 were worth 66s. 8d., whilst two at Wendover were valued at £10 in 1302, a considerable sum of money indeed.

Domesday Book mentions mills at seventy-eight places in Buckinghamshire, but it is likely that the record is incomplete. There are, for example, no mills at all in Mursley hundred. Most places had only one mill, but there were eight at Wooburn and nine at Wycombe, both on the river Wye, since Domesday mills are invariably watermills. The number of watermills in the county was never static. It continued to be added to in the centuries after Domesday Book was compiled, both to those parishes which do not appear to have had a mill at the time of Domesday, not forgetting that the Domesday record is unlikely to be complete, as well as to those which did. Thus in those parishes which do not seem to have had watermills in 1086, Chenies, Grove and Stowe each had one by 1200. That mentioned at Twyford in the beginning of the thirteenth century is called *Newmulne*. Whitchurch had one by 1263, Medmenham by 1264, Slapton by 1291, and a number of other parishes, including Emberton, Hardwick, Hughenden and Hulcott, by the end of the thirteenth century. At the same time the Domesday stock of mills was being added to.

Sherington had one mill in 1086, three by 1257. At Chesham a new mill is mentioned in the middle years of the twelfth century, an addition to the four already there in 1086. The building of new mills seems to have continued into the eighteenth century. The single Domesday mill at Stantonbury had become four by 1721, and the one at Thornton had become three by about the same time. The story is not however one of uninterrupted addition. It was said in 1666 that there was anciently a watermill in Great Horwood but now there was none. At Lillingstone Dayrell the old mill was, in 1610, being used as a cottage. At Water Stratford it was reported in 1349 that the watermill had been destroyed, whilst that at Aston Clinton was demolished when the grounds of Aston Clinton House were laid out towards the middle of the nineteenth century (see Fig. 9).

Domesday mills were of the undershot type, in which the wheel is turned by the current of water running underneath the wheel to catch the blades. A very small stream, with only a slight fall, suffices for a mill of this kind, and earthworks about the mill-race can be kept to the minimum. Colwick mill, in Waddesdon, on a stream near Binwell Lane Farm, must have been of this kind, as must those lying at the foot of the Chiltern scarp, as well as that at Broughton near Bierton, if the size of the stream flowing by the Millhouse today is any guide.

By the end of the twelfth century the overshot mill was appearing. In this type of mill the water is carried over the centre of the wheel before being allowed to fall onto the blades. The weight of the falling water then turns the wheel in the opposite direction to that of the undershot mill. Although a mill of this kind needs only about a quarter of the water required to turn a undershot wheel effectively, it does need an adequate fall. This means almost always some artificial earthworks, perhaps a weir across the river, or a diversion, a mill pond and sluices, in order that an adequate fall of water can be created. The millpond and sluices to Wolverton Mill are mentioned in 1251. There was a millpond at Loughton before 1210, and the watercourse to the mill at Broughton in Bierton is mentioned at the end of the twelfth century.

The effort and expense involved in the construction of millpond, dam and sluices meant that, once chosen, it was very unlikely that the site of a mill would be abandoned, and so it might continue in use for centuries. The buildings themselves, however, are much more subject to decay. The combined effects of timber rot, a consequence of the inevitably damp situation in which the mill was built, and the strains and vibrations created by the workings of the simple machinery, together with the very real risk of fire from the sparks showered into the heavily dust-laden atmosphere should the millstones ever be allowed to touch one another, meant that mill buildings were constantly in need of repair, and had to be rebuilt from time to time. Consequently, of the mill buildings once so common in the medieval Buckinghamshire landscape almost nothing survives today. Where watermills still stand their buildings are essentially eighteenth- and nineteenth-century, although it is likely that many incorporate older work. Some have been converted into industrial premises, as at Stony Stratford, and some into private residences, as at Amersham (Plate 13). Thus they bear little resemblance to their medieval precursors. Further, the buildings of many medieval watermills have disappeared without trace, and the recognition of the overgrown, perhaps now dry, earthworks of their ponds and sluices has scarcely begun. There is a likely site at Mursley. The straight cut leading from the south-west corner of the moat behind the church at Little Horwood is probably to be connected with the watermill pulled down at the end of the nineteenth century. There are other possible sites at Great Horwood and at Hughenden, but this is clearly an area of landscape archaeology in which much research remains to be done.

Watermills were common in the Buckinghamshire landscape by the end of the thirteenth century, and were to remain so until the end of the nineteenth. By the second half of the twelfth century their efforts to supply peasant and craftsman with flour for their bread were being supplemented by one of the most remarkable technological innovations before the Industrial Revolution. The origins of the windmill are obscure, but in a published document which its editor dates to the period between 1160 and 1170 there occurs the earliest mention of a windmill yet recorded in England, when a grant of land in Worminghall to the monks of St Frideswide in Oxford included half an acre *contra molendinum venti*.[14] Indeed this is one of the earliest references to a windmill for the whole of western Europe, they being recorded at Arles at just about the same time, 1162–80, and in Normandy in about 1180. The next reference in England is to a windmill at Weedley, in the East Riding of Yorkshire, in 1185.[15] Before the end of the twelfth century there was one in Steeple Claydon, and in the early years of the thirteenth century an acre of land in Hartwell was granted to the canons of Oseney with permission to build a windmill on it. By the end of the thirteenth century they were common in the landscape, and it was not unknown for there to be two or more in a parish. Thus the windmill at Brill was said in 1251 to be well-built, but in 1274 ten oak trees were granted by Edward I from the Forest of Bernwood for the building of a windmill in Brill, and so it would appear that Brill had its two windmills from this time. One was demolished in 1906, but the other, much rebuilt and restored, still survives (Plate 14).

Windmills are among the most ingenious and imaginative products of the skill of the medieval carpenter, but, like watermills, they required frequent repair and occasional rebuilding, so that, of the handful which remain today in the Buckinghamshire landscape of the scores which once were there until the end of the nineteenth century, the oldest is that at Pitstone, where some timbers date from 1627, and even this has been extensively restored and rebuilt (Plate 15). All that is left of so many medieval windmills is the artificial mounds upon which they were built. More than a dozen of these mounds have been recognised in Buckinghamshire, from Thornborough to Bradenham, and from Boarstall to Tattenhoe. Many more await recognition and recording.

[14] S. R. Wigram, ed., 'The Cartulary of the Monastery of St. Frideswide at Oxford', Vol. 2 *Oxford Historical Society* XXXI, (1896), pp. 142–143.
[15] K. J. Allison, *The East Riding of Yorkshire Landscape* (1976), p. 86.

The Church in the landscape

Its wealth and its continuity gave to the Church an even greater influence in the moulding of the medieval landscape than that of any lay lord, until Henry VIII despoiled it in the first part of the sixteenth century.

By the year 1200 the main features of a parochial organisation which would be recognised today had become established in Buckinghamshire, although it is important to appreciate that the pattern of parish boundaries has never been stable for very long. New parishes have continued to be carved out of existing ones down to the present to meet changing needs and to take account of population movements, whilst others have been amalgamated as their congregations diminished and their churches fell into ruins.

As population grew in the twelfth and thirteenth centuries and outlying hamlets developed into substantial villages it became increasingly more inconvenient for their inhabitants to continue to make use of a sometimes distant parish church. Thus a chapel of ease would be established, and this in time might evolve into a separate parish. This happened at Fulmer for example, where there was a chapel subordinate to Datchet by the end of the thirteenth century, becoming a separate parish in 1553. Similarly there were chapels of ease at Stony Stratford, St Giles, dependent upon Calverton, and St Mary Magdalen, dependent upon Wolverton, although it was the eighteenth century before they became separate parishes. Occasionally the situation could be reversed. In the middle of the thirteenth century Hanslope, which had hitherto been a chapelry dependent upon Castlethorpe, became the parish and Castlethorpe its dependent chapelry.

Not all of these chapelries developed into separate parishes. There was one at Littlecote, subordinate to Stewkley, by the second half of the thirteenth century, but enclosure of the arable fields of the hamlet led to its almost complete desertion at the beginning of the sixteenth century and the chapel had been destroyed by the middle of the sixteenth century. There was a chapel at Addingrove, dependent upon the church at

Plate 15 Pitstone windmill, some timbers of which may date from 1627. The chimneys in the background are those of a cement factory and illustrate the pressures to which ancient, traditional landscapes are now exposed.

Plate 16 Stewkley church built in about 1150 and the finest Norman church in the county.

Plate 17 The church at Fingest, with its massive Norman tower.

Plate 18 An aerial photograph of the deserted village at Burston, facing south. The stream and trees on the left-hand side are on the eastern edge of the map which forms Fig. 15. The village lay in Coppice Ground.

Plate 19   Littlecote from the air. The medieval village here was almost completely deserted by the middle of the sixteenth century, leaving behind a farm house fashioned from part of the manor house, house-platforms and extensive ridge and furrow.

Plate 20   Maids Moreton church, designed and built in the middle years of the fifteenth century.

Plate 21   The Cloisters at Eton College, from the north-east.

Plate 22   Chesham, nos 54 and 56 Church Street, once one medieval house with a hall and cross wing.

Oakley, at least by 1150, although it seems no longer to have been used by 1339. This pattern of contraction and decay is characteristic of many aspects of the later medieval scene in Buckinghamshire, as we shall see in the next chapter.

By the beginning of the thirteenth century the second of those Great Rebuildings which have from time to time washed over the English landscape was already well under way. By this date Saxon churches, whether in stone or in wood, were being rapidly replaced by new ones, in that most massive of architectural styles, the Norman or Romanesque, so that from now on the parish church becomes one of the most important and one of the most enduring features of the landscape, and for many centuries one of the principal focal points in the lives of those men and women whose labours, whether for pleasure or for profit, were moulding and changing the landscape at an accelerating pace. Nevertheless, as we shall see, in spite of their seeming permanence, even parish churches could be altered, pulled down, extended, moved, or abandoned to fall into ruins.

Of this earliest rebuilding of the churches of Buckinghamshire a splendid example survives almost intact. This is the church at Stewkley, built probably between 1140 and 1150, conceived as a whole and surviving as a whole (Plate 16). This is the most complete Norman church in the county. It is however closely rivalled by the church of St Lawrence at Upton, now part of Slough, where the south aisle, built in 1851, is the only major addition to what is otherwise a fine example of Norman parochial architecture. There is a fine Norman west tower to the church at Bradenham, and a magnificent one at Fingest, providing what must be one of the loveliest and best-known scenes in all the county (Plate 17).

The architectural history of the English parish church has been much studied and many excellent guides have been published. This is certainly not the place in which to recount in detail the changes in architectural style and technology which marked the passage of the medieval centuries as Norman gave way to successive phases of Gothic. The history of the fabric of individual churches in Buckinghamshire reveals that very few have remained untouched by these changes, and that the great majority are a palimpsest on which may be read the alterations carried out by successive generations. At Chilton, for example, the church as it stands today has a chancel and south transept of the thirteenth century, a tower built in the fourteenth, a nave erected in the late fifteenth century, and a south chapel added in the sixteenth. At Lavendon the nave and the tower are pre-Conquest. The aisles were added and the chancel rebuilt during the thirteenth century. Late in the fifteenth century clerestories were added to the nave and the north and south porches were built. Such histories are repeated over and over again in the great majority of Buckinghamshire churches. The parish church, a prominent feature of the landscape for at least the last thousand years, reflects in the history of its fabric something of the changes in the landscape which it once dominated.

The parish was only one form through which the Church carried out its functions, lay and spiritual, in the medieval centuries. As we have seen in chapter 2, there were several minster churches in Anglo-Saxon Buckinghamshire, but it is the twelfth century before we can be certain that there was a regular monastery in the county. Probably the first to be founded was the community of Augustinian Canons established by Walter Giffard at Notley, near Long Crendon, in the early years of the twelfth century. The Benedictine Priory of Luffield was founded in about 1118, and a second Augustinian house, that at Great Missenden, was established in about 1133. Within the next thirty years, that is by about 1160, a further seven monasteries had been established. After this the wave of enthusiasm for the monastic ideal began to subside, and only six more were added in the next hundred years. One only was founded in the late medieval centuries, the house of Franciscan Friars in Aylesbury, established in 1386. The original endowments of these houses were gradually added to, sometimes by purchase, more often by gifts from the pious, until eventually a monastery like Luffield owned property over much of the northern part of the county. However none of the Buckinghamshire houses was ever in the first rank for size, wealth or learning, and much property in the county was owned by monasteries outside. Thus the abbey of St Albans owned land in Winslow, Granborough and the Horwoods. Kenilworth had estates at Stewkley. Merton held lands in Hardmead, Taplow, Upton and Wexham. Oseney had lands in Stowe, Stone, Radclive and Chackmore. No less than eight religious houses had lands in Westbury in the thirteenth century. At the same time other ecclesiastical dignitaries were landowners in the county. The bishop of Winchester had lands at Ivinghoe and West Wycombe; the bishop of Lincoln had a palace and a deer park at Fingest. The overall influence of the Church upon the medieval scene must have been enormous.

Monastic estates were often extensive, but were frequently composed of widely scattered and quite small individual parcels of land. Arable land in particular was to be found distributed throughout the open fields of a village in just the same kind of pattern as that to be found in the holdings of the villagers, from whose devout ancestors the monastic lands had once come.

So far, the influence of monasteries upon the landscape could not have differed markedly from that of laymen, although it is possible that their estates were perhaps on the whole better managed and better cultivated. We know for example that when Ralf de Selveston was prior of Luffield, from 1263 to 1275, a real attempt was made to master the art and science of estate management, and the house acquired a copy of Walter of Henley's treatise, *Husbandry*. [16]

In other respects however, their effect upon the landscape was profound. They were in the forefront of those engaged in reclaiming land from waste, forest and marsh, and their continuity as institutions meant that their efforts in this direction could be sustained over long periods of time. In the north of the county Luffield, which was Benedictine, and Biddlesden, which was Cistercian, were particularly active in this respect. The monks of Luffield acquired acre after acre of woodland in Lillingstone Dayrell and Westbury during much

[16] G. R. Elvey, ed., 'Luffield Priory Charters', Part II, *Buckinghamshire Record Society* XVIII, (1975), pp. xxi, xxiv.

of the thirteenth century, with permission to enclose and cultivate. Indeed early in the thirteenth century it would seem that the priory actually preferred to hold woodland which it could clear and cultivate at will, since in about 1220 it exchanged almost all the arable, meadow and pasture it had so far acquired in Westbury for a tract of woodland for its exclusive use. The timber could be sold as it was felled, and provide a welcome addition to the revenues of the house, and there is some evidence to show that by the latter part of the thirteenth century some monasteries were cropping their woodland on a systematic basis. On the other hand the wood could be used directly in the monastery itself. We know for example that in about 1216 the monks of Snelshall priory were granted the right to cut timber from Tattenhoe Wood for firewood, to repair the conventual buildings, and to use as fuel in baking and brewing.

The final contributions of monastic houses to the medieval landscape were the conventual buildings, together with their attendant windmills, sheepfolds, barns and granges. It is important to appreciate that the first buildings erected when a monastery was founded were few, simple and made of wood. Only gradually were the first buildings rebuilt more elaborately in stone, so that it could take a century or more for a monastery to acquire the shape and layout that we now associate with a medieval religious community. Thus the church at Notley was originally built in about 1160. Aisles were added to the nave in about 1200, and a new east end was added at the beginning of the fourteenth century. The Chapter house and the Refectory belong to the thirteenth century, the dove cote was built of stone in the fourteenth-, and the Abbot's Lodging is partly fifteenth- and partly early sixteenth-century.[17] A similar story, of piecemeal building, rebuilding and extending, would be found in almost all the monastic houses of medieval Buckinghamshire.

But the conventual buildings themselves were not the only contribution of the monasteries to the medieval landscape of Buckinghamshire. In the early years of the thirteenth century

[17] W. A. Pantin, 'Notley Abbey', *Oxoniensia* VI, (1941), pp. 22–43.

the canons of Oseney abbey in Oxfordshire were granted an acre of land in Hartwell upon which to build a windmill and they had another on land in Claydon, perhaps where Windmillhill Farm is today. In Stowe the monks of Oseney had a sheepfold, which was surrounded with a ditch. In about 1206 Nigel, son of Osemund of Salden, agreed with the monks of Luffield to provide a barn for them to collect their tithes, as his father used to do. We can visualise something of what such a barn must have looked like from the accounts which have survived for the building of a new one on the estate of the bishop of Winchester at Ivinghoe. The barn was built in 1309–10 at a total cost of £83 8s. ¼d. Timber to the value of £33 2s. 3d. was bought. Lathes, 10,200 of them, came from St Albans and Dunstable, and 63,500 nails were used to fasten them. On the roof were 66,300 tiles in addition to 750 ridge tiles, and 70,000 wooden pegs were used to secure them. Six bushels of wheat were made into bread for the carpenter and his men, and ale, meat, herrings, eggs and cheese were also provided for them.[18]

Outlying monastic estates were farmed from a grange, at first a humble range of buildings designed to accommodate a group of lay brothers, their servants and supervisors. Two Grange Farms, one in Quainton and another in Saunderton, mark the location of granges of Thame abbey for its estates in those parishes. The abbey at Woburn had a grange in Stewkley, Snelshall priory had one in Beachampton, Lavendon had one at Haversham. These granges have all left their marks upon the landscape. The buildings themselves have long disappeared, but their memory is perpetuated, much more enduringly, in a place-name. For many more there is not even this. Gorrall Farm marks the site of a grange of Biddlesden abbey. The grange at Linslade of Woburn abbey has disappeared without trace.

Conclusion

It has taken two long chapters to deal with these early medieval centuries, but this is more than justified by the range

[18] J. Z. Titow, *English Rural Society 1200–1350* (1969), pp. 203–204.

and variety of the subjects they have had to cover, and by the importance of these centuries in the moulding of the Buckinghamshire landscape. The contributions made by generations of unknown men and women in the millenia covered in the first two chapters had of necessity to be described almost always in quite generalised terms, and the importance of this contribution has only recently come to be appreciated. But in these early medieval centuries we see that generalities give way increasingly to hard nuggets of detail. We can now point to fields and hedgerows still in the landscape today and know something of the lives of those who cared for them six centuries ago. Although their houses have long since disappeared or have been rebuilt, enough survives to enable us to piece together something of the conditions in which they lived. The churches where they worshipped still remain in the landscape and still retain that numinous aura created by the prayers of generations. The roads, streets and lanes used by a thirteenth-century traveller can, in the great majority of cases, still be followed by a traveller of the twentieth. The landscape of the middle of the fourteenth century carried very many more trees and far fewer people than that of the twentieth century, although in some parts of Buckinghamshire particularly in those parts of the north of the county outside the formally defined forests and chase, the landscape was probably little more tree-covered than it is today. Hedges would have been fewer, towns and villages very much smaller. Some buildings were of stone, especially the church and perhaps the manor house, and some had tile-clad roofs, but the great majority were timber-framed, of wattle and daub construction and with thatched roofs. Brick was largely unknown. Other parts of the county, particularly the forests, Whaddon Chase and the steeper slopes of the remoter Chiltern hills, were either still densely wooded, or else given over to heathland and rough grazing. But the woods did not form an untamed wilderness; they were divided up and exploited, although at a low level of intensity. Much has disappeared from the landscape in the centuries intervening between the middle of the fourteenth and the last quarter of the twentieth, and much has changed.

Bernwood forest is remembered only in the name of a farm, and the once ubiquitous windmill is now reduced to a handful of fossilised shells. Nevertheless, in spite of the changes, it is clear that the basic framework of the landscape of the middle of the fourteenth century is still the basic framework of that of the twentieth.

SELECT BIBLIOGRAPHY

Aberg, F. A., ed. *Medieval Moated Sites* Council for British Archaeology Research Report 17 (1978).

Addyman, P. and Morris, R., eds. *The Archaeological Study of Churches* Council for British Archaeology Research Report 13 (1976).

Bazeley, M. C., 'The English Forest in the Thirteenth Century', *Transactions of the Royal Historical Society* 4th Series IV, (1921), pp. 140–172.

Davison, B. K., 'The Origins of the Castle in England', *Archaeological Journal* 114, (1967), pp. 202–211.

Neilson, N., 'The Forests', in J. F. Willard and W. A. Morris, eds., *The English Government at Work, 1327–1336* Vol 1, (Cambridge, Mass., 1940), pp. 394–467.

Platt, C., *The Monastic Grange in Medieval England* (1969).

The Royal Archaeological Institute, *Five Castle Excavations*. Reports on the Institute's Research Project into the Origins of the Castle in England (1978).

Turner, G. J., 'Select Pleas of the Forest', *Selden Society* 13, (1899).

5. The break-up of the medieval landscape, 1350-1550

Enclosure and depopulation. Late medieval building in the landscape — Churches — Eton college. Late medieval secular building. The dissolution of the monasteries. Conclusion

Enclosure and depopulation

IN SPITE OF short-term fluctuations, the over-all impression of the centuries from the Norman Conquest to the coming of the Black Death is of a period of expansion, stimulated ultimately by population growth. The area of cultivated land continued to expand at the expense of wood, waste and marsh. Hamlets grew into villages, villages into towns. Churches were rebuilt, altered and enlarged. Trade developed, travel became easier. In contrast the centuries from the Black Death to the accession of the Tudors are characterised as years of decline and decay, with deserted villages, arable land tumbling to rough pasture, roofless buildings and falling population. Traditionally the reasons for this long period of stagnation and decline have been found in the effects of the ravages of the Black Death at its first coming in 1348–50 and in subsequent outbreaks of the disease later in the fourteenth century. More recently however, some historians would find the roots and origins of this period of decline in factors which were already becoming apparent in the half century before 1348. Population pressure, it is argued, had already stretched to their limits and beyond the capacities of medieval farming to produce sufficient food. Every available acre was under the plough, with soil exhaustion a real possibility and reserves of fresh arable, hitherto plentifully available in wood and waste, almost entirely consumed. Land-hungry peasants were prepared to pay higher and higher rents for smaller and smaller farms in their scramble to find a means of subsistence, however meagre. Other historians find this an exaggerated picture. Rents were not excessively high on every manor and estate. The subdivision of peasant farms seems often to have been carried to its greatest extreme in areas of ample waste and wood, with the implication that tenants could supplement the produce from their diminutive plots of arable by exploiting that of forest and common. At the same time industries were developing in both town and country, providing further sources of income.

The generalisations of historians often conceal very wide local and regional differences, and in any case the search for simple causal explanations for what was an immensely complex process can only be a spurious exercise. Nevertheless the evidence for late medieval decline is overwhelming, and across the landscape of these centuries lies the dark, terrifying shadow of the Black Death.

There is evidence to show that in some parts of Buckinghamshire the limits of cultivation may already have been reached before 1348, and that soils, especially along the Chiltern scarp, were exhausted. Returns to a tax of a ninth made in 1341 show that in a large number of villages in the county some arable land had been abandoned, although in only fourteen is soil exhaustion blamed for this.[1] Significantly, however, all save four of the villages concerned lay either along the Chiltern scarp or in the hills themselves. At Edlesborough 300 acres lay uncultivated, the soil exhausted. At Ivinghoe 400 acres and more lay uncultivated, and the parishioners were too poor to have animals with which to plough, or seed corn to sow. The major part of their land was white and hilly. In the north, at both Lillingstone Dayrell and Thornborough it was said that a carucate of sterile land used to be cultivated, whilst at Radclive the greater part of the village arable lay uncultivated, and that which was tilled was much debilitated.

[1] A. R. H. Baker, 'Evidence in the *Nonarum Inquisitiones* of Contracting Arable Lands in England during the Early Fourteenth Century', *Economic History Review* Ser. 2. XIX (1966), pp. 518–532. Reprinted in A. R. H. Baker, J. D. Hamshere and J. Langton, eds., *Geographical Interpretations of Historical Sources* (1970), pp. 85–100.

Now the 1341 record was prepared for taxation purposes, and so cries of poverty in such documents must be taken with a pinch of salt. Nevertheless abandoned arable land was widespread throughout the county and so it may very well represent a falling away from a peak. On the other hand we do not know sufficient about conditions in individual villages on either side of 1341 to be able to say whether or not this document represents normal conditions.

Occasionally other causes for the poverty are given or implied. At Great Crawley the pasture was poor. At Great Brickhill sixty acres lay uncultivated, the land of the parish being very sandy. At Fingest, where the major part of the land lay uncultivated, this was because it had been included in a new park and there was scarcely four virgates of arable land left. This would have been the park granted to the bishop of Lincoln in 1330. There was a similar situation at Stoke Poges, where the new park of Sir John Moleyns had swallowed up a carucate and fifty acres of land, all of which lay uncultivated.

There is no simple explanation to fit all circumstances, but clearly much land lay uncultivated throughout the county, and pleas of soil exhaustion occur too frequently for them all to be dismissed as attempts to evade taxation. That medieval farmers had overstretched their resources in many parts of the county in order to feed an ever-growing number of mouths is a very real possibility. At this point, however, an independent biological factor intervened. The bacillus *Pasteurella pestis* made sure that population pressure would not be a problem for the next two hundred years.

It is at this point too that two basically unrelated long-term developments at work on the Buckinghamshire landscape become increasingly intimately related and reach a peak in the years from about 1450 to about 1520. These two factors are first of all enclosure, particularly of arable land, and secondly the desertion of settlements. Both have, by the middle of the fourteenth century, been at work for a very long time in the Buckinghamshire landscape, but they enter into a causal relationship only in the fifteenth century. Both continued after the end of that century, but the total disappearance of villages comes almost to a standstill, whereas the process of enclosure continues to gather a momentum which is not exhausted until the second half of the nineteenth century.

We have seen in chapter 2 that the settlement pattern which had become established by the time of the Norman Conquest was a complex one in which a number of shifting hamlets might be subsumed under the name of an estate, the boundaries of which might be very ancient indeed. Some of these settlements have survived down to the present, others, an unknown number, have disappeared. The desertion of medieval villages has been much studied in recent years, [2] and it is now apparent that the reasons for the abandonment of settlements are very much more complex and that the time scale for their desertion is very much longer than has hitherto been appreciated. Excavations such as that at Walton near Aylesbury have revealed that hamlets could be abandoned and then re-occupied in Anglo-Saxon times. It is extremely likely that there was a steady trickle of desertions in the period from the Conquest to the Black Death, but their identification is made particularly difficult by the absence of comprehensive lists of villages and hamlets in the county before the beginning of the fourteenth century, so that for our knowledge of desertions before 1348 we have to rely upon chance references among relatively few documents. Thus in a taxation list drawn up in 1217 *Chalueleia*, *Aisses* and *Linlei* were all sufficiently large to be taxed separately, although they were among the smallest tax-paying villages. [3] As villages nothing is heard of them again after the end of the thirteenth century, although *Aisses* may be the Nash End which was paying 3s. 4d. for rights of common in the Forest of Bernwood as late as 1452. Today they are represented by Chawley Farm in West Wycombe, Nashway Farm in Brill and Lillyfee Farm in Hedsor.

The sites of at least sixty completely deserted villages are known in Buckinghamshire. They are marked on Fig. 14. They enjoy a wide variety of sites, soils and situations and so

[2] M. W. Beresford and J. G. Hurst, eds., *Deserted Medieval Villages* (1971).

[3] A. C. Chibnall, ed., 'Early Taxation Returns', *Buckinghamshire Record Society* XIV, (1966), pp. 110–116.

no simplistic explanation, such as that they represent a retreat from marginal soils, will suffice as a reason for the abandonment of them all. Several parishes contain two or more – Hardmead, Quainton, Waddesdon, Quarrendon – for which there is no known name. It seems clear that the great majority of desertions were of comparatively small hamlets and in perhaps no more than a dozen cases was the church village in a parish seriously affected. These sites date from every century, since the date of desertion of the majority of them is not known even approximately, and they include the eighteenth-century desertions of Wotton Underwood, Gayhurst and Stowe, so that Fig. 14, like so many distribution maps, is misleading in that it lacks a chronological dimension.

We can at present only guess at the reasons for the abandonment of villages before 1350. Their desertion in the later middle ages is probably due to two causes: the working out of the consequences of the high mortality from the Black Death and its later visitations during the course of the fourteenth century, and enclosure and the conversion of arable to pasture during the fifteenth. But there may well be a third reason, and this is climatic deterioration leading to soil degradation, something which may go part of the way towards explaining at least some of the desertions before 1350. Let us look at each in turn.

It is likely that the direct effects of the Black Death can be exaggerated. Certainly mortality was high in many places, but in Buckinghamshire at any rate it seems that no village was deserted permanently as a direct result of the plague. At Kimble it was stated in 1349 that all the tenants were dead and the lands uncultivated. But in due course the lands were taken up again and the village slowly returned to life. Nevertheless it is likely that a number of villages were seriously weakened as a result of the Black Death, never returned to their former vigour, and finally came to an end as much as fifty years later. There are several examples of deserted villages whose fate is best explained in this way. The taxation list of 1217 already mentioned shows the village of *Hasele* paying five shillings. It is described in Domesday Book, when

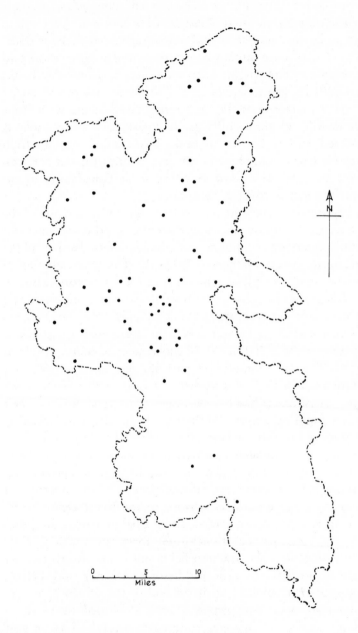

Fig. 14. Deserted villages in Buckinghamshire

it was said to have land for one and a half ploughs and meadow for the plough teams. It is last heard of in 1364, when it was said to be in Radclive. It has now disappeared without trace, its very site being unknown. A rather similar story can be told for *Halling*. This village does not appear in Domesday Book, although its name derives from *Heallingas*, one of the earlier forms of place-names. In 1217 it was taxed, along with Stoke Mandeville, at eight shillings. It is last heard of in 1382. A deserted site is known in Stoke Mandeville, not far from Timse's Farm. This may be the site of *Halling*, but we shall never be sure, since not even the most painstaking of excavations can uncover a place-name.

These two villages are not heard of again after the end of the fourteenth century, and are therefore good candidates for inclusion among the numbers of villages deserted as part of the long-term effects of the Black Death. The amalgamation of parishes may also tell us something of the long-term impact of the Black Death, since a parish would be very unlikely to lose its status if there were still a viable congregation. The parishes of Great and Little Loughton were amalgamated in 1409, and the two in Saunderton, St Nicholas and St Mary, in about 1450. The two Saunderton parishes had been severely hit before 1348 since it was reported in 1341 that in St Nicholas many parishioners had left because of their great poverty, their houses standing empty and their lands uncultivated, whilst in St Mary a carucate of land lay uncultivated. However, since the only other parishes in which depopulation was reported in 1341, namely Hambleden and Cublington, eventually re-covered, the decline and disappearance of Saunderton St Nicholas may perhaps be ascribed to the Black Death rather than to any preceding events. Later amalgamations are prob-ably the consequence of enclosure. Evershaw was a separate parish with its own common fields until the fifteeth century when it became part of Biddlesden. Okeney and Petsoe, independent chapelries until the end of the fifteenth century when they were amalgamated, were described in 1561, as having neither church nor congregation, and in 1650 they became part of Emberton.

Altogether it is likely that the desertion of no more than a dozen of the sixty sites marked on Fig. 14 can be ascribed to the consequences, however remote, of the Black Death. The second cause for the desertion of many medieval villages may well be the eviction of the villagers from their cottages and the enclosure of their arable fields for pasture.

The causes of this enclosure movement of the fifteenth century are to be sought in national, indeed in international, economic history. Rising demand for wool from the second half of the fourteenth century onwards made pastureland for sheep increasingly valuable, and the pressure to enclose open arable fields and turn them into pasture became irresistible in many areas of midland England, including north Buckinghamshire. This pressure was cyclical in its incidence, the first wave of enclosures falling between about 1450 and about 1480. It is poorly recorded, and as far as the surviving evidence allows us to judge, it seems to have passed off without a great deal of protest, due perhaps, to the fact that labour was still at a premium and dispossessed villagers and tenants found it comparatively easy either to find other holdings or else to find employment in the towns. By the early years of the sixteenth century however population growth was pressing hard upon available resources, and so ejected peasants and farmers found it very much more difficult to find alternative means of subsistence. Many contemporaries now saw enclosure and the subsequent depopulation as a serious threat to social stability. As Sir Thomas More wrote: "your sheep, that were wont to be so meek and tame and so small eaters, now, as I hear say, be become so great devourers and so wild, that they eat up and swallow down the very men themselves. They consume, destroy and devour whole fields, houses and cities."

The result was a vigorous pamphlet war, several government enquiries, in 1517–18, 1548–9, 1566 and 1607, and a number of ineffectual acts of Parliament. The overall impression from the surviving Buckinghamshire returns to these enquiries, none of which was prepared to look further back than 1488, is that in fact the really large-scale enclosures had already taken place, and that the great majority of those caught in the net of successive enquiries were only the small fry. Nor did they catch every encloser even then. In 1519 it was reported in an ecclesiastical visitation that Thomas Hawtry had enclosed the fields of Tetchwick in the parish of Ludgershall and refused to contribute to the repair of the mother church. None of the enclosure enquiries mentions Thomas Hawtry.

In the returns to the 1517 enquiry the total area reported as having been enclosed in Buckinghamshire was just under 9,000 acres, less than two per cent of the area of the county.[4] The largest single enclosure by far took place at Doddershall, where Thomas Pigott enclosed 960 acres for pasture in 1495. Twenty-four houses were destroyed and 120 persons were evicted. The landscape to the west of Quainton is still very empty, apart from the sheep. At Bradwell and Wolverton 425 acres were enclosed, of which twenty-five went to make Bradwell Park, forty-two acres went to arable, and the rest went down to pasture. At Castlethorpe, where 280 acres were enclosed to pasture, the manor house was destroyed and 88 villagers were evicted. The south of the county did not escape entirely, since at Stoke Poges 200 acres were enclosed for pasture and twelve persons evicted, and in Chesham 280 acres were enclosed, this time for arable. Nevertheless, although enclosure was widespread over the county only Burston, Littlecote and Lillingstone Dayrell were actually described as having been totally destroyed. Clearly the period from 1488 to 1517 was not the one which saw the desertion of the majority of the sixty known sites.

No returns survive for Buckinghamshire for the 1548 enquiry. The largest enclosure reported in 1566 was of 560 acres in Thornton, when twelve houses of husbandry were said to be decayed, as well as the parsonage house. At Twyford ninety-two acres were imparked by Sir Richard Wenman. At Castlethorpe 105 acres, parcel of the demesne of the decayed castle, were enclosed, presumably in addition to the 280 acres reported in 1517. At Stewkley it was said that twenty-six years

[4] I. S. Leadam, ed., *The Domesday of Inclosures 1517–1518* Vol. 2 (1897, 1971 reprint), p. 584.

ago a hundred acres in Stewkley Grange were enclosed, barns and other houses were utterly decayed and the mansion house was now occupied only by a shepherd. However the land had now been returned to tillage and the houses rebuilt.[5]

Up to the early years of the sixteenth century it is clear that the principal object of enclosure had been to provide grazing for sheep. From mid-century the motives change. The keeping of cattle and the improvement of arable farming become of equal importance. At the same time the years after about 1520 see a dramatic decline in the numbers of villages which are entirely depopulated as a result of enclosure. Enclosure continues to take place after mid-century, but its impact on villages and hamlets was less dramatic than it had been, and the result was often piecemeal enclosure with only very limited eviction of tenants.

In some villages the process of enclosure could be comparatively swift, its effects on the village, its landscape and its inhabitants, rapid and profound. In other villages it was a much more protracted affair, sometimes taking two or three generations to complete. Yet whatever the speed of enclosure the ultimate result was the same. All that is left today is a series of grass-covered mounds and hollows where once was a village, together with the ridge and furrow pattern of the arable fields, the result of centuries of ploughing by peasant-farmers, and so indelibly engraved into the landscape that only modern earth-moving machinery has been able to make any impression on it. The characteristic wave-like patterns produced by this ridge and furrow can still be seen today in many fields in the north of the county, underlying the hedges and ditches which were laid out over them to form the new field boundaries (Plate 19).

The full extent of the surviving earthworks of many deserted villages can best be appreciated only from the air, but it requires the combination of aerial photographs, documents and field work for individual villages before we can begin to grasp something of the variety and complexity of the factors

[5] P.R.O. E.178/424.

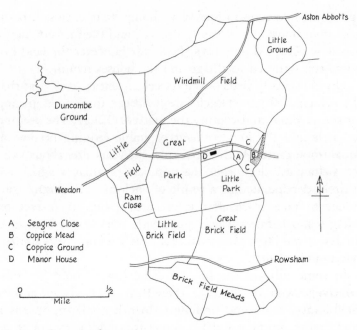

Windmill Field
Aston Abbotts
Little Ground
Duncombe Ground
Little Field
Great
Weedon
Park
Ram Close
Little Park
Little Brick Field
Great Brick Field
Rowsham
Brick Field Meads

A   Seagres Close
B   Coppice Mead
C   Coppice Ground
D   Manor House

0 ————————— ½
        Mile

Fig. 15. Burston after enclosure

making for change in the sixteenth-century landscape, as two examples may show.

At Burston in 1086 there were four plough-lands, with eight villeins, three bordars and a serf. It was taxed separately in 1217, but thereafter it appeared with Whitchurch, and we have no way of separating out the contributions of each. In 1489 eight ploughs were put down, sixty persons were evicted and 400 acres were enclosed for pasture. In 1517 it was said that the entire hamlet and manor had been converted to pasture. In the ecclesiastical survey of 1563 there were said to be only three families living there. In 1526 Robert Lee, who had bought the estate in 1516, received a royal licence to make a park at Burston. In 1620 his collateral descendant Sir Henry Lee was reported to have four enclosed grounds at Burston, the Park, Windmill Field, the Little Field and Brick Field. These supported 1,200 sheep and were worth £522 a year.[6] They are marked on a map of 1720 which is the basis of Fig. 15, and

[6] Bodleian Library, Oxford. Willis MS.30, f. 14.

154

they survive almost unchanged into the landscape of today (Plate 18).

At Burston enclosure and depopulation seem to have been swift and sudden, embracing the entire hamlet and its arable. At Littlecote however the process was much more prolonged. Some enclosure took place in 1494, more in the years immediately before 1507, and yet more in about 1540, and on each occasion by a different landlord, whilst one part of the hamlet lying in the Folding Field of Stewkley had to wait until 1811 for enclosure. Nevertheless the results were the same as at Burston. An isolated farm now stands surrounded by the tumbled house platforms and grass-covered ridge and furrow of a former village (Plate 19).

Burston and Littlecote are only two of the deserted villages in the Buckinghamshire landscape. Their histories show that enclosure could be a protracted affair, that it was not always the work of one landlord, that depopulation could come swiftly, or it could be spaced over a generation or more. Only much more detailed research can tell us how far their histories are characteristic of those of other deserted villages in the county.

The enclosures of the fifteenth and sixteenth centuries produced two kinds of fields: first of all comparatively small ones rarely much over twenty acres, and secondly immense pastures running into hundreds of acres (Fig. 16). At Aston Mullins enclosure produced one large field, the Great Ground, of 141 acres, and a number of smaller ones. At Creslow enclosure probably took place early in the fifteenth century. Here the Great Field extended over 310 acres. These huge fields were designed primarily to take large flocks and herds, whilst the smaller ones were sometimes arable. Changes in agricultural practice have produced two modifications into this landscape. First of all some of the smaller fields have been thrown into one another by having their boundary hedges removed, and secondly the larger fields have been divided up into smaller and more easily managed units. These changes have not always succeeded in removing all traces of earlier patterns. Fifteenth- and sixteenth-century field boundaries can often be recognised from their curving shapes. Later bound-

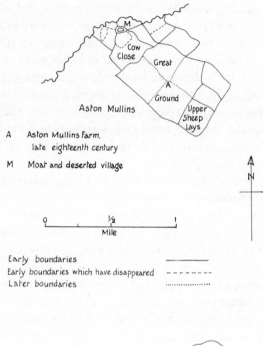

A   Aston Mullins Farm,
           late eighteenth century

M   Moat and deserted village

0   ½   1
             Mile

Early boundaries   ————————
Early boundaries which have disappeared   – – – – – – –
Later boundaries   ·················

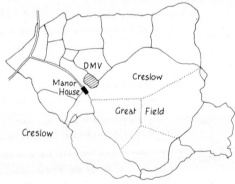

DMV   Deserted Medieval Village

Fig. 16. Aston Mullins and Creslow after enclosure

aries are usually quite straight. The contrast between the two sometimes serves to distinguish the older from the more recent. Thus the Great Ground at Aston Mullins has been divided into four by straight hedgerows, and the curving boundaries to the fields at Creslow betray at least the skeleton framework of the first enclosures, whilst the straight ones show where the huge Great Field has been divided up.

Almost all of the known Buckinghamshire deserted villages lie north of the Chilterns and it is clear that north Buckinghamshire was severely affected by enclosure and depopulation in the fifteenth and early sixteenth centuries. It is nonetheless apparent that we have accounted at the outside for no more than threequarters of the sites marked on Fig. 14. Neither enclosure for pasture nor the consequences of the Black Death can explain all of the desertions in Buckinghamshire. Recent research suggests[7] that the desertion of villages on clay soils could be due to a third reason, the implications of which are as yet scarcely explored for Buckinghamshire. From the early part of the thirteenth century to the early part of the fifteenth seems to have been a period of marked climatic deterioration and instability: floods alternating with long droughts, harsh winters and either wet summers or long dry ones. Bad weather and the soil mis-management which is the corollary of the common-field system could lead very rapidly to soil degradation and the formation of hard, impervious 'pan' just beneath the surface of the soil, with crop failure inevitable. Soil degradation of this kind is particularly likely to occur on the heavy clays found over much of north Buckinghamshire, although its effects would be localised by local variations in soil structure. It is very likely that more than one village on Fig. 14 foundered in a quagmire of its own making. Only the most painstaking excavation can produce corroborative evidence, but it is likely to be more widespread than we have so far suspected.

Neither Act of Parliament nor Commission of Enquiry

---

[7] G. Beresford, *The Medieval Clay-land Village: Excavations at Goltho and Barton Blount,* The Society for Medieval Archaeology Monograph Series No. 6 (1975), esp. pp. 50–52.

could halt for very long the tidal wave of enclosure which swept over the county in the fifteenth and sixteenth centuries, gradually transforming its landscape. But the word 'gradually' must be emphasised, since the process took four hundred years, from the middle of the fifteenth to the middle of the nineteenth century, before it was finally completed. The methods employed to bring about enclosure might change over the centuries, but the fundamental aim remained the same, to divide up into separate plots the open fields, common pastures and wastes of the medieval village. We have to return to enclosure again and again during the course of the remaining chapters of this book.

Late medieval building in the landscape – churches

It is possible that the social and economic dislocation consequent upon the plague epidemics of the second half of the fourteenth century can be exaggerated. There is plenty of evidence in Buckinghamshire churches to show that money and effort could be found for alterations and additions which in some cases were substantial and occasionally amounted to a complete rebuilding. Earlier in this chapter we have used evidence from ruined churches and amalgamated parishes to point to population decline. We cannot therefore logically avoid evidence of alterations and additions to churches as evidence of population growth, although it would require intensive research at microscopic level to prove satisfactorily any connection between additions to churches and increases in population. In any case it must not be forgotten that as there was a considerable time-lag between the decline and desertion of a village and the disappearance of its church, so there must have been a similar time-lag between a rise in population and the building of an extension to the parish church to cope with it. Nevertheless alterations and additions are so widespread as to be more than fortuitous or coincidental. It is likely too that in Buckinghamshire as in other parts of the country much of the money for this rebuilding came ultimately from the broad backs of sheep.

There are now approximately two hundred medieval

churches in the Buckinghamshire landscape. One of their most characteristic features is a tower. Less than thirty do not have one of some kind, however modest. Buckinghamshire churches are not famous for their spires, indeed only two are of any size and they seem to be the consequence of influences from neighbouring Northamptonshire. At Olney the spire is late fourteenth century. At Hanslope the spire was built early in the fifteenth century, the rector, Thomas Knight, leaving money in his will towards the cost when he died in 1414. It was once 200 feet high, but it collapsed in 1804 after being struck by lightning and was rebuilt slightly lower, although it still remains the tallest spire in the county and an impressive landmark in the village. There was also a tall, slender spire to the medieval church at Buckingham. This was blown down in 1699 and never rebuilt.

However, neither towers nor spires were once so common in the Buckinghamshire landscape as they are today. More than half were added in the later medieval centuries, from that at Great Kimble, built late in the fourteenth century, to that at Newport Pagnell, built between 1542 and 1548. These late medieval towers are found all over the county, from Stoke Goldington in the north, where the west tower was built in about 1430, to Horton in the south, and from Brill in the west to Linslade in the east. Almost all are fifteenth century, although those at Hitcham, Oving and Soulbury were added early in the sixteenth.

A new tower involved considerable expenditure of money on the part of the pious, but can scarcely be said to be a contribution towards accommodating the progeny of a fecund population. But when an aisle is widened, as happened at Turweston in about 1360, at Chalfont St Giles in about 1410, and at Hanslope a little later in the fifteenth century, or lengthened, as at Haversham in about 1360, or built in entirety as happened at Denham in about 1460, then we can be fairly sure that the work has been carried out in order to provide room for a growing congregation. Such alterations and additions are to be found all over Buckinghamshire. The nave was lengthened at Radnage and at Stokenchurch in the fifteenth century. The north aisle was widened at Great Hampden early in that century, whilst the nave at East Claydon was widened a little later. A similar pattern of piecemeal additions is to be found at Bow Brickhill, Great Horwood and Mentmore.

It is interesting to note that additions of this kind also took place at churches in villages which are now to be numbered among deserted or shrunken ones. Thus a south aisle was added at Stowe late in the fourteenth century, the south aisle at Hardmead was widened in the middle of the fifteenth century, whilst the church of St Mary at Linslade had a west tower built in the fifteenth century and its chancel rebuilt early in the sixteenth.

Occasionally however, additions and alterations gave way to a complete rebuilding or a full-scale restoration. Thus Nicholas Ledewick, who died in 1430, paid for an extensive restoration of the church at Little Marlow. The church at Drayton Beauchamp was almost completely rebuilt late in the fifteenth century, although much of the existing stonework was re-used. There was extensive rebuilding at High Wycombe early in the sixteenth century. An entirely new church was built at Cublington at the beginning of the fifteenth century when the site of the village was reoccupied after its desertion at about the time of the Black Death. But the two most important fifteenth-century church rebuildings in Buckinghamshire took place at Hillesden and at Maids Moreton. At Hillesden the west tower was built early in the fifteenth century, all the rest of the church being rebuilt shortly after 1493. The living belonged to the abbot of Notley, and the church had been allowed to fall into considerable decay. Eventually the abbot was persuaded to pay for a complete rebuilding, and the result is an impressive example of late Perpendicular architecture, all the more so from its remote and isolated position in a tiny hamlet.

The church at Maids Moreton is said to have been rebuilt in the middle years of the fifteenth century at the expense of two maiden sisters of the Peover family. Whatever the truth of the legend, the church itself (Plate 20) is a splendid example of fifteenth-century craftsmanship, showing a strong sense of overall design. Fortunately, since it was finished it has remained almost completely untouched.

Churches certainly form the commonest medieval buildings still surviving in the Buckinghamshire landscape, and the one at Wing which we looked at in chapter 2 takes us back into a period when there was no Buckinghamshire. The continuity of the Church as an institution, in spite of the immense changes which it had to endure during the sixteenth century, coupled with the affection and skill which men have lavished upon its buildings, means that the great majority of medieval churches are still to be seen in the landscape today. This is in complete contrast to medieval secular building. Only a small handful have come down to us from before 1350, and probably no more than two or three dozen from before 1500, but among these is one of the most splendid late medieval buildings to be found anywhere in England.

Eton college

The King's College of Our Lady of Eton beside Windsor was founded by Henry VI in 1440. He acquired a low-lying site in a bend of the river Thames, a site containing the old parish church. The building of the college church began in 1441, and by October 1443 it was possible to celebrate mass for the first time at the High Altar, although the church was by no means finished. By the end of 1448 it appears to have been almost complete, but in 1449 almost all of what had been erected was pulled down and rebuilding began on an altogether larger scale. In 1460 Henry was deposed and building came to a halt. Work began again on the church in 1469, but the plans for a large nave and aisles were abandoned, and the west end of the church was finished off instead with an ante-chapel, completed in about 1482, by which time the old parish church had been demolished.

Work had been going on at the same time on the college buildings, and by the time of Henry's deposition the cloister buildings, containing the lodgings for the Provost and

Fellows (Plate 21), a Hall with service rooms, and the Lower
School Building, which housed the scholars and their masters,
had been erected, forming the east and north sides of School
Yard, with the choir of the church to the south.

The church was built of stone, but the college buildings
were of brick with stone dressings. They represent one of the
earliest large scale uses of brick as a building material in the
country. The bricks were made at Slough, on a site acquired
specially for the purpose, and during the ten years between
1442 and 1452 something like two and a half million bricks
were supplied.

The church, school and cloister buildings were conceived as
a whole, and sufficient was built at one time, much of it under
the personal supervision of Henry himself, to give an excellent
idea of what a medieval collegiate establishment would have
been like. Changing standards of comfort in accommodation
have led to much remodelling of the interiors of the original
buildings, but they have been scarcely touched externally, save
for restoration work, and since so much was built in the same
style and with the same materials later additions are clearly
additions and do not appear at all incongruous.

Important additions were made whilst Roger Lupton was
Provost, between 1503 and 1535. The Kitchen was partially
rebuilt and Lupton's Chapel was added, and the range of
buildings between the cloister and School Yard was rebuilt.
Late in the seventeenth century the west range to the School
Yard was built, but proved to be of faulty construction and so
was pulled down and replaced by the Upper School building,
added between 1689 and 1691. The growth of the school and
the broadening of the curriculum has led to a long series of
additions, particularly from the middle years of the nineteenth
century, but the medieval buildings as conceived by Henry VI
still remain the heart of Eton. The story of the college and its
buildings has been told several times and in considerable
detail,[8] and nothing new can be added to that story here. It is

[8] Sir H. C. Maxwell Lyte, *A History of Eton College 1440–1910* (4th ed. 1911).
R. A. Austen Leigh, *Illustrated Guide to the Buildings of Eton College* (1904 and
later).

sufficient to say that their historical interest, architectural importance and aesthetic value make the collegiate buildings of Eton the most important group of medieval buildings in Buckinghamshire.

Late medieval secular building

When looking at fortified manor houses in the previous chapter we saw that there are perhaps no more than three or four houses now surviving in Buckinghamshire from before 1350. Since there are so few, and since there is no real break in the history of the medieval house it seems best to consider them here, in conjunction with later medieval building, rather than on their own. Before we begin, however, there is one important reservation to be made. In spite of much rebuilding and alteration, addition and demolition, we can still see a medieval manor house if we look hard enough. But our picture of medieval domestic building is nonetheless a very partial one. Those houses which have survived are the houses of the wealthy. Of the flimsy cottages in which lived the great majority of the inhabitants of medieval Buckinghamshire nothing is now to be seen save the grass-covered house-platforms of some long-deserted village.

Once we have made this reservation we can see that the story of the more substantial medieval English house is the story of the gradual modification and subdivision of what was once the principal, at first the only, room, the great hall. This was usually rectangular, open to the roof, and with a central hearth. In the eleventh and twelfth centuries the only way in which a great hall could be widened beyond the quite modest dimensions which the timber then available would allow was by building two parallel aisles, supported on arcades of wooden posts, in much the same way as the nave of a church was widened by the addition of aisles. Aisled halls continued to be built into the fifteenth century. One dating from the early fourteenth century is to be found at Savehay Farm, Denham, where part of one of the arcades to the hall still survives.

By the beginning of the fourteenth century the problem of providing a wide roof span without the obstruction of arcades had been solved by the use of the hammerbeam roof. There is a fine example of such a roof in the Rectory Cottages at Bletchley, built in the fifteenth century and now restored under the auspices of Milton Keynes Development Corporation.

The great hall was already being subdivided before the Norman Conquest, at first with nothing more substantial than a wooden screen, but in due course with stone. At one end of the hall was a dais, where the owner and his family took their meals, raised above that odoriferous litter in the main body of the hall so picturesquely described by Erasmus, whilst at the opposite end two further rooms were partitioned off, the pantry for storing bread, and the buttery for storing ale. The dais continued to be a normal feature of many substantial houses well into the sixteenth century, and one is to be found at the east end of the great hall at Dorney Court, a fine timber-framed house built in about 1510.

Behind the dais, partitioned off from the great hall, was the great chamber or solar, where the family slept. This was almost always a first floor room, with a ground floor store-room underneath. By the fifteenth century this ground floor room is being called the parlour, and has become another room for sleeping. The great hall at Huntercombe Manor, Burnham, has a solar at its eastern end, whilst at Bell Farm, Eton Wick, built in the second half of the fourteenth century, the solar is in the west end.

By the beginning of the fourteenth century the portions partitioned off at opposite ends of the great hall have developed into separate wings, each of two storeys, and roofed at right angles to the hall. This H-plan is characteristic of much domestic building until well into the eighteenth century, and houses erected according to this ancient, traditional, arrangement, are still to be found in the Buckinghamshire landscape. That Bell Farm at Eton Wick already mentioned is one of the most interesting of all medieval houses in Buckinghamshire. It is a timber-framed house, dating from the second half of the fourteenth century. The central block, of two bays, contains the hall. This runs east to west. The two wings are at right angles, the solar in the west wing and the kitchen in the east. Long Crendon Manor is a house of the early fifteenth century and still has its fifteenth-century stone gatehouse. There is a three bay hall, and a two-storey wing at each end, although the west wing was rebuilt in the second half of the sixteenth century.

However the H-plan is but one way in which rooms could be arranged and the weight of custom did not prevent others being tried. A rectangular block under one roof continued to be used, as at Upton Court, built probably late in the fifteenth-century. In other houses the plan was L-shaped, as at Dorney Court. Yet others were T-shaped in plan, as at the fifteenth century Codmore Farm, Chesham, where the great hall is orientated east to west, with the screens dividing off the service rooms at the east end, and the crossing with the solar at the west end. Nor were such houses necessarily conceived and built as a whole, even in medieval times. Alterations to take account of changing fashions, tastes and economic circumstances have always taken place and are factors underlying the evolution of any and every facet of the landscape. At Hill Farm, Chalfont St Peter, for example, the oldest part is a hall of two bays built in the fourteenth century. A timber-framed wing was added in the fifteenth century to the south-west end of the hall, whilst the wing on the north was not added until the seventeenth century.

The medieval house in Buckinghamshire with the most unusual plan is undoubtedly the manor house at Creslow. In spite of successive and extensive alterations it is still possible to discern its original design. It was built in about 1330 of squared limestone blocks. The principal room was the great hall of four bays open to the roof and running approximately north and south with the dais at the south end. The solar wing, at the south end of the hall, had two rooms on the ground floor with a crypt beneath, a first storey and, at its south-west corner, a three-storey tower and a stair turret. It is likely that this stone manor house was erected on the site of an earlier structure since close by is what was once a private chapel containing twelfth-century details. Almost the whole of the parish of Creslow was, as we have already seen in this chapter, enclosed during the fifteenth century and the village depopulated. The manor house, almost in the centre of the parish is, even today, one of the most isolated spots in all Buckinghamshire.

Of medieval houses in Buckinghamshire towns, only a handful now survive, again much altered and modified over the centuries. At Marlow the Old Parsonage was originally a high stone hall, built in about 1340. Two fourteenth-century stone windows still stare out over cool green lawns, startling reminders of those medieval antecedents to the twentieth-century landscape, antecedents which conspire together to give that landscape its rich historical density. At Chesham Nos 54–56 Church Street was originally one L-shaped house, built in the fourteenth century of timber-framing with wattle and daub in-filling. It comprised a hall, now No. 56, and a solar wing, now No. 54. In spite of later alterations to the house the timbers of the gable end to the solar wing still face into Church Street as they have done for six hundred years (Plate 22).

But the two most interesting medieval town houses in Buckinghamshire are to be found in Buckingham and in Aylesbury. At Castle House, West Street, Buckingham, a digni-fied, brick-built Queen Anne façade conceals a late fifteenth-century house built originally around a courtyard, although the buildings on the north and east were demolished in about 1835. The hall was probably in the western range of buildings and seems to have been on the first rather than on the ground floor. The King's Head Hotel in Aylesbury was built in about the middle of the fifteenth century. Although it has been much altered and restored, it still retains its original plan of four ranges of buildings surrounding an inner court-yard. The main hall of the house lay to the left of the archway into the yard. The original ten light window of the hall is still to be seen, as well as some of the medieval glass. In spite of much restoration and some rather incongruous advertisements, the cobbled entrance passage, the timber-framed gables and the inner courtyard still provide at least a fleeting glimpse of something of medieval Aylesbury.

Finally we must look briefly at some of the Buckinghamshire examples of cruck construction, that building technique which has intrigued and fascinated historians more than any other aspect of domestic vernacular building. There is considerable variety in its details, and an elaborate nomenclature has been developed to cover them,[9] but basically cruck construction involves the use of pairs of timbers, rising from ground level to meet, more or less, at a point overhead. These timbers then serve as the trusses for the roof of the building. This means that walls do not have to be of substantial, load-bearing construction (Plate 23).

Cruck construction is to be seen as an alternative to timber box-frame construction, developed as one answer to the problem of getting rid of the clutter of posts that an aisled hall necessarily entailed. Substantial manor houses of the fourteenth century embodying crucks are to be found all over southern England, including two in Buckinghamshire, at Creslow manor house and at Huntercombe Manor, Burnham. By the early fifteenth century cruck construction was being employed in the building of houses for well-to-do peasants, and it is from this period that the great majority of Buckinghamshire cruck built houses appear to date. It is likely that the technique had been abandoned in Buckinghamshire by the end of the sixteenth century.

The largest group of cruck built houses in the county is to be found at Long Crendon, where there are twelve. The demolition, alteration, patching and rebuilding so characteristic of Buckinghamshire vernacular building has undoubtedly swept many away without trace, and there is documentary evidence for at least one of those lost in this manner. The Queen's wardrobe in the royal palace at Brill, mentioned in 1245, was of cruck construction. The very site of this palace is now uncertain. At the same time further research among the surviving vernacular buildings of the county will

[9] see E. Mercer, *English Vernacular Houses* (1975), esp. chap. 7.

undoubtedly uncover more from beneath the layers of brick and plaster of subsequent generations.

The dissolution of the monasteries

The enclosure of the open fields of the medieval villages of north Buckinghamshire wrought a profound change in the landscape, although the change was at first very localised and its impact can be exaggerated. Enclosure would take four hundred years to complete. For the peasants turned out of their cottages in Hogshaw or Lillingstone Dayrell enclosure must have meant upheaval of the most dramatic kind, although we have no knowledge of their fate once they had left their homes. Nevertheless thousands of other villagers lived out their lives affected only indirectly by enclosure.

The late medieval landscape was altered by another change which came much more swiftly than enclosure and was worked out completely within a few years. We are not concerned with the political, religious and personal motives underlying the dissolution of the monasteries by Henry VIII. It is sufficient to say that one of the institutions most influential in the development of the landscape over the previous four hundred years came to an abrupt end on 19 September 1539, when the last religious house in Buckinghamshire, Burnham Abbey, surrendered to the king. Within a few years many conventual buildings lay in ruins, their roofs stripped of lead, their walls a quarry for neighbouring farmers, whilst others were already being converted into country houses.

Enthusiasm for the monastic ideal had by the fifteenth century long since flickered and failed, and no new house had been founded in Buckinghamshire since the Franciscan Friary at Aylesbury was established in about 1382. Instead the closure of monastic houses came early to Buckinghamshire. The alien cell at Wing was closed in 1416, and the estates of that at Newton Longville were granted to New College, Oxford, in 1441. In 1461 the priory at Chetwode was dissolved and its property went to the abbey at Notley. The house at Luffield, never very wealthy, became increasingly

Plate 23 A cruck-built cottage at Nearton End, Swanbourne.

Plate 24 The west tower of the Augustinian priory at Chetwode, built in about 1480 on to the chancel of the priory church. It became the parish church after the dissolution of the priory.

Plate 25 Part of a map of the Chequers estate made in 1629. South is on the right-hand side of the plate, and the house itself is almost in the middle.

Plate 26 A map of Upper Hall Farm, North End, Hughenden, made in 1673. Many of the boundaries survive unchanged. North is in the bottom right-hand corner.

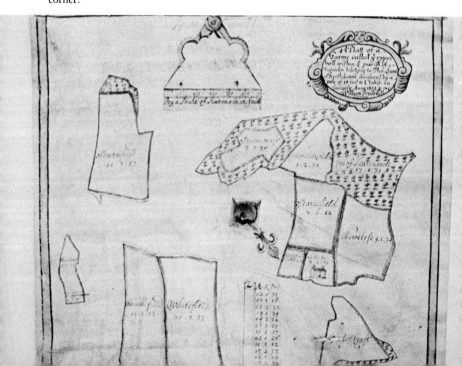

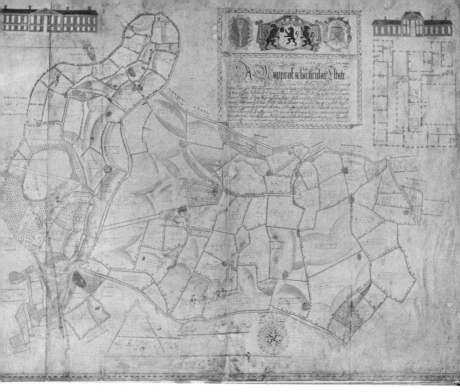

Plate 27 A map of the estate of Judge Jeffries at Bulstrode, made in 1686. North is at the lower edge of the map. The M40 motorway now slices through the middle of this landscape.

Plate 28 The late sixteenth-century house at Gayhurst.

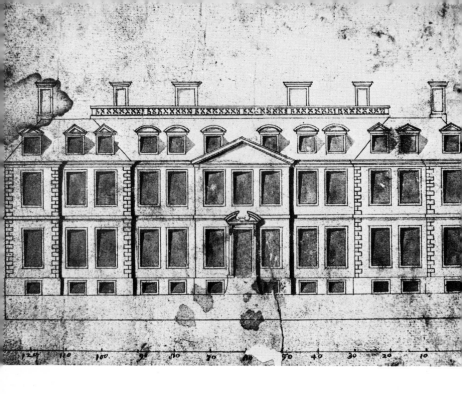

Plates 29 and 30 Late seventeenth-century drawings of the North and South Fronts of Sir Richard Temple's new house at Stowe.

impoverished during the course of the fifteenth century, and was eventually dissolved in 1494, its lands going to the abbey of Westminster. In 1524 Cardinal Wolsey procured the suppression of three more Buckinghamshire houses, Bradwell, Tickford and Ravenstone. Their estates went towards the endowment of his college at Oxford. The remaining houses were dissolved between 1535 and 1539. One of the most prominent strands in the fabric of the medieval Buckinghamshire landscape had run out.

Of the actual buildings of Buckinghamshire monastic houses very little now survives. Most remains at Burnham, where the east range of the cloisters, the chapter house, sacristy, parts of the infirmary and a stretch of the precinct wall are incorporated into a modern nunnery. At Notley the fine Abbot's Lodging, built in two stages, at the end of the fifteenth century and in about 1530, forms the basis of the modern house. At Missenden a house, now an Adult Residential College, was built over the cloisters and incorporates the fine fifteenth-century timber roof of the dormitory. At Bradwell the chapel and a great barn survive, and recent excavations have revealed much of the plan of the site. From the house at Ankerwyke some lengths of walling still stand. Tickford House incorporates fragments from the monastery, whilst of Medmenham abbey there is only a single pier still remaining. There is finally the church at Chetwode (Plate 24). By the end of the fifteenth century the parish church at Chetwode had decayed and fallen into ruin, whereupon the parishioners agreed with the abbot of Notley in 1480 that they might use the church of the dissolved priory of Chetwode, which, as we have seen, came into the hands of the abbot in 1461, as their parish church. The tall narrow west tower was then added. When Notley was in its turn dissolved its properties in Chetwode were acquired by the Risley family. There were acrimonious disputes between the family and the parishioners, during the course of which the old church of St Martin was finally demolished, together with the nave and transepts of the priory church.[10] Thus the church at Chetwode

[10] P.R.O. Star Chamber 4. 8/42.

as it survives today comprises only the choir of the old conventual church, the north chapel and the tower. Of the other priory buildings nothing now remains.

Conclusion

By the middle years of the sixteenth century the Buckinghamshire landscape had undergone more than a century of rapid change, probably the most rapid and far-reaching so far in its history in so short a period of time. Its monasteries had been dissolved. Some of the conventual buildings had been adapted for other purposes, but many others were already in an advanced stage of disrepair, and almost ruinous. The dissolution of the monasteries had led to a rapid turnover of the owners and tenants of land, leaving some of the Oxford colleges, together with Eton College, as the largest corporate landowners. The enclosure of land, which had been going on piecemeal for generations, suddenly accelerated dramatically during the fifteenth century under the pressure of international economic trends. Many open fields in the north of the county were enclosed, either in whole or in part, many peasants were dispossessed and several villages and hamlets were entirely destroyed. Enclosure must certainly occupy a central position in any account of this century, but we must be careful not to over-dramatise. Burston and Littlecote may have disappeared as hamlets and their open fields have been divided up into pastures for sheep, but Maids Moreton and Padbury were completely untouched, their great open fields still stretched to the horizon, and they were by no means unique.

The period ending in the middle of the sixteenth century is also of importance because it is really the first for which there is any significant survival into the twentieth century of elements from it, with churches providing the greatest element of stability. The later medieval changes which they endured are almost everywhere still to be seen, and this in spite of the often heavy-handed approach of Victorian restorers. Much ridge and furrow is still visible, and there are still many miles of late medieval field boundaries to be found in most parts of the county, as even the most superficial study of the trees and shrubs of their hedgerows will show. The county is not nearly so well endowed with surviving late medieval domestic buildings as is Kent, but there are several of great interest, whilst the buildings of Eton College are unique and of national importance.

But however important the changes of the preceding century may have been in some districts, the great majority of the woods, fields, lanes, towns and villages of Buckinghamshire remained almost entirely unaffected. The Forest of Bernwood was still largely wooded and given over to the deer. Wycombe Common and Iver Heath were still immense tracts of poor scrub and rough grazing. The pace of change in the last medieval centuries was as nothing compared with what was to come.

SELECT BIBLIOGRAPHY

Alcock, N. W., *A Catalogue of Cruck Buildings* (1973).

Faulkner, P., 'Domestic Planning from the Twelfth to the Fourteenth Centuries', *Archaeological Journal* 115, (1958), pp. 150–184.

Foster, P., 'Eton College Buildings', *Ancient Monuments Society Transactions* 18, (1971), pp. 23–35.

Hoskins, W. G., *The Age of Plunder* (1976).

Mead, W. R., 'Ridge and Furrow in Buckinghamshire', *Geographical Journal* 120, (1954), pp. 34–42.

Mead, W. R., 'The Study of Field Boundaries', *Geographische Zeitschrift* 54, (1966), pp. 101–117.

Pantin, W. A., 'Medieval English Town-House Plans', *Medieval Archaeology* 6–7, (1962–1963), pp. 202–239.

Taylor, C., *Fields in the English Landscape* (1975).

Wood, M. E., 'A Fourteenth Century House at Marlow', *Journal of the British Archaeological Association* 3rd Series 12, (1949), pp. 53–58.

6. Tudor and Stuart Buckinghamshire, 1550-1700

Introduction. The rural landscape — The common fields — Enclosure — The Chilterns — Woods and their management. The great rebuilding in town and country. The disafforestation of Bernwood

Introduction

WHEN JOHN LELAND in about 1540 crossed from Thame over Crendon bridge into Buckinghamshire on his way to Quarrendon we have for the first time a glimpse of the landscape through the eyes of a contemporary observer. From Quarrendon he went on for two miles "by great champaine, frutfull for pastures", to Burston, where Master Lee had a goodly house with orchards and a park. Here he would have found still raw and immature the newly enclosed landscape which we studied in the previous chapter (see Fig. 15). From Burston he travelled on to Aylesbury and then to Wendover, the road being a causeway almost all of the way because it crosses a low, stiff clay ground which in wet weather "were very tedius and ille to passe by".[1] He noticed that the Vale of Aylesbury was almost devoid of wood, whereas the Chilterns were well wooded and full of enclosures.

Perhaps forty years later William Camden came to Buckinghamshire. He thought the soil very fruitful and the inhabitants numerous. He too noticed that the Chilterns were covered with woods and that the Vale of Aylesbury was almost entirely open, the rich meadows feeding an incredible number of sheep. He described High Wycombe as a large and beautiful town.[2] Richard Blome, whose *Britannia* was published in 1673, also

---

[1] L. Toulmin Smith, ed., *The Itinerary of John Leland* Vol. 2 (1964 edition), p. 110.
[2] *Camden's Britannia* 2nd. ed. by Edmund Gibson (1695, 1971 facsimile reprint), p. 278 et seq.

remarked upon the large flocks of sheep to be found in the Vale, and he too thought High Wycombe a handsome town.

Celia Fiennes travelled through the northern part of the county at the very end of the seventeenth century. At Stony Stratford she found a little place, built all of stone, where a good deal of bone lace was made, people sitting and working all along the street. She much admired Sir Richard Temple's new house at Stowe, although she did not think the hall was very large in proportion to its height. She climbed up on to the roof through the recently added cupola and from there she had a fine prospect of the whole country.[3]

The last of these travellers we can mention is Daniel Defoe. He visited the county in the early years of the eighteenth century. He thought the Vale of Aylesbury, where all the gentlemen were graziers, although not all the graziers were gentlemen, was the richest land, with perhaps the richest graziers, in all England. Great Marlow was a busy river port, where goods from the neighbouring towns were loaded on to barges for London, especially malt and meal from High Wycombe, one of the greatest corn markets in this part of England. On the river between Wycombe and Marlow were many paper mills.[4]

The remarks of these sixteenth- and seventeenth-century visitors draw attention to what will be some of the principal themes of this chapter: pasture and sheep in the Vale of Aylesbury, enclosures and woods in the Chilterns, country houses and parks, whilst references to paper mills and bone lace indicate newly developing industries. Much of what they saw has changed beyond recognition. All that is left, externally at any rate, of the house that Celia Fiennes visited at Stowe is the porch to the door on the North Front. The comments of Camden and Blome on late twentieth-century High Wycombe would make interesting reading indeed. But it is the detail which has changed, the framework of their landscape still survives.

[3] C. Morris, ed., *The Journeys of Celia Fiennes* (1949), pp. 29–30, 119.
[4] D. Defoe, *A Tour Through England and Wales* (Everyman's Library ed., 1928 and reprints), Vol. 1, pp. 298–300, Vol. 2, pp. 14–15.

The rural landscape – the common fields

The enclosure movement of the fifteenth and early sixteenth centuries left many of the common-field villages of north Buckinghamshire untouched, so that immense open fields, cultivated in strips, continued to dominate their landscapes (Figs. 8 and 17). By the end of the sixteenth century a number of detailed written surveys had been compiled, and several large-scale maps made, giving us the most vivid picture that we can now ever have of what these common-field villages must have looked like. A very detailed survey of Chicheley was written out in 1557,[5] enumerating the tenants of several thousands of strips of arable land scattered over three huge fields, Heyfield of 516 acres plus meadowland, lying on the south side of the village, Barlong Field of 360 acres and meadow, and Brook Field of 480 acres and meadow. Cultivation had been pushed to the parish boundaries. The fields of Chicheley and Sherington were separated only by a balk. The survey reveals just how small the individual strips in the fields could be. Tyckfordeashe furlong in the Heyfield contained eighteen and a half acres, divided into forty-nine strips, and the Acrehed furlong in the same field contained within its thirty-nine acres no less than 109 strips. Some of the furlongs also contained patches of pasture and meadow which on occasion must also have been very small. Crosse furlong, still in Heyfield, contained three strips and a slade of grass next to the brook, and yet measured only three roods in area.

In Padbury (Fig. 17), almost the whole of the parish was given over to arable. There was no woodland at all, and only one area of any size of common and meadow, right on the northern boundary. Maids Moreton was perhaps a little better endowed. The Furzan Pasture, on the boundary with Akeley, extended over 144 acres, and Almeade Leas, on the boundary with Stowe, covered fifty-one acres, but there were only two areas of woodland, Moreton Park, of eight acres, and Mrs More's Wood Ground, of perhaps twelve acres. Both of these were enclosed and held in severalty. Moreton Park has long been cleared, but

[5] B.R.O. DC/2/11.

Mrs More's Wood Ground is still wooded, and called Long's Wood. As in Padbury, land less intensively used was furthest away from the village. At Thornborough (Fig. 8), there was an even greater area of common, perhaps as much as a quarter of the parish, but no woodland.

These maps and documents convey a detailed picture of the ragged, untidy landscape of a common-field village. But a picture is essentially static. The landscape could and did change, even in the most conservative of common-field villages, and it was enclosure that was one of the catalysts.

Enclosure

We saw in the last chapter that many villages north of the Chiltern scarp were affected during the course of the fifteenth and early sixteenth centuries by the enclosure of arable fields, almost always for pasture. The pace of enclosure probably slackened in Buckinghamshire in the middle decades of the sixteenth century, to gather a new momentum towards its close. At the same time the aims of enclosers became more diversified. They were as much concerned with improving stock raising and arable farming as with grazing sheep, since the decline of the cloth trade after 1551 began to reduce the profitability of wool, although it still continued to be of great importance. Nor was enclosure confined to existing arable, but was extended to pasture, meadow, wastes and woodland. Furthermore the impact of enclosure on the landscape after about 1550 differed from that of the fifteenth and early sixteenth centuries. The closes and paddocks it produced were generally smaller and often quite regular in shape when compared with those of the fifteenth century, whilst no village seems to have been completely depopulated during this period, although several show very real signs of shrinkage and almost stagnant populations as some holdings were abandoned.

Some enclosure was still being pushed through at the will of a single proprietor. In other villages it is clear that some kind of a bargain has been struck between a landlord and his tenants, whilst in yet others there has obviously been much discussion among the villagers themselves before eventually they have

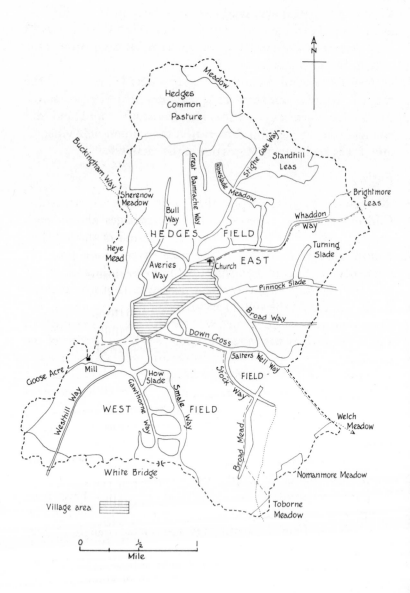

Fig. 17. Padbury before enclosure

agreed to enclose all or part of their lands, and enclosure by agreement becomes increasingly important as the seventeenth century draws on.

One of the earliest enclosures by agreement took place in Hartwell in May of 1551,[6] when it was agreed that Master Hampden should enclose twenty acres upon Abbots Hills, the Nether Caly Close, Kingham Acre and Southcote Acre. In return Master Hampden agreed to give up his warren of rabbits in Pipers and the Upper Caly Close. The inhabitants of Hartwell were probably more than willing to give up rights of common over the enclosed lands in order to see the last of the rabbits. Some enclosure agreements give very full descriptions of the reasons for the enclosure. At Great Linford in September 1658 the freeholders and leaseholders agreed to enclose their lands.[7] In the agreement it was stated that a great part of the lands of the village lay open, unenclosed and commonable, some parts at all times of the year, other parts yearly after harvest was 'inned'. The result was that many spoils, trespasses and destructions happened daily by escape of cattle into the corn and grass, whereby many actions, suits and troubles were raised and more were likely daily to arise if the fields and lands there should be kept open and continued in common any longer. It was therefore agreed that the land should be surveyed and enclosed, each person's proportion being marked forth and staked out as near adjoining to his dwelling as with conveniency might be done. The enclosure was confirmed by a Chancery Decree shortly after the Restoration.

There had been three common fields in Great Linford, Wood, Middle and Newport Fields, a common called Layfield, as well as meadow, and seventy-one acres of wood. Two seventeenth-century maps of Great Linford have survived, one made in 1641 before enclosure, the second made in 1678 after enclosure.[8] They form the basis for Figs. 18 and 19. They reveal how the landscape of the village was changed as a result of the enclosure. New roads were laid out, and old ones re-aligned. The meadow,

[6] B. A. S. Hartwell 402/39.
[7] B.R.O. D/U. 1/48.
[8] B.A.S. 632/43, 633/43.

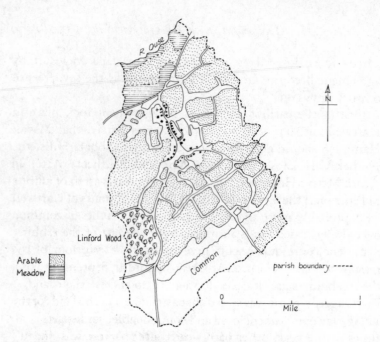

Fig. 18. Great Linford in 1641

Arable
Meadow

parish boundary -----

Linford Wood

Common

Mile

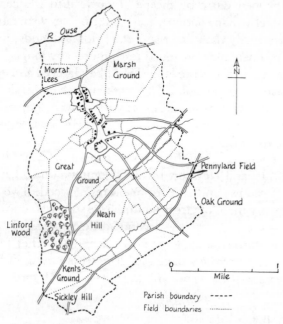

Fig. 19. Great Linford in 1678

R Ouse

Morrat Lees

Marsh Ground

Great Ground

Pennyland Field

Oak Ground

Linford Wood

Neath Hill

Kents Ground

Sickley Hill

Mile

Parish boundary -----
Field boundaries ·········

common and arable were enclosed and divided up. The new field
boundaries were drawn comparatively straight. The largest field
was the Great Ground, of 108 acres, whilst Neath Hill contained 102 acres. All together fifty-three new plots were carved
out of the old landscape, including a close from the north-west
corner of Linford Wood. Of these, thirty-five were under twenty
acres in size, and a further eleven were under fifty acres. The new
fields were altogether smaller in area and more regular in shape
than those produced by earlier enclosure.

Enclosure in the sixteenth and seventeenth centuries affected
woods and wastes as much as arable. It was said in 1588 that
woods and wastes in Steeple Claydon, Twyford and Quainton
had been enclosed within the last forty years, whilst about ten
years ago Thomas Piggot of Doddershall had enclosed Doddershall Wood and Common, Greatmore Woods and part of the
Lee Lawne. He had great hedges and ditches made, altered the
metes and bounds of the manor, depopulated the whole of the
town of Doddershall, destroyed all the farm houses, and erected
some few mean cottages upon Greatmoor to give colour of
satisfaction to the statute made against depopulation.[9] In 1611
Sir Edmund Verney, Sir Francis Fortescue and their respective
tenants agreed to enclose and divide up the common and waste
ground of the manor of Mursley, and in 1669 the waste on
Ovinghill was ordered to be surveyed so that it could be divided
up.

Enclosure was widespread over north Buckinghamshire
during the later sixteenth century and throughout the seventeenth century. Much of it cannot be dated at all precisely. It
was often piecemeal and frequently went unrecorded. For
example only a chance reference in a property deed of 1667 tells
us that parts of the Northfield and the West Mead in Lathbury
had been recently enclosed.[10] Nor did enclosure at this time
necessarily involve the whole of a parish, and so a number of
parishes in which enclosure did take place during the seventeenth century also needed an Act of Parliament in the
eighteenth or nineteenth centuries before their common fields

[9] B.R.O. D/P. AR. 23A/66.
[10] B.R.O. D/U. 1/137.

were finally extinguished. When Whaddon and Nash were finally enclosed in 1833 there were 429 acres of ancient enclosure in Whaddon out of a total area of 1468 acres, and 137 acres of ancient enclosure in Nash out of a total of 1161 acres, both exclusive of the Chase.

We have seen something of the direct and immediate effects upon the landscape of this enclosure when looking at its consequences in Great Linford. It could also have a more indirect, long-term effect, namely the gradual dispersal of farmhouses away from the village. This was sometimes deliberately encouraged by landlords so that tenants would be at the centre of their farms. Thus Sir Edmund Verney at Middle Claydon inserted in two leases of newly enclosed land made in 1624 clauses requiring the tenants to build two good and sufficient bays of dwelling house. When enquiries were being made in the same parish in 1634 concerning the conversion of tillage to pasture there, it was reported that about thirteen years ago thirty to forty acres, until then always in tillage, had been converted to pasture, but that there had been no decay of houses in the parish, "for thoughe ther bie some houses downe yett ther are more erected in theyr place".[11] Muxwell Farm and Knowl-hill Farm, both in Middle Claydon, contain as their oldest parts seventeenth-century brick and timber buildings. The same kind of pattern is to be seen at Lower Winchendon, where Muskhill Farm, Marsh Farm and Winchendon Hill Farm are all seventeenth century in origin.

The Chilterns

The contrasts between north Buckinghamshire and the Chilterns are no less marked in the sixteenth and seventeenth centuries than they were in medieval times. Common arable fields continued to be important, but there was much piecemeal enclosure, both of common arable lands and of woods and wastes, although it appears to have aroused much less opposition than in the north and its records are much more fragmentary. The contrasts between north and south are

[11] B.R.O. Claydon Correspondence, microfilm Reel 2.

brought out clearly in a number of detailed written surveys and estate maps for several Chiltern parishes.

It is estate maps which provide the most telling visual evidence of what the Chiltern landscape must have looked like in the seventeenth century. A very large, detailed map of Ellesborough was made in 1629 (Plate 25), and a map of a single farm in Hughenden was made in 1673 (Plate 26). A particularly fine map of the estate of Judge Jeffries at Bulstrode, made in 1686, includes plans and elevations of the house which was the centre of the estate (Plate 27). All three maps bring out very clearly that pattern of numerous, generally fairly small, arable fields, sometimes cultivated in common and sometimes enclosed and farmed in severalty, of woodland, pasture, commons and waste, often divided up into small parcels, but sometimes very extensive, and varying considerably in their distribution, which was to be found all over the south of the county except in the flood plain of the Thames valley where in villages such as Horton and Wraysbury a common-field landscape similar to that of many northern villages was to be found.

A written survey of Great Hampden made in 1653 describes the landscape of a large manor comprising 2253 acres.[12] Of this, just a fifth, 444 acres, was common, divided between five common arable fields, totalling 244 acres, and two pieces of common wood of which the larger by far was the Great Common Wood of 183 acres. Of the manor well over third, 874 acres, was in demesne, and this was entirely enclosed. Arable and pasture made up 496 acres of this, divided into twenty-seven pieces, the largest, Stony Field, no more than forty-six acres. There were only forty-one acres of meadowland, but 336 acres of woods and coppices. Like the arable and the pasture, the meadows, woods and coppices of the demesne were split into relatively small parcels, the largest, Barn Grove Coppice, no more than forty-four acres. As Barnes's Grove it still survives, directly to the west of Hampden House. Some of the woodland was in very small parcels, or shaws, little better than thick hedgerows, an acre or two at a time.

There were only two large farms, both held by tenants at will.

[12] B.R.O. D/MH. 28/2.

John Lydall occupied 208 acres, of which ninety-eight were enclosed arable and pasture, eighty-eight were arable in three of the five common fields, and sixteen were woods and coppices. Robert Morton held 181 acres, made up of 113 acres of enclosed arable and pasture, sixty-five acres scattered through all five of the common fields, and he seems to have been the only one of thirty-eight tenants to have held land in all five, together with a little coppice of two acres. The next largest farm was that of John Spyer, only seventy-six acres, all enclosed, with sixty-eight acres in arable and pasture. Thus not only was the landscape of the south markedly different visually from that of the north, but its social organisation was also very different. Farms may have been both larger and smaller than those in the north, and although it is clear that many were not enclosed within a ring-fence, their constituent parts were often better integrated and so more easily managed.

Piecemeal enclosure of every kind of terrain was widespread throughout the Chilterns in the sixteenth and seventeenth centuries, but it does not seem to have been on so large a scale as in the north. It is certainly far less fully recorded. This means that in some districts much more of the seventeenth century landscape has survived than in the north of the county. Almost the whole of the landscape portrayed on the map of Upper Hall Farm, Hughenden (Plate 26), remains. The only major changes are that the hedges dividing Middle and White fields have been removed, the two Searesfields have been thrown into one, and building along the lane on either side of the farm house has modified the shape of New Close. Similar piecemeal changes have taken place in and around Chequers to modify the landscape shown on the 1629 map (Plate 25). Mogestie Piece, Brooke Field and Chequers Pasture have been landscaped to form the park to the south of the house, but the Dene Field and Whorley Wood remain almost untouched, as does Long Field. In contrast the strips to the south of Ellesborough were swept away by enclosure following the Act of Parliament of 1805. Nevertheless for these two landscapes the seventeenth-century framework is still discernible. Judge Jeffries' estate (Plate 27) has, however, been transformed. His house has been demolished to make way for a nineteenth-century mansion, whilst twentieth-century suburban building and the construction of the M40 Motorway have obliterated almost every trace of the fields and woods shown on the 1686 map.

Woods and their management

Well before the beginning of the sixteenth century woods were recognised as valuable assets, to be carefully preserved and systematically exploited. It is only from this period however that detailed accounts of how this was to be done have survived.

Richard Grenville, writing in 1657, described how he proposed to manage his woods about Wotton Underwood in order that he might have a regular supply of timber.[13] By 1647 Grenvilles Wood, once 167 acres divided into two coppices, had been sadly diminished by the clearing of six closes, where the trees had been grubbed up and the land turned to pasture. What remained he now decided to divide up into eight coppices. The six closes were to be ploughed, and then planted and sown with timber. They were then to be rejoined to Grenvilles Wood to make up the existing coppices to twenty acres each. He already had another two coppices at the Grove of this size. This would give him ten coppices, one of which he would fell each year at ten years' growth. Once the coppices were established, and with proper management, he would then have a regular supply of timber for all his domestic and farm needs, and probably a surplus for sale. His woods still survive, much reduced in size, the paths through them evidence of their former division into coppices.

Large timber trees, for building and ship-building purposes for example, can of necessity be felled only once. Coppices, on the other hand, if carefully managed, with regular cutting at intervals of from three to twelve years depending on the size of the wood required, can produce almost indefinitely wood for a very wide range of purposes: broomstaves, hop-poles, faggots, hedge-stakes, hurdle rods, axle trees, chair-legs, the backs of

[13] B.A.S. 422/42. ff. 16–17.

brooms and brushes, and so on, and the bark can be peeled off and sold separately to the tanners. Estate documents make it abundantly clear that in the sixteenth and seventeenth centuries, as in medieval centuries, the chief economic value of woodland lay in the regular production of wood of this kind, and only very occasionally in the production of large, heavy timber. This must have had one important visual effect. There would have been very few fully grown trees and instead very many quite young, straight shoots growing closely together from stools which might be very old. Much seventeenth-century woodland must have been more open, less shady, but much denser, than that of today.

Woodland could, however, be made to yield even more than broom handles or beech mast. In October of 1622 Sir Thomas Temple let to John Knight and his son Robert two woodcock glades in Bushey Coppice in Biddlesden until March 1623. They were to pay in rent fifteen woodcock to Sir Thomas, and if they caught more then he would pay for them. Further glades in Gorral Wood and Boycott Wood were let upon similar terms, whilst Henry Davye and Edward Walcott were licensed to take larks and woodcock throughout Sir Thomas's liberties, but they were not to take partridges, and were to search for those who did. Their rent was two woodcock and two dozen larks a year.[14] Partridges, pheasants and woodcock were sent up from Stowe to the Temples' London house regularly throughout the seventeenth century.

Woods which were enclosed and in private ownership stood a reasonable chance of being properly cared for. Common woods however could be reduced to rough grazing by over-stocking and by indiscriminate felling. This is brought out vividly in two documents describing the Hillwork in Princes Risborough. In 1574 it was stated that the tenants of Princes Risborough had free common without stint in the wood called the Hillwork, and that the lord of the manor of Horsendon had the right to a load of wood every day of the year.[15] But although it was called Hillwork Wood it was in fact described as common or brush-

14 H.H.L. Stowe Papers. Temple Lease Book. ST 41. f. 53d.
15 P.R.O. E.134. 16 Eliz. Easter 1.

wood, and in his survey of the woods of the manor of Horsendon in 1662[16] John Herne wrote as follows:

> I have viewed that great Common called the Hellocks, where I find abundance of smale bushy stuff ffitt for no other use then to heat Ovens, sew Bucks for washing, and brewing, and unlike to be any better, for that every mans hand is against it.

The great rebuilding in town and country

Beginning in the second half of the sixteenth century and impelled by a rising population, by improvements in domestic comfort and by changes in taste that came ultimately from Italy, a mounting wave of building and rebuilding swept over the English landscape. At first this building was in traditional Tudor-Gothic patterns, but these were increasingly diluted by foreign influences so that in the second half of the seventeenth century there came a fundamental break in the continuity of English building with the erection of country houses designed after continental models either by talented amateurs or else by professional surveyors and master-masons who increasingly called themselves architects. The emergence of what may be called 'polite architecture', as opposed to traditional, vernacular building, is matched by an increasing use of much more substantial techniques and materials at a lower level of society than hitherto, so that from the middle years of the sixteenth century the farmhouses and cottages of yeomen and husbandmen begin to survive as well as the manor houses of the gentry.

In Buckinghamshire the building and rebuilding of country houses shows no real break with the past for much of the sixteenth and seventeenth centuries. Occasionally an existing house was completely demolished and a new one built on the site. Others were built on entirely new sites, whilst at yet others a late medieval core was altered and extended, and sometimes more than once. Gayhurst House, for example, probably the finest late sixteenth-century domestic building in Buckinghamshire (Plate 28), seems to have been built on earlier

[16] B.R.O. D.42 A1.

foundations. It was begun in 1597 by William Mulso, continued by his son-in-law Sir Everard Digby, executed in 1606 for his part in the Gunpowder Plot, and completed by his son Sir Kenelm Digby. It was altered in the eighteenth century when the area between the projecting wings on the North Front was filled in. This pattern of alteration, rebuilding and adaptation is characteristic of the history of the great majority of Buckinghamshire country houses, a pattern illustrated admirably by the example of what is perhaps the most famous of Buckinghamshire's country houses.

Chequers owes its name to the family of Elyas de Scaccario, or of the Exchequer, present there by the end of the twelfth century. The male line came to an end in the middle of the thirteenth century, and William Hawtry married one of the co-heiresses. A house was built on the present site by the end of the fifteenth century, probably replacing an earlier one. This new house was much altered and rebuilt in about 1565 by Sir William Hawtry, descended from the thirteenth-century William. Further alterations were carried out at the end of the eighteenth century, when much of the exterior was covered with stucco and given battlements in the most approved 'Gothick' manner of the period. Further extensive alterations were carried out by Lord Lee of Fareham between 1909 and 1912, when much of the stucco and most of the battlements were removed, and the central courtyard was roofed over to make a hall. When Lord Lee died the house and estate passed to the nation as a country house for the Prime Minister. Since that time it has been further restored and carefully maintained, so that now, at least from the road, it more nearly represents what an Elizabethan country mansion must have looked like than perhaps any other comparable house in Buckinghamshire.

Houses like Gayhurst and Chequers were deeply rooted by design and by materials into a traditional mould, a mould which had been evolving slowly for generations. There are many other similar houses, perhaps less well-known and perhaps less pretentious. The Manor House at Swanbourne, for example is a substantial stone-built house of the last half of the sixteenth century, whilst Crawley Grange is a brick-built one of about the same date. All share an intangible aura of having grown out of the landscape in which they stand.

But the seeds of change were already present. Sir Thomas Smith, author, statesman and scholar, Secretary of State under Queen Elizabeth, graduate of the University of Padua and vice-chancellor of the University of Cambridge, lived during the reign of Mary at Ankerwyke, in the far south of the county, close to the Thames, where he built a house of which nothing survives. In his library were no less than six editions of the writings of Vitruvius on architecture. The enthusiasm and interest of men like Smith for the principles of classical architecture led eventually, in the years after the Restoration, to a profound transformation in domestic building. Country houses built in the last decades of the seventeenth century are characterised by two main storeys, with further rooms in basement and garret, often with flanking wings, a pedimented central entrance, and a hipped roof, sometimes surrounded with a balustrade and surmounted with a cupola. Such houses, neither too large nor too small, set in a carefully contrived, elegantly informal, park, have for subsequent generations been of the essence of the English rural landscape, but their inspiration is ultimately Italian in origin.

Buckinghamshire contains a number of these new, late seventeenth-century, houses, at Hall Barn, at Denham Place, at Great Hundridge. At Winslow, William Lowndes, a native of the town and Secretary to the Treasury from 1695 until his death in 1724, spent £6,585 10s. 2¼d. on building Winslow Hall, in Sheep Street, only just off the centre of the town. Over a million locally made bricks were used, and at least three of the craftsmen who worked on the decoration of the interior came from the Office of Works and had worked under Sir Christopher Wren's direction in the rebuilding of St Paul's Cathedral. Wren may not actually have designed the stately, rather prim, house, but he certainly checked the accounts and reduced some bills when he thought them excessive.[17]

Yet another late seventeenth-century house survives in a

[17] see A. T. Bolton and H. D. Hendry. eds., 'Designs and Drawings Supplementary to Vol. XII', *Wren Society* XVII, (1940), pp. 54—75.

rather unexpected place. The great eighteenth-century mansion at Stowe, with its four hundred acres of gardens, has for so long dominated the landscape of north-western Buckinghamshire that it is very easy to lose sight of its predecessors. The sixteenth-century house of the first of the Temples was eventually demolished to make way for an entirely new house designed in the new fashion. Sir Richard Temple was appointed a Commissioner of the Customs in 1672 with an annual salary of £2000. With so ample an income he felt able to embark upon an ambitious building programme. Accordingly he drew up a contract with John Heynes of St Martins in the Field, London, carpenter, and Thomas Miller of London, bricklayer. For £2600, payable in instalments, they were to build "a greate messuage or mantion House of Brick", according to the design provided by William Cleare, gent., surveyor to Sir Richard (Plates 29 and 30). A draft of the contract, dated 1676, survives,[18] and gives us an immense amount of information about the size of the house and the structural details. In its overall design it follows the contemporary fashion, the feature which appears to be unique is the forward 'break' in the wings. The contractors had leave to dig for sand, stone and for clay for bricks on Sir Richard's estates, and he was to sell them such timber as they might need from his woods in Stowe, Westbury and Biddlesden. Part of the basement floor was to be paved in local stone, and the hearths were to be set in the local fashion. Thus although the new house introduced a foreign, Italianate, note into the quiet, wooded landscape of north-western Buckinghamshire, it was still built of local materials, making for a measure of continuity and a softening of its impact. Not until the second half of the nineteenth century, when improvements in transport make such alien materials as Welsh slate readily available, do new buildings become harshly obtrusive in the landscape.

Sir Richard died in 1697 and was succeeded by his son, also Sir Richard, and eventually Lord Cobham. Under his direction the gardens were transformed, but Sir Richard's house was never demolished. Instead it was gradually engulfed as extensions

[18] H. H. L. Stowe Papers. Articles of Agreement for Rebuilding Stowe. L9 D2.

were added, and it is still possible to recognise at least its outline in the plan of the great mansion. All that remains externally is the door on the North Front.

We have spent some time looking at country houses, since they form the most conspicuous survivals of the sixteenth- and seventeenth-century building boom. But two points need to be made. First of all we have been able to look at only a small handful of those that have survived. Similar houses, solidly built from local materials, form an integral part of the landscape of most parishes in the county. Secondly, many have disappeared, often without trace, destruction and demolition taking place in the seventeenth and eighteenth centuries as well as in the twentieth. The great house at Salden, said to have cost its builder, Sir John Fortescue, Chancellor of the Exchequer to Queen Elizabeth, £33,000 to build, and to have measured 175 feet across the principal front, was probably the nearest approach in Buckinghamshire to the great 'prodigy' houses such as Theobalds, Burghley and Holdenby put up by the statesmen and courtiers of Elizabeth in the latter years of her reign. Almost the whole of Salden House was demolished by 1743, part of the eastern wing surviving, much altered, as Salden House Farm. Of the mansion built by Sir Henry Lee at Quarrendon nothing now remains.

The houses we have been looking at so far have been large, sometimes very large, but there is no real break in the continuum which stretches from the most splendidly extravagant mansion of the fortunate possessor of a lucrative office under the Crown to the most wretched hovel of an impoverished farm labourer. There has been much destruction of houses and cottages at the lower end of this continuum by quite indiscriminate and unnecessary demolition but there are few villages in the county which do not have at least a handful still standing. There appears to be nothing unique to Buckinghamshire in their design and layout, although this is an area of the landscape history of the county in which much field work remains to be done. The smallest cottage may have had no more than two or three ground floor rooms and perhaps an attic, whilst the largest and most substantial farmhouses had little to distinguish them from the country houses we have just looked at.

Farmhouses and cottages in Buckinghamshire are usually timber-framed with brick infilling. It would appear that in the sixteenth century the timber frames were normally infilled with wattle and daub or plaster, but there are only a handful of cottages throughout the county in which something of this kind of infilling is still to be found. From the last years of the sixteenth century brick is increasingly used, and the wattle and daub was gradually replaced. The bricks themselves were often set in a herring-bone pattern, providing, even when seventeenth-century bricks have been replaced with nineteenth- and twentieth-century ones, a particularly attractive texture to wall surfaces (Plate 31).

From the last half of the seventeenth century brick is used increasingly on its own as a building material, without any timber framing, although it is not until the eighteenth century that the decorative effect to be obtained by using different coloured headers and stretchers is exploited to any degree.

The use of other building materials such as stone, flint and wichert is very localised and is clearly determined by the difficulty and expense of transporting them any distance. Buckinghamshire lacks any really good building stone and its use as a building material in houses and cottages is largely confined to three fairly well-defined areas. The first belongs to the outcrop of the Cornbrash, a shelly limestone that was quarried from quite small and shallow pits. There is an isolated exposure at Marsh Gibbon, and then it is found in a string of villages along the valley of the Ouse, from Chetwode in the west to Lavendon in the north-east, and including Tingewick, Leckhampstead, Thornborough, Beachampton (Plate 32) and Calverton. Secondly a number of villages are conveniently close to spots where the Great Oolite limestones can be quarried. These lie to the north of the river Ouse and include Shalstone, Water Stratford, Hanslope and Gayhurst. Finally there are stone cottages to be found where the Portland and Purbeck beds occur, at Oving and Whitchurch, Cuddington and Haddenham, Long Crendon and Ickford.

In all three areas there are sixteenth- and seventeenth-century houses and cottages built of stone rubble and thatched with straw, together with timber-framed brick infilled ones, and sometimes the two kinds of materials are to be found in the same building, as at Beachampton (Plate 32).

Other building materials are very exceptional and their use is very localised. Flint is used extensively in the southern part of the county in churches, but only occasionally in domestic buildings, and then in fairly substantial farmhouses such as Wellwick Farm in Wendover rather than small cottages, although it is used in several cottages in Hambleden. Sir William Borlase's school at Marlow, built in 1624, is also of flint. Flint is a particularly hard and durable building material, but it is difficult to work, and nowhere in Buckinghamshire is it used with the virtuosity to be found in Norfolk and Suffolk.

There is finally, the building material which is unique to Buckinghamshire, and this is wichert. Wichert is a hard, chalky earth to be found only at Haddenham, Cuddington and Lower Winchendon. It is mixed with chopped straw and a little water, and then built up in layers of about two feet in thickness into walls about two or three feet in width. Each successive layer has to be allowed to dry out before the next is added, and so it can take some time to reach a suitable height for a house. Provided it can be protected from the weather it gives a durable building material that, if anything, tends to harden with the passage of time. In order to protect it from the damp it is erected on stone rubble footings, and boundary walls are given their own thatched or tiled roofs. It is also often rendered with plaster or rough cast. Several houses in and around Cuddington and Lower Winchendon are built of wichert, but it is used extensively only at Haddenham (Plate 33). Here it was once used on a large scale in houses, cottages and barns. It is particularly suited to the building of long, gently curving walls, and this has given to Haddenham a series of winding lanes which, enclosed between their pale yellow walls topped with terracotta tiles, have an air of detachment tinged with mystery that is unique to Buckinghamshire.

Churches were almost entirely passed by during the Great Rebuilding. The wealth and energy which went into the building of church towers in the fifteenth century had almost petered out by about 1540 and was being diverted into other channels. Churches had to wait until the nineteenth century for their Great Rebuilding. Nevertheless some work was done in Buckinghamshire churches during this period, and scarcely a decade passed without some alteration to a church somewhere in the county, even during the years of the Commonwealth.

Some of this work was little more than repair and restoration, as when the nave of Adstock church was reroofed in 1597, but occasionally there was more extensive rebuilding. The tower at Horton church was much rebuilt, using brick and flint, in about 1580, and brick walls were built around the churchyard at about the same time. The west tower at Padbury church was almost entirely rebuilt in the middle years of the seventeenth century. Sometimes additions were made, as at Langley Marish, where the north-west tower was added in 1609 and the south porch enlarged in about 1630 to take the library of Sir John Kederminster.

Several additions to Buckinghamshire churches took the form of mortuary chapels, designed to hold funerary monuments. The most outstanding of these is the Bedford chapel, added in 1556 to the church at Chenies. Here is the richest and most sumptuous assemblage of funeral monuments to be found in any parish church in England, ranging in date from that of the first Earl of Bedford, who died in 1555, to that of the ninth Duke, who died in 1891. The chapel itself has been rebuilt since 1556. Another, similar, chapel, remains almost untouched. This is the Hastings chapel, built in brick in 1558 to the church at Stoke Poges. It was intended to serve two purposes, as a chapel for the inmates of an almshouse built nearby at about the same time, and as family mortuary chapel (Plate 34). The associations of this church and its churchyard with Thomas Gray must make it one of the most visited and most photographed churches in the whole of England.

Mortuary chapels and rebuilt towers are only additions and refurbishings to existing churches. No new churches were built anywhere in Buckinghamshire between 1550 and 1700, but two were completely rebuilt. At Fulmer the church was rebuilt in brick and consecrated in 1610. At Willen the ancient church had by the middle of the seventeenth century become ruinous and so a new one was built between 1679 and 1680. It was designed by Robert Hooke, who had worked closely with Sir Christopher Wren on the rebuilding of London's churches after the Great Fire, and this experience is reflected in his design for the church at Willen, his only independent work. The tower is in three stages. The lowest is in limestone, the upper two in brick with tall Corinthian pilasters rising the full height of the tower to a deep moulded cornice with pineapple-shaped pinnacles at the corners. The whole effect is rather stiff and awkward. Hooke may well have worked closely with Wren, but he absorbed nothing of Wren's marvellous control over mass and movement in architecture.

This is probably the most appropriate place to mention briefly another building for religious worship added to the Buckinghamshire landscape in the late seventeenth century. The Friends' Meeting House at Jordans was completed in 1688. It was designed and built, of brick with a hipped roof, specifically for the purpose, and has a caretaker's house under the same roof (Plate 35). Set in a quiet, well-wooded spot in the heart of the Chilterns, its plain brick exterior and the austere simplicity of the meeting room inside add to the landscape a dimension which cannot be measured or plotted on a map, but which is as tangible as much that can.

Finally, during the course of the second half of the sixteenth century and on into the seventeenth, the Great Rebuilding also became the medium through which religious and charitable zeal, until about 1540 expressed in the building and adornment of churches, was directed into new, more severely practical, purposes. Several schools and nearly a dozen almshouses were founded in Buckinghamshire before the end of the seventeenth century and a surprising number of the buildings in which they were housed have survived into the landscape of the twentieth century. The usual pattern seems to have been a single row of one-storeyed buildings, built of brick, simply and without fuss. There are, exceptionally, two rows to the almshouses at Ravenstone, an upper floor partly in the roof in the Winwood

Almshouses at Quainton, a particularly good example of late seventeenth-century brickwork complete with Dutch gables, and two full storeys to those at Worminghall. The single storey almshouses at Amersham, built in 1657 by Sir William Drake, form three sides of a square (Plate 36).

Several schools were established in Buckinghamshire during the sixteenth and seventeenth centuries. The oldest building used as a school must be the Chantry Chapel at Buckingham, which housed the Royal Latin School, founded, or refounded, in 1540. The Chapel itself was built in about 1475, but it incorporates a Norman doorway. The simple stone building put up in about 1650 for William Elmer's school at Beachampton is still standing, as is that built in 1656 at Steeple Claydon at the instigation of Sir Thomas Chaloner. The original two storey flint and brick building erected in 1624 for Sir William Borlase's school at Marlow is still recognisable in spite of later additions. At Amersham, however, Dr Challoner's school, founded in 1620, was not provided with a new building but was housed in the Church House, a timber-framed building of the early sixteenth century just to the south of the church.

Almshouses and schools mark the first beginnings of a new development in the landscape, a development which will eventually transform it. Hitherto, the buildings we have been looking at fall into two broad categories: they are either houses, whether country mansions or the cabins of the rural poor, together with associated farm buildings, or else they are churches. This division has a long tradition. Medieval castles were also at least in part used for residential purposes, and monasteries were religious in their intent. Almshouses and schools, together with town halls, represent the first appearance of buildings designed to fulfil a newly emerging, secular, need. They are the harbingers of nineteenth-century railway stations and twentieth-century office blocks.

The disafforestation of Bernwood

By the end of the sixteenth century many areas within the formal bounds of the Forest of Bernwood had been enclosed and turned into arable or grazing land. A survey of the Forest made in 1586 recorded that in Boarstall alone over five hundred acres had been converted into pasture and so mounded about with great ditches and quickset hedges that the deer could not get in to have their feeding.[19] Mr Denham had enclosed in Godstow Woods almost two hundred acres under pretext of making a park for the Queen's pleasure, but the trees had been grubbed up, the deer turned out, a keeper's lodge made into a shepherd's cot, and the land stocked with five hundred sheep. All together it was estimated that there were at least 7,600 sheep grazing where once Her Majesty's game had roamed.

The same survey then goes on to list the numbers of tenants and cottagers in the three main villages in the Forest, together with the livestock for which they had common of pasture. In Boarstall there were eleven tenants, supporting ninety-one persons in all, with rights of common for eighty-four pigs and 1,260 sheep. In the same village there were twenty-two cottagers, sustaining 110 persons in all, and with the right to pasture forty-four pigs and an unknown number of sheep. In Brill there were twenty tenants and eighty-three cottagers, supporting 148 and 314 persons respectively, and with rights to pasture a total of 246 pigs and 1,020 sheep. Finally in Oakley there were twenty-two tenants, sustaining 111 persons, and thirty-four cottagers, supporting 137 persons, and able to pasture 269 pigs and 2,010 sheep. It is likely that at least ten thousand sheep were being grazed within the bounds of the Forest. The pressure on the woodland must have been considerable.

Nevertheless, in spite of this enclosure, there were still very extensive woodlands within the Forest. In Panshill there were 792 acres unenclosed, with an estimated 600 deer. In the Frith nearly 1,200 acres were open, supporting over a thousand deer, and in Ixhill 301 acres were unenclosed, with 200 deer. Nearly two thousand deer roamed almost unchecked through the Forest, often doing considerable damage to the corn, hay, grass, meadow and pastures of the inhabitants of the Forest.

In 1624 an Exchequer Commission set about the formal

[19] British Library. Lansdowne MS.47, Nos. 3, 5, 6.

disafforestation of Bernwood.[20] The Commissioners took evidence from the inhabitants of the forest towns of Brill, Boarstall and Oakley, and decided to allocate ten acres within the Forest for every hundred acres held by freeholders, and three acres to every cottager. But there were many objections to the terms, and a second Commission decided that the allotments to the poorer sort of men should be hedged and enclosed at the king's expense. The 'poorer sort' remained unsatisfied, and in September 1630 many took the matter into their own hands, pulling down the fences and gates of the new enclosures and turning their cattle in to feed.

Eventually however the matter was settled in 1633. A total of 346 acres of Crown land and 231 acres belonging to Sir John Denham were allocated to the inhabitants of Oakley and Boarstall. The remaining Crown lands, amounting to 1394 acres, were to be enclosed and provided with roads, gates, posts and rails, and bridges, at the king's expense.

Sir John Denham was Forester, and he had 1,200 acres in the Forest subject to common of pasture. It was agreed that he should give 231 acres to the poor of Brill and Oakley, 104 acres to the Crown, and some waste ground to his tenants in Boarstall in lieu of their rights to common. The remainder of his land was to be freely disafforested, freed from any right to common that others might have, and with leave to improve and enclose. Of this latter he had already begun to avail himself. In 1632 he leased out for twenty years a pasture called Frith Field containing eighty-five acres, together with another close of pasture called Bardalls, of seven acres. He reserved to himself all oak, ash and elm trees, together with the moat or fishpond in Bardalls, the underwood growing on the banks of the moat, the right to fish in it and to plant an orchard on its banks. He also reserved a walk from the churchyard rails to the moat and the right to plant rows of trees on both sides. The rent, £97 a year, was to be paid in the dining hall of Boarstall Place House.[21] The pasture called Frith Field has now been divided into three. The close of pasture called Bardalls perpetuates Bardolphys Garden,

[20] B.R.O. D/AF. 2/1, 2/3.
[21] B.R.O. D/AF. 3/19.

mentioned in a document of 1449. It is the field that lies just to the south of the school. In one corner lies the moat, its banks now heavily overgrown. The walk from the churchyard to the moat, marked by the hedge and wooden fence between the school and the field, has all but disappeared, the trees on either side, if ever planted, have long been felled.

By the end of the seventeenth century the only fragments of the Forest of Bernwood still remaining in the parish of Boarstall were the woods now called Boarstall Wood and Oriel Wood. The rest had been divided into fields and closes, and the village itself had been depopulated. As late as 1676 there were seventy-seven communicants in the parish, a total population of perhaps 130 people, but a map of 1697 marks no more than seven cottages in addition to the manor house. The village fields had been divided up, the duck decoy built, the road which once formed the southern boundary to the Frith Field had been stopped up. It was probably at this time that the road through the village was re-aligned to run to the east of the church. This would give more room for the grounds of the manor house, and would have entailed the demolition of several cottages, although the inhabitants may not have gone far, since enclosure also led to the gradual dispersal of isolated farmsteads into the newly created fields. Old Arngrove Farm, Pasture Farm and Upper Panshill Farm are seventeenth-century, New Arngrove Farm, once called Boarstall Farm, is eighteenth-century, whilst Red House Farm belongs to the second half of the nineteenth century. The pattern of field boundaries created during the course of the seventeenth century remains largely unchanged. In Boarstall it is the gatehouse which is the most substantial survival from the medieval landscape (Plate 11), since even the church itself was rebuilt in 1818.

SELECT BIBLIOGRAPHY

Barley, M. W., *The English Farmhouse and Cottage* (1961).
Broad, J. P. F., Sir Ralph Verney and his Estates, 1630–1696.
    Unpublished D.Phil. thesis, University of Oxford, 1973.

Finberg, H. P. R. general editor. *The Agrarian History of England and Wales*, Vol. 4, 1500–1640, edited by Joan Thirsk (1967).

Fry, P. S., *Chequers* (1977).

Godfrey, W. H., *The English Almshouse* (1955).

Hill, O. and Cornforth, J., *English Country Houses: Caroline 1625–1685* (1966).

Jordan, W. K., *The Charities of Rural England* (1961).

Leonard, E. M., 'The Enclosure of Common Fields in the Seventeenth Century', *Transactions of the Royal Historical Society* New Series XIX, (1905), pp. 101–146.

Peysner, N., *Buckinghamshire* (1960, 1973 reprint).

Royal Commission on Historical Monuments, *Buckinghamshire* 2 vols (1912).

Smith, J. T. and Yates, E. M., 'On the Dating of English Houses from External Evidence', *Field Studies* 2 No. 5, (1968), pp. 536–577.

Whitehand, J. W. R., 'Traditional Building Materials in the Chilterns', *Oxoniensia* 32, (1967), pp. 1–9.

7. Georgian Buckinghamshire

Parliamentary enclosure.   Improvements in communications and transport – The Thames – The Grand Junction Canal – Turnpike roads.   Georgian building in town and country

THE EIGHTEENTH CENTURY sees some particularly important developments in the history of the making of the Buckinghamshire landscape. First of all the enclosure of the remaining common arable fields and wastes slowly gathered momentum and was finally completed in 1865. This, the last phase of one of the most important movements in the entire history of the landscape, created a new and quite unmistakable landscape, of straight hedgerows, broad grass verges to roads and isolated farmsteads. While this enclosure movement was reaching its climax two new features were being introduced: the turnpike road and the canal. Turnpike roads have been much rebuilt since the turnpike trustees finally gave up their responsibilities, and so little evidence of their labours now remains. Canals, however, have become a permanent feature of the landscape, although they have long ceased to be used by barges laden with coal and bricks and instead are often silted up and overgrown.

Perhaps however the eighteenth century makes an even more significant contribution to the history of the making of the Buckinghamshire landscape. Parliamentary enclosures, turnpike roads and canals are in many respects no more than continuations of trends which have been working in the landscape for generations, their visual consequences brought about almost unconsciously, with very little attention given to long-term effects. By the end of the seventeenth century there was almost for the first time a conscious awareness of the landscape, a growing appreciation of natural beauty and, most important of all, increasingly ambitious attempts deliberately to mould the landscape to conform with preconceived notions as to what the ideal natural landscape should look like. The aesthetics of landscape design were first embodied in the work of landscape gardeners in the grounds and parks of country houses. The work of all three great eighteenth-century gardeners, Charles Bridgeman, Lancelot Brown and Humphrey Repton, is well represented in the county, and at Stowe the gardens are a unique palimpsest on which is recorded every change in taste and fashion through much of the eighteenth century. At the same time, by the end of the century, traditional styles of building finally disappeared even at the lowest level of the social structure, as architects, conscious of Italian, classical and even Gothic precedents, replaced masons and carpenters in the building of houses. Few towns and villages in Buckinghamshire are without a number of Georgian houses whose symmetry of façade and porticoed entrances owe more to Renaissance Italy than they do to medieval England.

Parliamentary enclosure

We have seen in previous chapters that the enclosure of arable, wastes and commons had been taking place almost without break certainly from the early decades of the fifteenth century. The consequence of this was that by the middle years of the eighteenth century only thirty-five per cent of the county remained unenclosed, a figure which disguises wide regional variations, from the fifty-eight per cent of Cottesloe Hundred still unenclosed, through the twenty-seven per cent of Ashendon to the seven per cent of Burnham Hundred. At the same time the proportion of enclosed to unenclosed land in individual parishes could also vary considerably. Very few parishes anywhere in the county seem to have escaped ancient enclosure entirely and in a number Parliamentary enclosure was little more than a tidying up process after a long period of piecemeal enclosure extending back perhaps several centuries.

From the first decades of the eighteenth century the advantages of enclosure by private Act of Parliament over enclosure by agreement were becoming increasingly recognised: it was speedier, more effective and it could be extended to the

Plate 31   A late sixteenth-century timber-framed cottage at Swanbourne, with brick nogging in-filling.

Plate 32   A partly stone and partly timber-framed cottage at Beachampton.

Plate 33 The use of wichert as a building material means long, gently curving walls, as here at Haddenham.

Plate 34 The church at Stoke Poges. On the right, the flint-built tower and on the left the brick Hastings chapel, built in about 1560.

Plate 35   The Friends' Meeting House at Jordan, built in 1688.

Plate 36   The almshouses at Amersham, founded by Sir William Drake in 1657.

Plate 37 This thick, over-grown line of trees marks all that is left of the Buckingham branch of the Grand Junction canal near Thornton.

Plate 38 The Temple of British Worthies in the gardens at Stowe, with one of the lakes of the Serpentine River.

whole of a parish. The first private Act of enclosure for Buckinghamshire was obtained in 1738 for Ashendon, a parish in which Richard Grenville had already been able to enclose some lands by agreement. There were two more Acts in the 1740s, for Wotton Underwood in 1742 and for Shipton in Winslow in 1744. There was then a break before the next, for Swanbourne in 1761, after which they follow in increasing numbers to reach a climax in the years between 1790 and 1820. By 1845 enclosure was complete north of the Chilterns and in the Thames valley. After that date activity was confined entirely to the enclosure of commons and wastes within the Chilterns themselves. The last two Acts, for Fulmer and High Wycombe, were obtained in 1865 under the General Enclosure Act of 1845. In other words, although Parliamentary enclosure made an early start in Buckinghamshire, the main period of activity came fairly late within the enclosure movement as a whole. Recent research[1] has shown that this unusual chronological pattern was due to the presence in many Buckinghamshire parishes of large numbers of small proprietors, proprietors whose opposition to enclosure could sometimes cause considerable delays and who were too numerous to be bought out. This opposition often voiced itself through counter-petitions to Parliament to have the enclosure bills rejected. Such counter-petitions were sometimes successful and occasionally enclosure could be delayed for many years as a result. Perhaps the extreme example of this is Quainton, where a petition for enclosure was first presented in 1801, but the Act did not pass until 1840.

The passing of an enclosure Act would lead to a radical transformation of the landscape of an individual parish, and the total impact of Parliamentary enclosure upon the landscape of the county as a whole was permanent and profound. Much of the detailed planning of a particular enclosure was entrusted to a surveyor and a group of commissioners, in early Acts as many as seven but in later ones only two or three, appointed under each enclosure Act. The influence of these men upon the evolution of

[1] M. E. Turner, Some Social and Economic Consequences of Parliamentary Enclosure in Buckinghamshire, 1738–1865. Unpublished University of Sheffield Ph.D. thesis, 1973, pp. 89, 114, 184–185.

the Buckinghamshire landscape has been grossly under-estimated. A man such as John Fellows of Foscott, surveyor to the enclosures at Tingewick, 1773–5, Hartwell and Stone, 1776–7, and Preston Bissett, 1781–2, and then, between 1788 and 1825, serving on twenty-nine enclosure commissions in Buckinghamshire, fifteen in Bedfordshire, seven in Northamptonshire, and one each in Oxfordshire, Hertfordshire and Somerset, must be counted among the most influential upon the formation of the modern landscape, seeing as he did the final demise of the last remnants of the medieval and being intimately concerned with the shaping of the new.

We can study the transformation which Parliamentary enclosure could bring to an individual parish by comparing Fig. 17, a map of Padbury before enclosure, with Fig. 20, a map of the same parish after enclosure. The Act for the enclosure of the village was passed in 1795. The surveyors were Richard Davis of Lewknor in Oxfordshire, who also served as surveyor for the enclosure of Little Brickhill, and Michael Russell of Brackley, in Northamptonshire, who served as surveyor on no less than twelve other enclosures in Buckinghamshire. Davis and Russell laid their rulers straight across the map of Padbury, producing a landscape of long, unbending hedgerows and rectangular fields. Even the service roads to the new farms, such as the Grange and Low Farm, had to follow the same stiff, angular pattern. The old Whaddon Way, which had served as the boundary between East Field and Hedges Field, was reduced to the status of a footpath. Stock Way and Smale Way were stopped up entirely, and straight, trim roads marching purposefully across the landscape replaced broad, straggling ways, whilst the great majority of old field and furlong names were swept into oblivion. The only part of the ancient landscape to survive outside the village itself is the hedgerow that marked off Hedges Common pasture from a strip of meadow. The only relaxation allowed in the grim, sternly utilitarian landscape was a small block of woodland, Padbury New Covert. Gradually new, isolated, farms appeared in the landscape, but the old, loosely textured landscape has gone.

A similar transformation of the rural landscape is to be found

Fig. 20. Padbury after enclosure

wherever Parliamentary enclosure took place, and not only over what was once arable but also over wastes and commons. New roads were made and old ones re-aligned. Many miles of hedges and ditches were planted and dug out. Common arable fields, wastes and commons were divided up, some to be set to the plough, others to be converted to pasture and meadow. These changes in their turn brought about changes in the pattern of settlement. The dispersal of farmsteads, noted as a consequence of sixteenth- and seventeenth-century enclosure, was further stimulated and became much more pronounced. Occupiers of the new, consolidated, farms created by enclosure found it more convenient to build new farmsteads in the middle of their new fields and to move out into comparative isolation rather than remain in their old houses clustered together with their neighbours along the village street. Solidly built Georgian and Victorian farmhouses began to appear in the landscapes of many parishes. In Great Horwood for example Common Farm, Fir Tree Farm, Grove Farm, Briarsbank Farm and Sunnyhill Farm were all built after enclosure.

Thus the last overt, large-scale fragments of the medieval landscape disappeared for ever from Buckinghamshire, although in fact the old still lies only just beneath the surface of the modern. Ridge and furrow is still to be seen curving gently across many fields and meadows in north Buckinghamshire, and ancient hedgerows in quiet Chiltern valleys reveal something of their long past through their rich vegetation. Even the landscape which has replaced the medieval one is in its turn being eroded by the red rust of twentieth-century suburbia. But, as we shall see in the next two chapters, speculative house-builders have been confined by the fields they buy, and avenues and crescents of three-bedroom semi-detached houses are even today shaped by the patterns drawn by John Fellows and his contemporaries.

However the older landscape has not gone entirely, since some of the larger commons and wastes still remain open and unenclosed. Perhaps the most famous of these is the area now known as Burnham Beeches, over 500 acres of open woodland owned since 1880 by the City of London. Common grazing had come to an end by this date, and what was then largely rough pasture and scrub has, by a process of natural succession, become wooded, in some parts quite densely. The area contains a wide variety of animals and birds, plants and trees, of which perhaps the most spectacular are the massive, gnarled, distorted beech trees, many nearly four hundred years old, their grotesque shapes the result of three centuries of pollarding for fuel. This pollarding came to a stop early in the nineteenth century and much of the growth since then is now too heavy for the trunks of the trees, which are often hollow, to support. Much has been done to preserve them, but time and disease will inevitably bring them down. Burnham Beeches is an area very popular with visitors, especially in the summer months. Fortunately however the roads and footpaths, signs and barriers which their coming make necessary have been kept to a minimum, and it is still possible, deep among the trees, to catch a thin, clear echo from a much older landscape.

Improvements in communications and transport

The eighteenth century sees for the first time since the end of Roman power in Britain important and substantial improvements in communications. A long series of river improvements led eventually to the cutting of entirely new waterways. These developments are reflected in the Buckinghamshire landscape along the line of the river Thames and in the building of the Grand Junction Canal and its branches. The Thames was controlled from 1695, at least nominally, throughout much of its length by a body of Commissioners, and the building of the Grand Junction Canal was a major undertaking requiring considerable capital and the vision of a national network of navigable waterways. Road improvements on the other hand were carried out piecemeal by turnpike trustees who were rarely responsible for much more than twenty miles of road. Nevertheless, in spite of these limitations of scale, the main roads out of London had been almost completely turnpiked by 1750, and by the end of the eighteenth century a remarkably well-integrated

network of turnpike roads had evolved. Each of these organis-
ations made its own distinctive contribution to the making of
the Buckinghamshire landscape.

The Thames

For centuries the Thames had been an important highway, but
its significance increased markedly from the beginnings of the
sixteenth century as growing quantities of agricultural produce
moved downstream to feed London's rapidly mounting population and a steadily widening range of merchandise such as
coal, bricks and groceries moved upstream to the towns strung
along its banks. But there were serious obstacles to the navigation of the river. The river bed was entirely unimproved, a
series of rapids and shallows alternating with deep pools,
through which the current ran swiftly and strongly. To stand on
the footbridge over the weir at Hambleden, with the water
rushing and tumbling only two feet below, is to get some faint
idea of just how swiftly the current must have run. The river was
likely to be impassable for long periods, during the winter
months because of flooding or freezing, and during the summer
months because drought could reduce it to a trickle. The natural
obstacles were matched by the man-made ones. In about 1578 it
was reported that there were twenty-three locks, sixteen floodgates, seven weirs and over twenty watermills on the stretch of
the river between Maidenhead and Oxford.[2] The owners of these
locks, weirs and mills charged stiff tolls for the right of passage,
even charging for the use of the towing path. The locks were
flashlocks, that is to say they had only one gate. When this was
opened the flash of water would sweep forward boats going
downstream with considerable force, whilst boats trying to pass
upstream had to be winched up against the current. Many boats
were overturned, their passengers drowned and their cargoes
lost. After a flashlock had been opened so much water was
wasted that for as long as twenty-four hours afterwards the river
was almost dry. It was said in 1793 that after Marlow flashlock

[2] F. S. Thacker, *The Thames Highway* Vol. 1 (1914, 1968 reprint), p. 45.

had been opened it was possible to walk across the river dry-foot.[3]

In 1694 an Act of Parliament was passed to attempt to remedy some of these abuses. The Justices of the Peace of every county through which the river passed were appointed Commissioners to set reasonable tolls for the passage through locks, weirs, winches, turnpikes, dams and floodgates, and to fix the charges for the carriage of goods by bargemasters. However this Act was to expire after nine years, and its effects could have been only very short-lived. It was revived in 1730, and re-enacted in 1751, when the river was divided into six districts, of which the third ran from Boulter's Lock to Mapledurham. The Commission was very much enlarged, and consisted of almost six hundred persons. But its powers were very limited. In 1770 a more successful attempt was made to provide for the managment of the river. The Commission was still further enlarged, but the quorum was fixed at eleven. The Commissioners had power to build towpaths and acquire the rights of way, to buy flashlocks and to replace them with poundlocks. The effects of these powers were felt almost immediately. The poundlock at Boulter's Lock was built in 1772, and those at Hambleden, Hurley and Marlow were opened in 1773. A small wooden lock-keeper's house was built at Hambleden in 1774, to be replaced by a brick-built one in 1777. Marlow Lock had its first lock-house in 1815. An unpretentious, square brick house, it is still there.

In 1866 the Thames Conservancy was established, replacing the Commissioners, and private tolls along the river were abolished. From 1878 the Conservancy took increasing powers to control pollution, not only in the Thames itself but also in its tributaries. In 1883 all steam launches navigating above Kew Bridge were required to register with the Conservators, and from 1885 this was extended to all pleasure craft. The late nineteenth century saw a remarkable growth in boating and sailing on the river as the extension of the railway network

---

[3] *Report of a Committee Appointed to Enquire Into the Progress Made towards the Amendment and Improvement of the Navigation of the Thames and Isis.* House of Commons Sessional Papers Reports Vol. XIII No. 109 (1793), p. 7.

brought many small riverside towns such as Bourne End within easy reach of London. Boating for recreation and pleasure at this period finds its best and most permanent memorial in the pages of Jerome K. Jerome's book, *Three Men in a Boat*, first published in 1889, in which Marlow is described as a bustling, lively little town, with lovely country around it.

As the river became increasingly tame, more predictable and less liable to flood, so from the first years of the nineteenth century onwards its banks were slowly built up with houses, villas and cottages. Many still survive, cool, white and elegant, at Taplow, Marlow and elsewhere along the river, ducks and moorhens at home on their smoothly shaven lawns and in the weeping willows at the water's edge. The watermills have now ceased to grind corn. That at Hambleden has lost its millwheel, but the mill-race is still to be seen, a quiet, narrow backwater, boats of every description moored to its banks. At Marlow the mill has been demolished and replaced with blocks of terraced houses clad in white weatherboarding, a not entirely unsuccessful attempt to fit the new in with the old. The mill-race still plunges beneath as it must have done for a thousand years.

The Grand Junction Canal

Canals were comparatively late in coming to Buckinghamshire. The success of the Duke of Bridgewater's canal from his Worsley coalmines to Manchester stimulated the construction of many miles of canals so that by the 1770s the Trent, Severn and Mersey were all connected by a network of inland waterways. But it was 1790 before this network was linked to the fourth major river in England, when the canal from Coventry to Oxford and the Thames was finally completed. However this route from Birmingham to London was nearly 248 miles long and included 109 locks (Fig. 21). Plans were almost immediately drawn up for a more direct route. In July of 1792 a public meeting in Stony Stratford enthusiastically supported the line which had been surveyed by James Barnes of Banbury, whose expenses had been met by the Marquis of Buckingham. Construction work began in the following year, both at Braunston

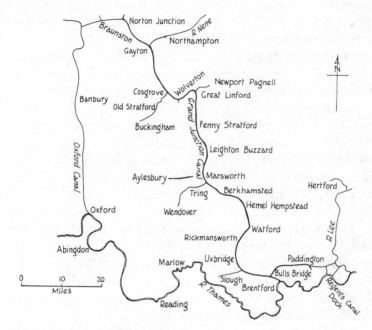

Fig. 21. Canals in Buckinghamshire

in Northamptonshire, where the canal was to join the Oxford Canal, and at Brentford, where it joined the Thames. By October 1800 most of the work was finished save for the Blisworth tunnel section. There were seemingly endless problems here and it was March of 1805 before the tunnel was finally completed and the canal was open for through traffic.

The crossing of the valley of the Ouse also caused problems. At first it was intended that the drop from the Tring summit should be accomplished by means of thirty-one locks, and the rise to Braunston by a further twenty-eight. In December 1799 however it was proposed that the canal should be carried over the Ouse by means of an aqueduct.[4] Construction work did not begin until January of 1803, and it was August 1805 before it was open for traffic. In February 1808 it collapsed, and a temporary wooden structure was built to replace it until the

[4] A. H. Faulkner, 'The Wolverton Aqueduct: A Case Study in Canal Engineering', *Transport History* 2, (1969), pp. 155–166.

present iron aqueduct could be erected and opened in January 1811. The lakes on the north-east side of the foot of the canal embankment were formed when material for the embankments was excavated. At the same time two tunnels were built, one on either side of the river and under the canal to allow cattle to pass from one side of the canal to the other.

It was intended from the first that there should be a number of branch cuts off the main course of the canal. That to Wendover was the first to be built, because of its importance as a feeder for the Tring summit. The next to be finished was that from Cosgrove, at the north end of the Wolverton aqueduct, through Old Stratford and Deanshanger to Buckingham, and largely at the instigation of the Marquis of Buckingham, who lent the Company the money to build the stretch from Old Stratford to Buckingham. Its effects were immediate and beneficial. The price of coal in Buckingham fell dramatically, and a brisk trade in this and other commodities quickly developed, so that within a few years 20,000 tons of goods were being moved along this branch (Plate 37).

The Aylesbury branch had been authorised as early as 1794, but it was not opened until 1815, after considerable delays and many changes of plan. It was soon realised that this branch would impose a severe strain on the water supplies in the main canal, and so new reservoirs were built on the Tring summit, at Tringford and Startopsend. A small portion of the latter is just inside the county boundary. This branch was also a commercial success. The story of the Newport Pagnell branch is one of similar delays, and it was January of 1817 before the canal, a mile and a quarter long with seven locks, was finally opened. Traffic developed quickly, and wharves were built at Newport Pagnell and at Great Linford, where the branch joined the main canal, to handle the coal, stone, bricks, timber, grain and malt which were the principal commodities carried along it. In 1845–6 it was proposed to build a railway from Wolverton through Newport Pagnell to join the Bletchley to Bedford line near Ridgmont, and it was suggested that the line should use the canal bed for part of the route, but this plan was dropped. In 1862 a similar scheme, again for a line from Wolverton to

Newport Pagnell, was put forward, and this was eventually adopted. The canal was closed in September 1864 and the railway built. An extension to Olney, authorised in 1865, was in fact never finished, although extensive earthworks were built, including a series of embankments which can still be seen curving away across the north Buckinghamshire landscape.

The Newport Pagnell branch canal was not the only one to be closed. The Wendover feeder was rarely free from leakages, which at one time were so severe that water was actually being drawn off the main line. Eventually, in 1897, stop planks were inserted at Little Tring, cutting it off from the main canal. These were in due course replaced by a lock, but in reality the branch was never reopened. In 1904 the water level was lowered, the stretch between Drayton Beauchamp and Wendover was re-puddled and diverted into Wilstone reservoir, and the length between Drayton Beauchamp and the stop lock abandoned.

The last branch canal to be built was that to Slough. The Act of Parliament was passed in 1879 and the canal was opened in 1882. It needed three aqueducts and a big cutting, at Iver. As with the Buckingham and Aylesbury branches, it was a great commercial success.

Within less than thirty years of the opening of the Blisworth tunnel the very existence of the Grand Junction Canal Company was threatened by the building of the London to Birmingham railway. The Canal Company was among the leaders of the opposition to the Act for the building of the railway, allocating £2,000 towards the cost of opposition. Even after the Act passed, the Canal Company refused to co-operate at all willingly with the Railway Company, whose line followed very closely that of the canal. Indeed at one stage canal employees deliberately demolished the temporary railway bridge at Wolverton and it took a court injunction to stop them doing it again.

Once the railway was complete a fierce battle rapidly developed. The canal very quickly lost its passenger trade to the railway, and only by savagely cutting its tolls on goods did it maintain something of its position. Further steps to fight back included the duplication of the narrow locks at Marsworth in order to increase the speed at which barges could pass through, and by mid-1839 the locks had been duplicated as far as Stoke Hammond. This also meant rebuilding no less than six bridges over the canal, to give them a double arch. The double locks have since been filled in, but the double-arched bridges still remain, testimony to the fierce struggles that once raged over the use of these now silent, rather muddy, waters.

The Grand Junction Canal and its branches have now become so much a part of the Buckinghamshire landscape that their impact is very difficult to appreciate. The building of the canal itself meant cuttings and embankments, locks, bridges, towpaths and aqueducts, wharves and warehouses. In its wider impact the coming of the canal often stimulated industrial and commercial development. At Fenny Stratford the gas works, an iron foundry and a sawmill, several rows of cottages, the White Hart Inn, the police station and a Navigation Inn, now the Bridge Hotel, were all built in direct response to the new opportunities that the canal presented.[5] The Grand Junction Canal was once one of the main communications links of industrial England, raw, brash and intrusive. Long stretches are now overgrown with rushes, meadow-sweet and water crow-foot, disturbed only by moorhens and the occasional angler (see Plate 37).

Turnpike roads

From 1555 until 1835 responsibility for the repair and maintenance of roads rested with the parish. This meant that money for repairs was grudgingly given, and engineering knowledge and experience entirely lacking. Thus the condition of the roads was never very good, and often very bad. The establishment of turnpike trusts by private Act of Parliament to take over a defined stretch of road, to raise capital for its improvement and to charge tolls to cover maintenance costs and to repay the capital, was a method of road improvement increasingly adopted during the course of the eighteenth century,

[5] E. Legg, 'Canal Settlement in Fenny Stratford', *Records of Buckinghamshire* XIX Part 1, (1971), pp. 67–72.

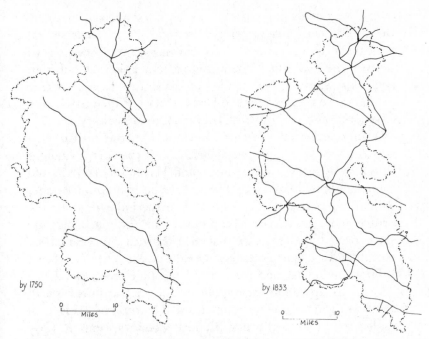

by 1750

Miles
0   10

by 1833

Miles
0   10

Fig. 22. The development of the turnpike road system in Buckinghamshire

and Fig. 22 shows the way in which they spread across Buckinghamshire. One of the first stretches of road turnpiked anywhere
in the country was that part of Watling Street, the London to
Holyhead road, between Fonthill in Bedfordshire and Stony
Stratford, for which the Act was passed in 1706.

Turnpike trustees were usually empowered to widen roads,
except where they ran through certain types of land, such as
towns and villages, orchards, gardens and parks, and the width
of turnpike roads was often specified in the Act. This meant that
wide grass verges became as much a feature of turnpike roads as
they were of Parliamentary enclosure ones. The commissioners
could also straighten roads, make cuttings and embankments,
build and repair bridges and fords, and all were, from 1720,
obliged to measure their roads and erect mileposts and sign
posts. It is probably in these areas of their activities that they
made their most permanent contribution to the landscape.
These points are brought out particularly clearly in the history

of the Wendover to Buckingham trust, established in 1721. Before the trust finally expired in 1879 it had made several radical realignments in the roads it managed. In the seventeenth century the road from Aylesbury to Buckingham ran out from Aylesbury through Quarrendon to Blackgrove Farm, where it picked up the Roman road to East Claydon. It then crossed the Claydon brook at the White Bridge south of Padbury (see Fig. 17) before eventually reaching Buckingham. But the turnpike trustees chose for their route what is now the A413, running through Winslow, Whitchurch and Hardwick, and the old route fell into decay. In 1838 they rebuilt Shipton Bridge, which had partially collapsed, and in the following year the bridge at Hardwick was also rebuilt. The Shipton Bridge has since been bypassed, but that at Hardwick has again been rebuilt and still carries the heavy traffic on the A143.

In 1864 it was decided that all turnpike trusts should be allowed to lapse, and the last one in Buckinghamshire came to an end in 1881. In 1889 all main and disturnpiked roads came under the care of the new County Councils, and in 1895 responsibility for all other roads was assumed by the newly formed Rural and Urban District Councils. These administrative changes usher in a new era in road construction and in road transport. As trusts came to an end it was usual for them to demolish their toll houses and sell the materials. As a consequence there appear to be no turnpike toll houses left in the county. However a number of their mileposts still survive. They are, for example, still to be seen along much of the Aylesbury to Buckingham road, of stone, carefully painted white with black letters and numbers.

Georgian building in town and country

Sir Richard Temple, when laying out the gardens around his new red brick house at Stowe in the last two decades of the seventeenth century, chose, if Plate 30 is at all a reliable guide, the formal, enclosed, elaborately organised design that was the fashion at the time. But already tastes were beginning to move in the direction of a more relaxed, naturalistic approach to gardens and to landscape. The new gardens, bounded by the horizon rather than by a brick wall, sought to combine a carefully contrived simplicity with a studied elegance, and it took all the skills of the newly emerging professional landscape gardeners to achieve such a combination successfully. The story of the progressive breaking down of the formal, rigid lines of the late seventeenth-century garden is epitomised in the history of Stowe, "the outstanding monument of English landscape gardening"[6] (see Plate 39).

Old Sir Richard Temple died in 1697 and was succeeded by his son, also called Richard. In 1702, on the outbreak of the War of the Spanish Succession, he was appointed Colonel of an infantry regiment, and served with distinction under Marlborough in his Continental campaigns. He rose to be Lieutenant-General, but, strongly Whig in his political views, he was cashiered by the Tories in 1713. However on the accession of George I in the following year he was re-instated, and created Lord Cobham. In 1715 he married a wealthy heiress, and in 1718 he was made a viscount. In 1719 he commanded the Vigo Expedition to Spain, from which he returned immensely rich. But this was his last important military command, and he had increasing leisure to devote to his house and gardens. He was created Field Marshall in 1742 and died in 1749.

Certainly by 1711 he was taking a keen interest in the gardens and house but the first significant changes were not executed until 1715, when, it seems, Charles Bridgeman was called in. By the end of 1718 the first ha-ha, the complete antithesis to an enclosing garden wall, was being built. From the end of 1720 Lord Cobham was working on an altogether very much larger scale and gradually over the next fifty or sixty years the gardens and house were altered and enlarged, without obliterating entirely all trace of what had gone before.[7] By 1731 William Kent was at work designing buildings for the gardens, including the Temple of Ancient Virtue, at once the centre of the Elysian Fields, the terminus of the Great Cross Walk and

[6] C. Hussey, *English Gardens and Landscapes 1700–1750* (1967), p. 89.
[7] G. Clarke, 'The Gardens of Stowe', *Apollo* 97, (1973), pp. 558–565.

the reflection of the Temple of British Worthies (Plate 38) lying across the narrow lakes which make up the Serpentine River. The scale is small and intimate, the Shell Bridge over the stream emphasising the air of delicate fantasy which is scarcely affected, today at any rate, by the overt political symbolism of the buildings. From the 1740s Lord Cobham's nephew and heir, Richard Grenville, was taking an interest in the development of the gardens, although much of the actual work fell to the new head gardener, Lancelot Brown. Brown had arrived in Stowe by 1740, and was head gardener by March of 1741. He married in Stowe parish church in November of 1744 and finally left Stowe for good in the autumn of 1751. By 1744 the Gothic Temple, designed by James Gibbs, and one of the earliest examples of 'Gothick', was complete. The view from this Temple out over the countryside to the east was further embellished by the building of a keeper's lodge disguised as a medieval tower, and by a farmhouse masquerading as a castle. Both were probably designed by Gibbs.

In 1749 Lord Cobham died, to be succeeded by his sister Hester, who had married Richard Grenville of Wotton Underwood. She became Viscountess Cobham in her own right, and was created Countess Temple. At her death three years later her son Richard succeeded, becoming Earl Temple. Under his direction the relaxation of the formal layout (Plate 39) gathered momentum. The Octagon Pond was reshaped into a more natural lake. The great parterre on the southern vista had already been grassed over (Plate 40), and the thinning out of the trees planted by Bridgeman continued. In 1765 Temple's cousin, Thomas Pitt, designed the splendid Corinthian triumphal arch, at last replacing the long-lost spire of Buckingham church as the focal point on the southern horizon.

The gardens themselves were now almost complete. In spite of the long period during which they were evolving they had, and still have, a marvellous overall unity of spirit. The design is the embodiment of movement, in which buildings, when seen from a distance, serve as a point of rest, but when reached they open the way to new avenues and vistas, inviting the visitor to

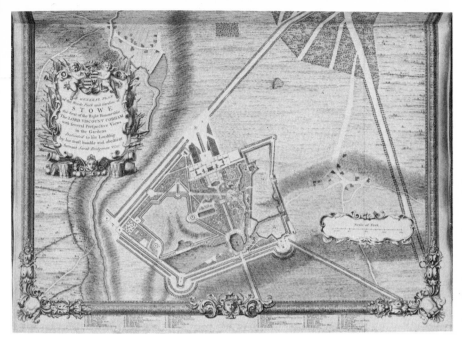

Plate 39 A plan of the gardens at Stowe. This was published in 1739 by Sarah Bridgeman to accompany the volume of engravings of views of the house and its grounds made by the French artist Jacques Rigaud.

Plate 40 The South Parterre at Stowe, from the engraving by Jacques Rigaud. It should be compared with plate 41.

Plate 41 The South Front at Stowe as it is today, from designs by Robert Adam modified by Thomas Pitt. It was finished in about 1775.

Plate 42 The South Front to the house at West Wycombe Park. This façade was remodelled in about 1760. The golden ball on the top of the church of St Lawrence can just be seen above the trees.

Plate 43 The Temple of Music, on an island in the lake at West Wycombe, with the church of St Lawrence just visible.

explore still further, whether along tree-shaded walks or across open turf, with water, still or moving, never far away. But the invitation is always a gentle one. There is nothing hurried, restless or strident at Stowe.

Lord Temple now turned to providing a fitting climax to the whole undertaking by rebuilding the North and South Fronts to the house itself in an appropriate manner and on a suitable scale. The house of 1676 was in fact never pulled down. Instead it was added to and extended in a rather piecemeal fashion, for a long time lagging behind the gardens in concept and scale. Eventually, in 1770, Lord Temple approached Robert Adam, who supplied a design which served as the basis for the magnificent South Front (Plate 41) although some significant alterations were made to this design before it was eventually completed in 1775, about three years after the reshaping of the North Front by the addition of colonnades half enclosing the forecourt had been finished.

By this time Earl Temple was elderly and very infirm. His gardens were the admiration of Europe and the exterior of his mansion now had an overall splendour of design, balanced and dignified without being pompous or dull, to match its quite astonishing setting, a setting upon which so much time, labour, talent and money had been lavished.

The subsequent history of Stowe can be told more briefly. Lord Temple died in 1779. He had no children and so his titles and estates descended to his nephew, George Grenville, created first Marquis of Buckingham in 1784. He married Mary Nugent, and his son was created first Duke of Buckingham, having married Anna, sole heiress of the last Duke of Chandos. The family was now at its apogee, immensely rich, with estates extending over 52,000 acres, with 25,000 in Buckinghamshire alone, and a gross rental of £66,000 a year.[8] But disaster was not far away. The first Duke died in 1839, to be succeeded by his son, whose sense of his own importance could be sustained only by grotesquely extravagant expenditure. By 1847 the interest on his debts exceeded the annual rental of his estates. In August

[8] D. and E. Spring, 'The Fall of the Grenvilles, 1844–1848', *Huntington Library Quarterly* 19, (1956), pp. 165–190.

of 1848 the contents of the mansion at Stowe were sold by public auction, an event which drew huge crowds to look over the house and aroused much excited and sometimes malicious comment. Almost everyone who was anyone bought something in the sale, even Queen Victoria. The spendthrift Duke died in 1861. His son was an altogether much more admirable character, but Stowe still remained empty. He died in 1889, leaving a daughter, and the estates eventually passed to her son. The house was finally sold in 1923 and its demolition and the destruction of the gardens was averted only by the establishment of a school. The development of the school has led to the erection of buildings out of sympathy with their setting, and some are undoubtedly intrusive. For many years little was done to conserve the gardens and their buildings. However since 1945 a determined attempt has been made to make up for years of neglect. No less than seventeen of the garden buildings have been restored, and much time and effort has been spent in the garden, where dead and decayed trees have been removed and new ones planted. Perhaps the saddest loss has been the felling of the magnificent avenue of trees leading up to the Corinthian Arch, but the trees were in a dangerous condition and there was no alternative. The avenue is being progressively replanted, so that it looks at present as it must have done when first laid out, but two generations will pass before it again reaches maturity.

We have spent a long time looking at the development of the house and gardens at Stowe, but this is more than justified by their significance as a record of the development of eighteenth-century ideas on landscape. The most spacious single monument to the eighteenth century in Buckinghamshire, they are of national, indeed European importance, deserving, and repaying, the closest study. Their history brings together on one site four of the most significant trends in the landscape of eighteenth-century Buckinghamshire.

The enclosure of Stowe was completed by 1649 and it seems likely that its final depopulation had been accomplished by the end of the seventeenth century, leaving behind only the church discreetly screened from the great house by encircling trees.

Depopulation in order to make way for extensions to gardens is echoed both at Wotton Underwood and at Gayhurst, where the church was also rebuilt, in 1728, within a hundred yards of the house. These three villages are the last of those marked on Fig. 14 to be deserted.

Secondly, as we have seen, the mansion at Stowe as Lord Temple left it at his death in 1779 encased a late seventeenth-century house which in fact had never been demolished. The same pattern is repeated at other Buckinghamshire country houses. At West Wycombe the splendid mansion of Sir Francis Dashwood incorporates the shell of the house built by his father at the very beginning of the eighteenth century (Plate 42), whilst at Hartwell the substantial Jacobean brick house was considerably altered and enlarged by Henry Keene for Sir William Lee in the middle of the eighteenth century. Similarly, the second Earl Verney spent lavishly on his house at Middle Claydon for nearly thirty years in an attempt to outdo the Grenvilles, but he never demolished entirely the unpretentious Jacobean house with which he began. This is not to imply that there were no completely new houses built during the century. One of the most attractive of all of the country houses in Buckinghamshire, that at Chicheley, was entirely new when it was built in the years after 1719.

Thirdly, much of the significance of Stowe in the history of the landscape attaches to its gardens, the various stages of the development of which mirror changing aesthetic attitudes towards art and nature. Other gardens reflect the same changes, although not so accurately nor so fully. There were for example very formal rectilinear gardens at Hartwell, reputed to have been swept away by Lancelot Brown in the second half of the century. At West Wycombe the gardens at the beginning of the century were as formal as anything devised by Bridgeman at Stowe and, as at Stowe, the broad structure then laid down still forms their fundamental framework, and, again as at Stowe, their history is one of the progressive softening of clear-cut lines and the introduction of garden buildings into a deliberately composed landscape. The Temple of Music, designed and built by Nicholas Revett, is unsurpassed by anything even at Stowe as an essay in pictorial composition (Plate 43). The gardens at Cliveden appear to have gone through the same process.[9]

Finally, the buildings in the gardens at Stowe reflect those shifts in taste and attitude summed up in the words Gothic and neo-classical revivals, and again these movements are echoed elsewhere in Buckinghamshire. The Temple of the Four Winds at West Wycombe, completed in 1759, is the earliest attempt to reproduce a classical building in England, the Tower of the Winds in Athens. The Old Gaol at Buckingham, built as an imitation castle, was finished in 1748 and paid for by Lord Cobham. On a hill to the north of the church at Hedsor is another mock medieval castle and a very substantial one, with three flint towers. From the middle years of the century enthusiasm for things 'Gothick' led a number of country gentlemen to add battlements to their houses, as at Hampden House, Liscombe Park and Missenden Abbey. At Lower Winchendon what was fundamentally a late fifteenth-century house was enthusiastically Gothicised by its owner, Scrope Bernard, between about 1797 and 1803, and to his own designs. In the building of Tyringham House, between 1793 and 1797, in the first work of his maturity, Sir John Soane made one of his uniquely personal contributions to the neo-classical revival, although unfortunately only the gateway and the bridge now survive unchanged.

We have spent some time looking at country houses and the parks and gardens which were deliberately created as their setting. This is only fitting, since it was in building and in gardening that much of the spirit of the eighteenth century finds its most characteristic expression, as that of the medieval centuries finds it expression in churches and monasteries, and that of the twentieth in motorways and office blocks. However, building was not confined exclusively to the country or to domestic and secular purposes. A sober prosperity, based upon trade in agricultural produce, especially cattle and grain, together with that brought by growing traffic upon the main thorough fares of the county, coupled with a rising population, led to much building and rebuilding in Buckinghamshire

[9] see B.R.O. Ma. 271/1.T and Ma. 271/2.T.

towns in the eighteenth century. Indeed in the face that they present to the street, Buckinghamshire towns are essentially of the eighteenth century. Unfortunately, the attentions of property developers in the years after 1945 have all too often destroyed so much in the centres of Buckinghamshire towns that was of historical, architectural and aesthetic value that very little survives of the pre-industrial townscape.

Perhaps the best-preserved eighteenth-century townscape in the county is that at Olney. The High Street curves gently away to the north from the Market Place, and there is almost nothing incongruous to be seen anywhere. Most of the houses are faced with stone and there are no side streets off the High Street to interrupt the succession of reticent, well-bred houses, each different and yet each sharing the same fundamentals of form and design. One of the few brick houses in the town is that in the Market Place where William Cowper lived for twenty years of his sad, quiet life. It is now a museum and, together with the summer house and the garden he loved so well, open to the public.

Of other Buckinghamshire towns, Stony Stratford, Marlow and Amersham are those where most remains of the eighteenth century. At Stony Stratford the majority of houses and shops facing the main street, the High Street, part of Watling Street, are of brick and stone, rebuilt in the eighteenth century after two particularly disastrous fires in 1736 and 1742. There is more here than at Olney which is incongruous, although a new shopping centre has at least been kept to scale, even if the colour of its brickwork jars with the mellow stone work of much of its neighbours. The new Public Library fits in much more sympathetically. In the Market Place are several very pleasant Georgian houses of stone or stucco, and yet more in Horsefair Green. Stony Stratford was a town in danger of being choked by the volume of traffic on the A5, Watling Street. The building of the M1 motorway has brought a welcome relief and it is now possible to admire the layout of a very pleasant market town without one's life being constantly in jeopardy.

The High Street at Marlow must be the happiest blend of old and new in any town in the county. Almost every building is eighteenth century and those few which are not have been designed sympathetically and keep to the same human, civilised scale. Marlow has clearly not been intimidated by its past, since the town is busy and lively, nor has it made a cult of it, although everything is carefully maintained. At No. 79, High Street is a delightful example of a nineteenth-century shop-front, small square panes of glass set in delicate Gothic tracery in double bow windows. The Post Office is a handsome five-bay mid-eighteenth-century house which has been adapted to its present use with the minimum of alteration. Other buildings are plainer and simpler, one, No. 65, plain to the point of severity. It has not been adapted as a shop, and has the air of standing slightly aloof from the trivial gossip of its neighbours. The climax of the High Street is the old Town Hall, built in about 1807, and now, its façade cleaned and restored, the Crown Inn. This stands at the point where High Street and West Street meet, and West Street for much of its length has the same cheerful, bubbling atmosphere as the High Street.

Amersham, however, is perhaps a trifle too self-conscious of its past. It cannot be denied that the town is very attractive in a rather static way, but east of the Market House there are some very unsightly buildings and the gas works is a disaster, whilst to the west the High Street lacks that sense of vitality that runs through Marlow High Street. There is in the High Street at Amersham one very large house, Elmodesham House, eleven bays wide and, on the other side, a group of very small ones, only one bay wide, No. 113 being built, rather unusually for Amersham, of flint as well as brick. Although the High Street is predominantly from the eighteenth century, there is more visible here from earlier times than in Marlow. The King's Head, Nos 26 and 39 are clearly sixteenth century and earlier, whilst the almshouses, built round three sides of a square, date from 1657 (Plate 36).

In Aylesbury an awareness of what was being lost by post-war property development came only at the eleventh hour, but it was in time to save Church Street, Temple Square, Castle Street and St Mary's Churchyard. The original Grammar School, built between July 1718 and August 1720, still stands at the end of

Church Street and overlooking St Mary's Churchyard. It is now part of the County Museum. On the other side of the street three adjacent houses illustrate very neatly the organic quality of the townscape. First is a sixteenth-century timber-framed house with over-hanging jetty, recently carefully restored. Next is a house with an eighteenth-century façade, and next to that is the Chantry, with a very pretty Gothic front of about 1840. Behind both are sixteenth-century timbers, and all three sites were certainly occupied in medieval times (Plate 44).

It is High Wycombe however which has lost most in post 1945 rebuilding. The High Street is very busy, and the Guildhall, built in 1757 to designs by the same Henry Keene who worked for Sir William Lee at Hartwell, and the Market Hall, rebuilt by Robert Adam in 1761, are almost swamped in heavy traffic. The High Street itself still contains a handful of Georgian buildings, of which three are banks, but it is hedged about with concrete multi-storey car-parks and shopping centres, and all that is left of the Red Lion Inn is the entrance porch and the red lion itself sitting on top.

Olney, Amersham and Marlow still contain sufficient from the eighteenth century to enable the visitor to recreate something of the atmosphere, even if not the odour, of an eighteenth-century country town. In other towns, Buckingham, Chesham, Stony Stratford and Aylesbury, much survives in rather disjointed fragments, whilst in High Wycombe only isolated buildings remain. However, until quite recently, change has been less radical in towns than in the countryside, so that in very many towns in Buckinghamshire the medieval past lies very close to the surface, no more than the thickness of two bricks or perhaps a coat of plaster away, as a glance at Lum's Yard in Chesham, or the back of Castle House in Buckingham, will quickly reveal.

The building of churches came almost to a standstill in Buckinghamshire in the eighteenth century, and what was done was either essential repair work, or else it was undertaken deliberately as part of the landscaping of the grounds to a country house.

At Buckingham, the old church in Prebend End, shorn of its

spire, fell increasingly into disrepair and eventually became too dangerous to be used. A new site was prepared, a little to the north, on the motte of the former castle, and the new church was built between 1777 and 1781, making use of some of the stone work from the old church. Unfortunately this new church was particularly heavily restored by Sir George Gilbert Scott, so that very little remains of the eighteenth-century structure. At Bow Brickhill the church standing high on a hill looking out over the valley of the Ousel, had also been allowed to fall into disrepair. Here the restoration work was carried out in 1756, at the instigation of Browne Willis. He was also responsible for the building of the church at Fenny Stratford between 1724 and 1730.

In addition to that at Gayhurst, two other Buckinghamshire churches were substantially altered or rebuilt in the interests of the aesthetics of landscape gardening. At Hartwell Sir William Lee commissioned the building, at a cost of £2,595 17s. 1½d., of a new church to serve as a focal point for a view from the house. Henry Keene was the architect, and Mr Henry Keene, senior, was the joiner. He provided an altar of wainscot carved "in the Saxon manner", and a rich 'Gothick' altar piece. The fine plaster work was executed by Thomas Roberts. He charged £250 for stucco work on the ceiling, completely finished with 'Gothick' mouldings and ornaments.[10] That so splendid an example of eighteenth-century architecture, and a church at that, should have been allowed to fall into ruin is a silent indictment of twentieth-century values.

The other church remodelled in order to improve the view from a house is that at West Wycombe. Here the church crowns a hill overlooking the mansion and park of Sir Francis Dashwood (see Plate 42). He had the tower raised and finished off with a huge golden ball, which has seats inside. The nave was rebuilt and given arched windows, whilst the interior was richly decorated and paved with marble. At the same time the main road out of High Wycombe was straightened and aligned on the church. On the eastern edge of the churchyard an extraordinary family mausoleum was built, of flint, in 1763–4. It is

[10] B.R.O. D/Le. D.13/1–22.

hexagonal in shape, open to the sky. The three sides backing on to the churchyard are solid, but the other three are themselves open screens, with Tuscan columns. The whole composition, perched high on its hill, is visible for well over a mile, forming a quite astonishing landmark as the traveller approaches from High Wycombe, and a suitable climax to this account of the eighteenth-century landscape.

SELECT BIBLIOGRAPHY

Chibnall, J., The Roads of Buckinghamshire with special reference to turnpike roads. Unpublished University of London M.Sc. thesis 1963.

Faulkner, A. H., *The Grand Junction Canal* (1972).

Hussey, C., *The Picturesque* (1927).

Hussey, C., *English Country Houses: Early Georgian, 1715–1760* (1955).

Priestley, J., *Navigable Rivers and Canals* (1831, 1969 reprint).

Stroud, D., *Humphrey Repton* (1962).

Stroud, D., *Capability Brown* (1975).

Turner, M. E., 'The Cost of Parliamentary Enclosure in Buckinghamshire', *Agricultural History Review* 21, (1973), pp. 35–46.

Turner, M. E., 'Enclosure Commissioners and Buckinghamshire Parliamentary Enclosure', *Agricultural History Review* 25, (1977), pp. 120–129.

Willis, P., *Charles Bridgeman and the English Landscape Garden* (1977).

8. Victorian Buckinghamshire

Introduction. Population change. The coming of the railway. Urban development. Victorian building in town and country

Introduction

THE HISTORY OF the landscape of Victorian England is dominated by the immense changes brought about by rapid industrialisation. Buckinghamshire, however, was one of those parts of the country less dramatically affected. In spite of the building of two main-line railways across the county and numerous branch lines, and the rapid growth in size of several of the towns in the county, Buckinghamshire remained essentially and overwhelmingly rural throughout the nineteenth century. This is not to deny the effects of industrialisation, but its impact was more muted, more delayed, than in South Wales, south Lancashire or Staffordshire.

Buckinghamshire shared with the rest of the country in that rapid growth of population of the first third of the nineteenth century, but by 1841 it is apparent that rural depopulation is already taking place, and this accelerates as the century draws on, so that by 1901 many villages had fewer inhabitants than they had in 1801. In contrast, a number of Buckinghamshire towns show a marked growth in population, particularly in the second half of the century. The greatest single stimulus to this growth was undoubtedly the coming of the railway. An entirely new town, Wolverton, was the creation of the London and North Western Railway Company, and several others, Bletchley and Linslade for example, grew rapidly once the railway was built. In the south of the county residential development prompted by the railway began at Slough in the 1840s, but other towns, Beaconsfield, Amersham and the

Chalfonts, show no real signs of expansion until commuter lines were built out of London in the 1890s, making access to the capital very easy and bringing very rapid residential development in their wake. By 1914 that contrast between north and south which has been so pronounced a feature of the county's history had taken an entirely new direction, and has become even more noticeable. For the first time more people lived in the south than in the north, with all that this entailed of new houses, streets, schools, churches and railway stations.

Population change

The mainspring of change in both the rural and the urban landscapes of Victorian Buckinghamshire is to be sought in an overall growth of population, coupled with radical shifts in the patterns of its distribution. As we have seen in previous chapters settlement drift is nothing new in the history of the Buckinghamshire landscape. What gives Victorian changes their significance is their speed, scale and consequent impact upon the fabric of society and its environment.

The population of the county almost doubled between 1801 and 1901, from 107,900 inhabitants to 197,000, whereas over England and Wales as a whole the population multiplied three and a half times. These figures serve to mask very wide divergences of experience in individual parishes and at various points of time through the course of the nineteenth century. The largest intercensal population increase occurred in Buckinghamshire between 1811 and 1821, when the increase was something over fourteen per cent. Thereafter the rate of increase declined steadily to its lowest point, less than one per cent, between 1871 and 1881. It then turned upwards, to reach a little over eleven per cent, a rate larger than the national average, between 1901 and 1911, and one presaging the rates of increase, and the consequent changes in the landscape, of the twentieth century.

Hitherto Buckinghamshire north of the Chiltern scarp has been the more populous half of the county, and although the principal valleys of the Chilterns contained towns of some size, the hills themselves were only thinly settled. The nineteenth century saw the relationship between north and south progressively reversed. The great majority of parishes across the north of the county show a steady increase in population through to mid-century, the years between 1831 and 1851 seeing them at their most populous. But thereafter the story is one of decline, a decline which in some parishes accelerates dramatically in the last decades of the century, so that Leckhampstead for example lost almost a quarter of its inhabitants between 1871 and 1881, and a third of the remainder between 1881 and 1901. The result was that many rural parishes in the north of the county had fewer inhabitants in 1901 than they did in 1801. Shrunken villages are by no means exclusively a medieval phenomenon.

The causes for this rural depopulation in the north of the county are not hard to find. Even during the golden years of agricultural prosperity in the mid-nineteenth century there simply was not sufficient work for all of these extra villagers and it is clear that by 1841 many were already beginning to leave their homes in search of work elsewhere. The misfortunes of the villagers of north Buckinghamshire were exacerbated by the Great Depression in agriculture of the last quarter of the nineteenth century. At the same time the mechanisation of those rural handicrafts, such as lace-making and straw-plaiting, which were the support of so many under-employed labouring families, gave them no alternative between starving in their homes or migrating to find alternative employment. Fortunately, however, for the first time in history, alternative means of support were available, as the histories of Wolverton and Bletchley show.

These factors were reflected in the growth of towns in the north of the county. The population of Aylesbury almost trebled, from 3,186 in 1801 to 9,099 in 1901, and Newport Pagnell grew steadily throughout the century, from 2,048 in 1801 to 4,028 in 1901. But it is Wolverton and Bletchley which saw the most startling increases, due directly to the coming of the railway. In 1801 Wolverton's population was 238, fewer than that of Woughton-on-the-Green, Castlethorpe or Great Linford. In 1831 it was 417, but by 1841 it was 1,261, almost a three-fold increase in ten years. It almost doubled again by 1861, and again by 1901. At Bletchley however the real increase came in the last thirty years of the century, when the population more than doubled, from 1,619 in 1871 to 4,068 in 1901. The nineteenth century is marked in north Buckinghamshire by a flight from the countryside to the towns, a flight which scarred the landscape deeply.

Rural depopulation south of the Chiltern scarp was much less severe than north of it. Only a handful of parishes, Bradenham, Lee, Chenies, Monks Risborough, had fewer inhabitants in 1901 than in 1801. Agriculture was hit less severely by the Great Depression of the last quarter of the century than it was north of the scarp. The spread westwards across Middlesex of the built-up areas of London pushed market gardening into the fertile soils of the Thames valley. Richard Cox, a retired brewer living at Colnbrook, had perfected the Cox's Orange Pippin apple by 1836, by which time lilies, pinks, roses and watercress were being grown commercially around Slough. The insatiable demands of London meant continued prosperity for farmers who, in parishes like Denham, concentrated on growing oats and hay for the large numbers of horses still kept in London. At the same time the spread of the railway across the southern part of the county speeded communication with the capital, arrested the decline of several towns and villages, and brought the first of the commuters to those places within easy reach of a railway station.

Although rural parishes in the south did not experience the same dramatic decline in numbers that those in the north endured, there was the same growth in the population of towns. Of the older towns it is High Wycombe that shows the most spectacular development, from 4,248 in 1801 to 19,282 in 1901. Amersham, in contrast, after consistent growth from 1801 to 1851, was clearly on the decline thereafter, and the town was only saved from complete stagnation by the coming of the railway in 1892. It was however in the parish of Upton-cum-Chalvey that the most rapid growth of all took place. Here the population doubled between 1801 and 1841, doubled again by 1861 and again by 1901, figures heralding the arrival of Slough.

More people meant more houses, and in due course shops, offices, factories, railway stations and gas works. The impact of these additional people and the changes their presence brought about is compounded by the arrival of one of the most important inventions in human history. For the first time in our account of the making of the Buckinghamshire landscape we must begin a new chapter, not with the rural landscape, but with a technological innovation.

The coming of the railway

The geographical location of Buckinghamshire, lying across the main communication routes between London and Birmingham and the north-west, meant that the railway came early to the county (Fig. 23). By 1825 there were proposals for a line from London to Birmingham, but it was 1830 before a Bill was presented to Parliament. This proposed a route, surveyed by Francis Giles and approved by George Stephenson, which would have run through Uxbridge, the Wendover Gap, Aylesbury and Coventry to Birmingham. However the opposition from landowners, coach and waggon proprietors, the Grand Junction and Oxford Canal Companies and turnpike trustees was so bitter that it was rejected in the House of Lords. A new route was surveyed, and the Act of Parliament authorising its construction was passed in 1833. The new line ran to the east of the one first proposed, using the Tring Gap and, passing between Marsworth and Ivinghoe, it went through Linslade and Bletchley and so on to Birmingham. Work was completed by September of 1838. It involved two major engineering feats in Buckinghamshire. The first was the excavation of the Ivinghoe Cutting (Plate 45), two and a quarter miles long and, for a quarter of a mile, over fifty-seven feet deep. Immediately to the north of the cutting a six mile long thirty feet high embankment was necessary. The second remarkable piece of engineering was the Wolverton embankment, a mile and a half long, and at forty-eight feet, the highest on the entire line.

Fig. 23. Railways in Buckinghamshire by 1914. The dates are of the opening of the lines.

Locomotives were not at first capable of making the full journey from London to Birmingham. They had to be changed about half way. The choice of the directors of the Company for this stopping point fell on Wolverton, then a small village of about 400 inhabitants. The consequences of this choice are studied in more detail later in this chapter. The other parish where population growth was early stimulated by the coming of this railway was Linslade, where an entirely new town grew up rapidly, immediately opposite to Leighton Buzzard, in Bedfordshire, and some distance away from the old village of Linslade, in the north of the parish.

Even while the London to Birmingham railway was being built, two further lines were being planned and constructed in the county.

The Act for the Great Western Railway Company's line from London to Bristol was passed in 1833, in spite of fierce opposition, in Buckinghamshire from the Colnbrook turnpike trustees and from the Provost and Fellows of Eton College, afraid of the deleterious impact upon the morals of their pupils of the building of a railway line. Isambard Kingdom Brunel was the engineer for this line, and he chose to use the broad seven feet gauge. The line, completed through to Bristol in 1841, ran across the southernmost part of the county, and, for the crossing of the Thames just to the south of Taplow, Brunel built a splendid, soaring, arched bridge of brick (Plate 46). The line passed through Slough, but the opposition from the College authorities at Eton prevented the building of a railway station there until 1840, and tickets at first had to be bought at the Crown Inn. The coming of the railway stimulated residential development at Slough, where the Upton Park estate was laid out in 1843 to designs by Joseph Paxton. His plans led to the erection of what were called 'handsome villa residences'. Victoria Terrace, of three- and four-storeyed terrace houses in three blocks, in a mildly 'Jacobethan' style and a medley of purple, yellow and red bricks, was built to form the north side of the park. On the west semi-detached villas were erected (Plate 47), and on the east a large house in its own grounds, the Mere. The park itself was given an ornamental lake. The estate

Plate 44 Church Street, Aylesbury. These façades, ranging in date from the sixteenth to the twentieth centuries, all mask medieval sites and illustrate very clearly the organic nature of the landscape.

Plate 45 The cutting at Ivinghoe, excavated during the building of the London to Birmingham railway in the 1830s.

Plate 46 The brick-built bridge at Taplow, designed by Isambard Kingdom Brunel to carry the London to Bristol railway, and still in use.

Plate 47 Semi-detached villas at Upton Park, Slough, built in 1843 to designs by
Sir Joseph Paxton.

Plate 48 Oxford Street, Wolverton. One of the more fanciful blocks of terraced
houses built in the 1880s.

Plate 49 The Victorian Tudor hospital at Amersham built in 1838 as a workhouse to designs by Sir George Gilbert Scott, with an intrusive modern addition in the background.

Plate 50 St Peter's Roman Catholic church at Marlow, built of flint in 1845-8 to designs by Pugin.

was bought by Slough Borough Council in 1949. Some demolition took place, principally one of the blocks to Victoria Terrace. The remaining houses were divided up into flats, and the park was renamed Herschel Park, an oasis of quiet just off the busy main road to Windsor and the M4 Motorway.

The second line building before the London to Birmingham line was finished was that from Cheddington, where it joined the main line, to Aylesbury. This was opened in June of 1839, terminating in Aylesbury at a station built in the newly laid out Station Street, to the west of the new gas works. A new station was built in 1889, this time to the east of the gas works and fronting on to the High Street (see Fig. 24). The line was finally closed in 1963. The tracks have been taken up, the station demolished and replaced with a car park and an office block.

The London to Birmingham and London to Bristol lines, when completed, formed the backbone of the railway network in Buckinghamshire (Fig. 23). These first lines were aimed primarily at joining London to major cities and little thought was given to providing intermediate stops or cross-country links. Much of the history of the railway in Buckinghamshire from 1840 until the very last decade of the nineteenth century was concerned with providing just these stops and links. Bletchley was the town to profit most from these developments. It became the junction for a railway line to Bedford in 1846, and for lines to Buckingham and Oxford in the five years following. The growth in its population is really to be dated from the completion of these lines.

The final stage in the growth of the railway network in the county opened in 1892 with the completion of the first part of the Metropolitan and Great Central line from Sheffield to Marylebone, and closed when the last major undertaking, a new line from Paddington through High Wycombe to Birmingham, was completed in 1910.

The coming of the railway to Buckinghamshire accelerated markedly the pace of change and introduced many new and alien elements into the landscape. Welsh slate was being used on Company houses in Wolverton before 1840 was out. The number of coaches through Newport Pagnell dropped from 188 a week to thirty a week between 1838 and 1844. Although coach traffic declined rapidly and irretrievably once a railway had been built, country carriers prospered and multiplied, bringing in goods and passengers to railway stations from surrounding villages, to be replaced in their turn by bus services immediately prior to 1914. One of the first motor bus services in the country began in 1898 to run between Newport Pagnell and Olney.[1]

Once the railway had been built, rapid residential development followed, at Beaconsfield, at Gerrards Cross and the Chalfonts, at Denham and, as we have just seen, at Slough. The railway station at Winslow was built a little to the north of the old town, and its coming promoted the building of several streets of houses to fill the gap. Even in Buckingham, the town least affected by the coming of the railway, there was some development. The Marquis of Chandos laid out Chandos Road in 1861 to lead to the station, and a number of Italianate villas were built. At the same time the wooden railway station was replaced with a brick one.

The building of the railway itself meant cuttings and embankments, stations, approach roads, signal boxes, level-crossings, bridges and tunnels. New hotels, inns and public houses were built. There was a Railway Hotel built in Great Western Street in Aylesbury in 1898, and at Verney Junction a fine red brick inn was built, with extensive stabling at the rear, especially for the accommodation of passengers using the railway to visit the country houses in the neighbourhood, their servants and horses. Stations were built and rebuilt, sometimes several times as at Aylesbury, Buckingham, and Wolverton. That at Slough, rebuilt in 1882, of red brick, has a wide central pavilion and two smaller ones at the ends, crowned with heavy, tile-hung domes and fancy wrought-iron railings. Others always remained small, simple wooden affairs, as at South Aylesbury Halt, not opened until 1933.

The railway was at its peak by 1914. By this date no part of the county was more than five miles from a railway line. Its

[1] A. Everitt, 'Country Carriers in the Nineteenth Century', *Journal of Transport History* New Series 3, (1975–1976), pp. 179–202, esp. p. 182.

influence upon the landscape, and upon the men and women who were making it, was all-pervasive, ineluctable and beyond measurement.

Urban development

We have seen earlier in this chapter that population change in Buckinghamshire in the nineteenth century meant growth in the size of towns and stagnation if not decline in the country-side. The concentration of increasing numbers of people in towns meant the laying out of new streets, the building of new houses, shops, churches and chapels and factories. We can study the effects of this new building on the landscape of towns by looking in some detail at just two examples, a very old town, Aylesbury, and an entirely new one, Wolverton.

Aylesbury (Fig. 24) at the beginning of the nineteenth century was a marketing and commercial centre of just over 3,000 inhabitants, a settlement concentrated on a hilltop site, development into the surrounding lowlands being severely restricted by bad drainage. The ancient Market House and a block of very old shops occupied the centre of the Market Square. The principal cattle market was in Kingsbury, which in wet weather could be knee deep in mud. No less than twenty-eight country carriers, their horses, carts, passengers and goods, left Kingsbury in mid-century on Wednesday and Saturday afternoons for the surrounding villages, eleven of them from the Angel Inn and nine from the Black Swan.[2] Congestion, confusion and noise are no new thing in Kingsbury.

That slow, almost leisurely pace of change which had refaced many of the houses in Church Street and Temple Square with pleasant, brick, Georgian façades (see Plate 44), accelerated only very gradually through much of the nineteenth century. A new Market House was built in about 1806, to be replaced in 1876 by the present Clock Tower. The White Hart Inn was demolished in 1865 to be replaced by the present Corn Exchange. The High Street, at first called New Road, was not

[2] Mussen and Craven, *Commercial Directory of the County of Buckingham* (1853), pp. 23–24.

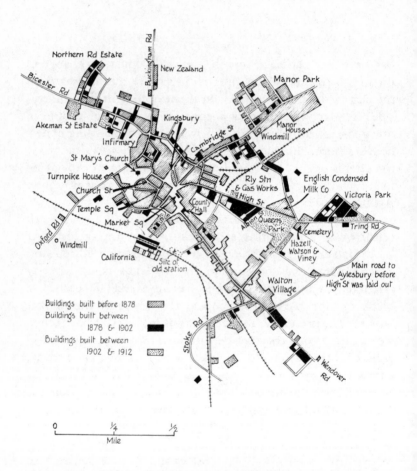

Fig. 24. The growth of Aylesbury

Labels on the map:

Northern Rd Estate
New Zealand
Buckingham Rd
Manor Park
Bicester Rd
Akeman St Estate
Kingsbury
Cambridge St
Manor House
Windmill
Infirmary
St Mary's Church
Turnpike House
Rly Stn & Gas Works
English Condensed Milk Co
Victoria Park
Church St
High St
Temple Sq
County Hall
Oxford Rd
Market Sq
Albion
Queens Park
Cemetery
Tring Rd
Windmill
California
Site of old station
Hazell, Watson & Viney
Main road to Aylesbury before High St was laid out
Walton Village
Stoke Rd
Wendover Rd

Buildings built before 1878
Buildings built between 1878 & 1902
Buildings built between 1902 & 1912

0   ¼   ½
Mile

laid out until 1826, much improving access to the town from the south-east. But it filled up only very slowly, and as late as 1867 there were only seventy-five houses along its entire length. Two completely new kinds of building appeared very early in the town, both in Station Street, immediately to the north of the High Street. The gas works were built in 1834, so that gradually the streets of the town could be properly lit, and the railway station was built in 1839. In the 1840s a number of small houses and cottages were built out along the Buckingham Road, their name, together with that of their public house, New Zealand, pointing nicely to the date of their building. Two small developments of houses took place to the west, along the Bicester Road, at Akeman Street and Northern Road, but again they were built up only very slowly. Drainage was poor, and it was 1890 before Northern Road had a piped water supply.

In 1844 a Union Workhouse was built on Bierton Hill, and a new prison was built close by shortly afterwards. These were the first substantial extensions of the town out on its north-eastern margins. To the east, along Tring Road, a new cemetery was laid out in 1857 on a site nearly a mile from the church and well out in open fields. In 1870 the English Condensed Milk Company and in 1879 the printing firm of Hazell, Watson and Viney built factories, on opposite sides of the road, between the cemetery and the town, but again it was long before building crept out along the Tring Road to link them to the town.

On the southern side of the town Great Western Street was laid out in 1863 to the new railway station just built for the line from Princes Risborough. This new railway line in fact proved a great barrier to the further expansion of the town on this side, and the district known as California was for long linked to the town only by a footbridge.

These were the principal developments in Aylesbury in the first three quarters of the nineteenth century, and by 1871 the population of the town had little more than doubled since 1801, not a spectacular rate of growth at all. It is really only in the last quarter of the nineteenth century that the pace of change begins to accelerate to any marked extent, when three new residential areas were laid out and largely built up before 1914. In 1882 a single field in Manor Park was bought for building and this was taken up only very slowly for a small number of larger houses set in fairly extensive gardens. Queen's Park, however, a development of houses of the middling sort, grew very rapidly between 1902 and 1907. Victoria Park, along the Tring Road, was laid out in the last part of the nineteenth century as an estate of comparatively small houses. Its triangular shape and the pattern of its streets were dictated by the shape of the fields upon which it was built, a common enough phenomenon in Aylesbury and in other towns in the county. The ghost of the old landscape has continued to haunt the new long after it has itself passed away. By 1911 the population of the town was just over 11,000. Some industrial development had taken place, but the old function of the town as a marketing and commercial centre still remained and had only marginally been altered.

Aylesbury is an ancient town. Wolverton is very new (Figs. 25 and 26). But there is a long tradition of new towns in Buckinghamshire, Olney and Winslow, for example, being centres of urban development in the thirteenth century. Nor is it the only modern new town in the county. Linslade also developed remarkably in the nineteenth century as a direct result of the coming of the railway, as did Amersham-on-the-Hill and Beaconsfield later in the nineteenth century, whilst Milton Keynes is but a late twentieth-century continuation of the same theme, albeit on an altogether unprecedented scale.

The London and Birmingham Railway Company acquired eight acres of land at Wolverton in 1837 from the ground landlords, the Radcliffe Trustees, and began to build a railway repair depot, a red brick square building. Early in 1839 the Company started to put up houses for its employees, laying out Bury Street to the west of the repair works, Walker, Cook and Garnett Streets to the north, Gas Street, and a gas works, to the south. A total of eighty-four houses were built by local builders in this first stage, terraced, of red brick with slate roofs. All houses opened straight on to the street, and all had a small garden or yard at the rear. There were no back-to-back houses in Wolverton. A Reading Room was built, and in 1839 a public house, the Radcliffe Arms. This first phase of building at Wolverton is worth more than a passing glance because it has all since disappeared under later extensions to the railway engineering works.

In June 1840 the Railway Company bought a further fourteen acres of land from the Radcliffe Trustees, to the south of the site. By 1847 this had been completely built over. A new railway station, four times as large as the old, was erected at some distance to the south. In 1844 the turnpike trustees re-aligned the road from Stony Stratford to Newport Pagnell so that it passed right through the centre of the new town, bypassing the old village of Wolverton, which now rapidly declined. In due course this new, Stratford Road, emerged as the boundary between the engineering works and the commercial and residential parts of the town. A second public house, the Royal Engineer, was built, and the Radcliffe Trustees gave two acres of land for a church, St George's, finished in 1844. Three new streets, Creed, Ledsam and Young, named after directors of the Company, and Glyn Square, named after the banker and chairman of the Company, were laid out, again in a stiff rectilinear pattern. Glyn Square now contains a single-storey shopping centre, whilst the school on the west side of Creed Street is used as a market.

In 1846 the London and Birmingham Railway Company amalgamated with four other railway companies to form the London and North Western Railway Company. This brought a great increase of work to the railway engineering workshops at Wolverton, and increased pressure on housing. For a number of years the Radcliffe Trustees refused to sell any more land, and so in 1852 the Railway Company bought a fifteen acre field some distance away, at Bradwell, and built there. This new estate, again grimly rectangular in shape, came to be known as New Bradwell.

Eventually, in 1858, the Radcliffe Trustees were persuaded to sell a further twenty acres of land to the west of the town. They sold another fourteen acres in 1866, and 15 more in 1892, until eventually they decided in 1904 to sell building plots on lease direct to the public, and a further forty acres were set aside

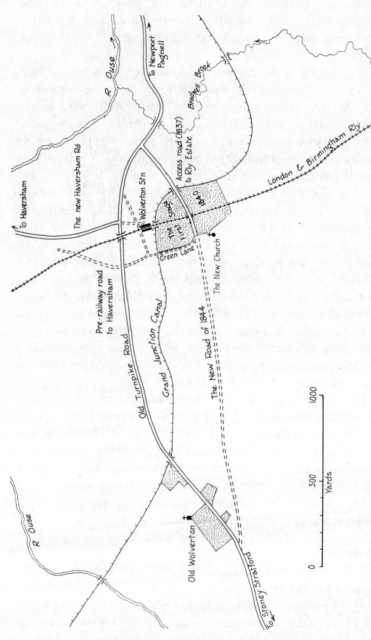

Fig. 25. The site of Wolverton

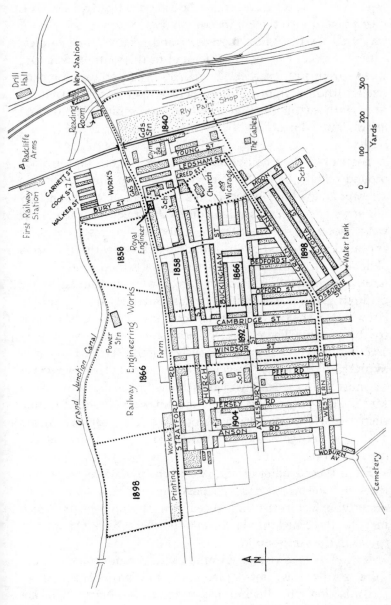

Fig. 26. Wolverton by 1914

for this purpose, quickly being laid out as Peel, Jersey and Anson Roads. All these successive purchases of land were on the west side of the town. North of the Stratford Road the land was incorporated into the engineering works. South of this road it was used for residential purposes, and a second main street, Church Street, running parallel and to the south of Stratford Road, gradually emerged. From 1860 the Railway Company itself withdrew from building houses, and instead contented itself with laying out the plots, and then selling the building leases, but controlling the type and standard of the houses built.

Some of the first houses built in Church Street, on the block of land bought in 1858, were very plain and simple, with no attempt at any kind of decoration. They had slate roofs, no bay windows and opened straight on to the street. Further to the west along this street more elaborate houses eventually appeared, one, dated 1897, is double fronted, with a profusion of decoration applied in rows of red tiles. On the second block of land, bought in 1866, four new streets were laid out, again in a gridiron pattern. These filled up comparatively slowly, and, as elsewhere in the town, this is reflected in the variegated designs to the houses. There was no large-scale speculative builder erecting long rows of monotonously uniform terraced houses in Wolverton (Plate 48). Between 1890 and 1914 the town was at its most prosperous. Two new schools, a cinema, a Working Men's Club and a new sewage system were all added during these years. The population in 1901 was 5,323. By 1911 it was 7,384, with over 2,400 men employed directly in the railway carriage works.

From these studies of just two towns in nineteenth-century Buckinghamshire it may be possible to isolate some of the underlying factors that influenced their development and which may be discerned in the history of other Buckinghamshire towns in the same period.

It is clear that change in nineteenth-century Buckinghamshire towns was slow, piecemeal and on a small scale. Urbanisation, in Buckinghamshire at any rate, was not accompanied by the mass development of rows of terraced houses and cottages of a deadening uniformity. If any Buckinghamshire town must be sought as the quintessence of nineteenth-century urban development then it must be Wolverton, the child of its age if ever there was one. The layout of its streets may at first glance appear to be monotonously regular, but in fact this pattern reflects closely the history of the gradual acquisition of building land, a theme underlying the morphology of all Buckinghamshire towns, from Newport Pagnell and Bletchley to Slough and High Wycombe. At the same time the buildings erected in those streets, houses and cottages, churches, schools, clubs and public houses, through subtle differences in the shapes of windows and doors, in the changes in the decoration over porches or under eaves, or the lack of it, in the increasing variety in the designs of house fronts, bay windows, front gardens, gable ends and barge boards, in the colour of bricks, tiles and slates, and the height and shape of chimney pots, together with the happy Victorian habit of putting dates on everything, reflect the gradual unfolding over time and space of a complex urban landscape in which is embedded the record of its own development. To walk from east to west through Wolverton is to make a serendipitous journey through time. The longer history of the other towns in Buckinghamshire such as Aylesbury, Buckingham and Marlow, means an even richer texture, but the differences are of detail and experience, not of substance.

Victorian building in town and country

Building in the landscape before the closing decades of the eighteenth century conformed fundamentally to two or three basic forms. The pace of change was slow. New designs and patterns came in very gradually so that buildings in traditional designs continued to be put up along side innovatory ones. The range of materials used in construction was strictly limited, and almost always produced locally. In the decades about the turn of the century all of this changed with startling and dramatic suddenness. The range of styles available to builders and architects expanded enormously, so that elements and patterns from Byzantium, from fifteenth-century Italy and sixteenth-century France, from ancient Greece and Rome, even from Egypt and China, jostled those from medieval England as well as from what has been called 'Jacobethan' England. Much nineteenth-century building is grossly overcrowded with machine-cut decoration drawn from several, sometimes all, of these sources and applied sometimes with a naive exuberance that disarms criticism and sometimes with a lack of balance or discrimination which is almost pathological. Improvements in technology and in communications put a greatly enlarged range of building materials at the disposal of builders, architects and engineers, particularly cast iron, sheet glass and Welsh slate, and provided the means of imitating almost everything in something else. New styles, new materials and new kinds of buildings meant a complete breakdown in previously accepted standards of taste, form and balance so that much Victorian building is entirely indefensible upon purely aesthetic grounds, its only merit being a certain impudent ugliness. On the other hand much Victorian building impresses because of the scale, the self-confidence and the zest with which it was carried out.

At the same time there was by the end of the eighteenth century a reaction against the landscape gardening of Lancelot Brown. He had abandoned almost entirely the use of statuary, of garden buildings and of flowers, concentrating instead upon grass, water and a handful of species of forest trees arranged in simple, harmonious, almost sensual patterns in which line was all important. By the end of the eighteenth century flowers were being readmitted to the garden, not only traditional English ones, but also an increasingly wide range of exotics, from North America, from China and from South Africa. Such flowers and trees had to be protected, from cattle and from the weather. Garden walls, fences and garden greenhouses became a necessity. Special gardens, set aside for the cultivation of a set group of plants, alpines, heaths or water plants, begin to appear, together with different styles of gardens, French, Dutch, Italian, Chinese, formal and informal, and all too often all together in the same garden. Victorian gardens became overcrowded with terraces and statues, balustrades and urns, fountains, clipped trees and a profusion of half-hardy flowers in violent colours planted out from massive greenhouses into beds of elaborately convoluted shape rivalling any Elizabethan knot garden. The gardens at Waddesdon, Ascott, Cliveden and Hughenden illustrate some or all of these trends in Victorian gardening.

From the last part of the eighteenth century an increasingly wide range of different kinds of buildings was being called for, prompted by technological, commercial and social change and specialisation. A gas works was built in Aylesbury in 1834, in Stony Stratford and Newport Pagnell in 1837 and in Chesham in 1847. Railway stations were built and rebuilt. The police station at Stony Stratford, of a particularly startling red brick and with a crude rose window, illustrating that confusion of form and function which marks so much Victorian building, was erected in 1865. A County Lunatic Asylum was built in Stone between 1850 and 1853. The reorganisation of the poor law following the Act of Parliament of 1834 prompted the building of Union Workhouses, a field of enterprise in which the young George Gilbert Scott first found employment. Those at Winslow and Buckingham, both of 1835, were designed by him in a plain, classical Georgian style, free from decoration. That at Amersham, however, which he designed three years later, is in imitation Tudor, of brick and flint, with pinnacles, pointed arches and diaper brick-work. It is now a hospital, dominated by the massive concrete block of the nurses' hostel (Plate 49).

Railway stations and gasworks are entirely new kinds of buildings, making their first appearance in the landscape. The nineteenth century was also the great age for the building of new churches and for the restoration of old ones, a building form which had long been present in the landscape. Population growth and movement placed an increasing strain upon the ancient parish as an organisation, and that growth and decline of settlement which led to parochial reorganisation in the later middle ages was repeated, but on a much larger scale, in the nineteenth century. The census of 1891 lists twenty parishes as having been created in the previous fifty years, all save three, Walton near Aylesbury, Wolverton St George and Wolverton St Mary, being in the south of the county, adding point to that suggestion made earlier in this chapter that the nineteenth century sees an accelerating shift in the balance of population as between the north and the south of the county. Thus Hazlemere and Seer Green became separate parishes in 1847, Prestwood in 1849, Penn Street in 1850, Lacey Green in 1851, Cadmore End in 1853, Chesham Christchurch in 1867 and Ashley Green in 1875.

New parishes meant new churches and new parsonages. At Prestwood E. B. Lamb designed the new church and the new vicarage, built shortly after the new parish was created. At Gerrards Cross Sir William Tite designed the really quite extraordinary church, using yellow, red and white bricks, in an overpowering medley of Byzantine, Italian and Early English motifs, although it was built two years before the separate parish was created, in 1861. The church for the new parish of Ashley Green was built by G. E. Street. His finest church in the county, however, is that at Westcott, a chapel of ease to Waddesdon.

The growth of nonconformity in the latter part of the eighteenth century, led to the building of a large number of chapels of every denomination, the exuberant ugliness of some of which must surely be the justification of Matthew Arnold's criticism of those who commissioned them. The Methodist church in Buckingham Street in Aylesbury, built in 1893, is in that debased Italianate style which is almost the hall-mark of late nineteenth-century nonconformity. It is found in the Baptist chapel at Fenny Stratford, built in 1892, the Primitive Methodist chapel at Stokenchurch of the following year, whilst the Congregational chapel of 1879 at Olney defies description.

The passage of the Catholic Emancipation Act in 1829 meant that Roman Catholic churches began slowly to make their appearance in the landscape. At Marlow the church of St Peter was built between 1845 and 1848 to designs by Pugin, who was responsible not only for the building itself, not very distinguished architecturally, but also for the interior metal work, the stained glass, the churchyard gates and the school and school-master's house adjoining (Plate 50).

The spread of entirely new churches, whether Anglican, nonconformist or Roman Catholic, was matched by an equally enthusiastic restoration of existing ones. Indeed only a minority of the county's medieval churches, including, fortunately, Stewkley and Maids Moreton, escaped the attentions of the restorers. Some of the most distinguished names in Victorian architecture restored at least one church in the county. Sir Arthur Blomfield rebuilt Hughenden and William Butterfield restored Wavendon, where he probably also built the parsonage, while the most notorious of all the restorers was in fact born in the county. George Gilbert Scott was born in 1811 at Gawcott, near Buckingham. His father was the incumbent and also responsible for the designing of the very attractive classical Georgian church, built there in 1827. The churches which Scott restored, sometimes so extensively that his work amounted to an almost complete rebuilding, include those at Aylesbury, Buckingham, Chesham, Shalstone and Steeple Claydon. He has been much criticised for his apparently ruthless and heavy-handed approach, but it should not be overlooked that in fact a number of the churches he restored had been so neglected that they were a danger to their congregations.

By the middle years of the nineteenth century the country house was at its apogee as a centre of cultural, political, social and economic power, which is why the great sale at Stowe in 1848 seemed so scandalous to so many contemporaries.

Of the two threads noted in the last chapter as running through eighteenth-century building of country houses, namely additions and alterations to old ones, and the building of new, it is the latter which receives more attention in the nineteenth century. Perhaps the most spectacular alteration of this period was the aggressive, almost painful reshaping by E. B. Lamb of the plain eighteenth-century manor house at Hughenden in 1862 for Disraeli. However a number of splendidly over-ripe new country mansions were built in the nineteenth century, some on a scale the equal of Stowe, and with an extravagance of expenditure far beyond anything the Temples could do.

By far the most magnificent of Buckinghamshire's nineteenth-century mansions are the Rothschild group, at
Waddesdon, Halton, Ascott and Mentmore. With these should
be associated that at Tring, in Hertfordshire.

The Rothschilds burst in upon central Buckinghamshire in
the 1830s, when Baron Meyer began to buy land on a lavish
scale at Mentmore, buying the manor itself in 1850. In the
following year his brother Lionel bought Halton, and his other
brother Anthony bought Aston Clinton. Anthony's son Nathan
bought Ascott in 1874 and made it over to his brother Leopold
in the following year, whilst a cousin, Ferdinand, bought
Waddesdon in the same year. These five properties rapidly
became the centres for extensive landed estates, whilst the
principal house on each was rebuilt on a prodigious scale and
stuffed with pictures, furniture, books and works of art of a
quality in keeping with the setting.

The first was built at Mentmore, where Baron Meyer de
Rothschild called in Sir Joseph Paxton and his son-in-law
G. H. Stokes to design a house that was based upon Wollaton
Hall, near Nottingham, an Elizabethan prodigy house which
Mentmore consciously outdid. It has Wollaton's square angle
towers and the same elaborate Jacobean decoration, only very
much more profusely applied. A 700 acre park was laid out, the
parish church was over-restored and many houses and cottages
in the village of Mentmore were built or rebuilt. As far as
possible an entire landscape was redrawn to a Victorian ideal. To
compare it with Stowe is to discover just how much, and how
little, the ideal landscape has changed in the intervening years.

Then there is a pause for over twenty years, until the 1870s
and 1880s, when Ascott, Waddesdon and Halton were built.

At Ascott Leopold de Rothschild bought a timber-framed
house with the date 1606 over the front door. He employed George
Devey to enlarge and extend this quite modest early seventeenth-
century house in the same style, and the result is an immensely
overgrown mock Tudor cottage, set in forty-five acres of gardens
which illustrate Victorian gardening at its best and its worst.
The house was used for many years as a hunting lodge, and so
was occupied mainly in the winter months. This led Sir Harry

Plate 51 The main entrance to Waddesdon Manor, built in the French
Renaissance château style for Baron Ferdinand de Rothschild and finished in 1880.

Plate 52   Factories along the Bath Road, Slough.

Plate 53   The new city at Milton Keynes under construction, a view looking north over Fishermead.

Plate 54 Part of the Aylesbury to Buckingham railway line near Twyford, now completely dismantled.

Plate 55 The M40 motorway south of High Wycombe.

Plate 56   This photograph, taken in the late summer of 1978 near Waddesdon, shows the disastrous impact of Dutch elm disease upon the fabric of the rural landscape.

Plate 57   The County Buildings at Aylesbury, an epitome of the twentieth-century contribution to the making of the Buckinghamshire landscape.

Veitch, who planted the gardens, to make extensive use of evergreen trees and shrubs. He reversed the usual pattern in Victorian garden design in that he placed the more casual elements nearer to the house and the more formal further away. There is a long, rather narrow, Dutch garden, marked off by high banks of shrubs, with a Victorian grotto at one end as the focal point. There is also a circular garden surrounded with yew hedges and containing a magnificent fountain of Venus in a shell-chariot drawn by horses.[3] Such profusion of disparate elements means that the gardens at Ascott lack that overall unity of spirit which is so marked a feature of the gardens at Stowe, nearly ten times the size.

At Waddesdon Baron Ferdinand de Rothschild employed Hippolyte Destailleur, who had already built the Vienna town house for another member of the Rothschild family, to design a quite astonishing house in the style of a French château (Plate 51). Much is deliberately imitated from Chambord and Blois, but there is much else beside and, as with so much Victorian architecture, the decoration is at times very over-crowded, but Destailleur handled his material with real skill and the house has a remarkable overall unity transcending its various parts. The main walls of the corner towers are quite simple and free of decoration, their plain, gently curving Bath stone serving only to emphasise the exuberant turrets, friezes, pinnacles and immensely tall chimneys at rooftop level. The house itself is not over-large. Its interior is not a rabbit warren of cold, stone corridors, but is remarkably compact and convenient in its layout. Most of the ground floor rooms are lined with eighteenth-century French wooden panelling, salvaged as the Baron Haussman drove his boulevards through Second Empire Paris, and it was eighteenth-century France which contributed most to the furnishing of the house. To have lived in it could only have been unalloyed delight. By an odd coincidence Thomas Gainsborough's painting 'The Pink Boy' is here at Waddesdon, and his 'Blue Boy' is at the Huntington Library in California.

[3] A. G. L. Hellyer, 'A Garden of Strong Contrasts: Ascott, Wing, Bucks.', *Country Life* 159, (1976), pp. 662–664.

The gardens were laid out by another Frenchman, Lainé. The bare hilltop site with which he and Destailleur began had to be levelled, walks and driveways had to be carved out, and fully-grown trees planted. The design of the gardens bears a remarkable resemblance to that at Cliveden, another splendid Victorian mansion. Both houses are approached by long curving drives through belts of mature trees. Both drives then come to a halt at elaborate fountains, and then both turn sharp left into a breath-taking vista of the house, set on a slight eminence at the end of a long, broad, gravelled avenue. Only on the South Terrace at Waddesdon are there any formal flower gardens, and these are, for Victorian standards, very restrained. Instead Lainé made great use of groups of trees and broad curving sweeps of grass, all carefully designed to give views out over the surrounding countryside, with the Chiltern hills on the southern horizon. Two things distinguish his use of grass and trees from that of an eighteenth-century landscape gardener. First of all he has introduced, and very skilfully, into the immediate vicinity of the house, more than a dozen pieces of seventeenth- and eighteenth-century French and Italian statuary. Secondly he has used a far wider range of species of trees than any eighteenth-century gardener would have planted, including Indian Cedar, Sequoia, Spanish Fir, Tulip Tree, Macedonian Pine and Ginkgo. In contrast to Stowe, there is only one garden building, an aviary, designed by Destailleur, and unlike Ascott there is only one specialised garden and that is for daffodils.

Baron Ferdinand died in 1898, barely ten years after his house and its grounds had been finished. The property then passed to his sister, and after her death in 1922 to her great-nephew, James de Rothschild. At his death in 1957 it went to the National Trust.

The last Rothschild mansion to be built was that at Halton, erected between 1882 and 1888 for Alfred, an eccentric bachelor who loved to drive about the estate in a carriage drawn by two zebras and to conduct his own orchestra in the sumptuous Winter Garden. As at Waddesdon Manor, Halton House is based, although more freely, on French château style. The interior decoration was particularly splendid, a white and gold Central Hall going through two storeys with an enormous chandelier suspended from the centre roof. During the 1914–18 war the Halton estate became a great military camp, as many as 20,000 troops being there under training at any one time. After Alfred's death in 1918 the estate was taken over permanently by the Royal Air Force. In the years between 1914 and 1939 it became the central establishment for the training of all R.A.F. apprentices in the mechanical trades as well as housing the R.A.F. Institute of Pathology and Tropical Medicine. This has meant that much of the estate has become built over with military installations, although the House itself still stands, being used as the Officers' Mess. The Winter Garden was demolished in 1935 to make way for a more suitable building. Halton has now lost all trace of that aura of sunset splendour that still surrounds two of these Rothschild mansions, Ascott and Waddesdon. Sir Anthony de Rothschild's mansion at Aston Clinton has been demolished. The saddest is Mentmore Towers. Its contents were sold in 1977, and the fate of the house itself is uncertain.

In complete contrast to the magnificence of the Rothschilds, agricultural labourers were often housed in particularly bad conditions. Cottages at Waddesdon were described in 1842 as being built of mud with earthen floors and thatched roofs.[4] Lack of any kind of drainage meant that fevers of every kind were endemic in the village. A little later in the century, in 1867,[5] cottages at Shabbington were said to be extremely bad, mud built, often with only two rooms, and no drainage. At Stewkley the cottages were said to be totally inadequate. The straw plait trade had brought nearly nine hundred people into the parish this century. This had caused considerable overcrowding and much sub-division of tenements. One old malting house had been divided up into seven cottages, each with only one small bedroom, and an open drain ran close to the doors. On the other hand, by the 1860s some landlords had done much to rebuild

[4] *Local Reports on the Sanitary Conditions of the Labouring Population of England*. No. 6. On the Sanitary Conditions of the counties of Berks, Bucks and Oxford. (1842). p. 89.
[5] *First Report From the Commissioners on the Employment of Children, Young Persons and Women in Agriculture*. Parliamentary Papers (1867–68) XVII, p. 479.

and improve housing in the villages on their estates. What a good landlord could do in a village can be clearly seen at Waddesdon, where Baron de Rothschild, who bought the estate in 1874, rebuilt almost the entire village. Rows of cottages, more substantial semi-detached and detached houses all bear the family crest, five arrows, as does the fine Five Arrows Hotel, built in 1887. Historians may regret the disappearance of so many sixteenth- and seventeenth-century cottages which rebuilding of this kind entailed, but they do not have to endure the privations which living in such cottages until quite recently could mean.

The nineteenth century was an age of great contrasts, between the luxurious elegance of Waddesdon Manor and the squalor and stench endured by those who were rearing ducklings on the mud floor of a hovel less than a mile away. It was also an age which saw great changes in the Buckinghamshire landscape. Old towns grew considerably and new ones were established. Railways brought disruption and dislocation to ancient landscapes and to traditional ways of life. The completion of the enclosure movement brought finally to an end the last vestiges of medieval Buckinghamshire. Even churches, much more solid reminders of the medieval past than common fields, were restored, often over-restored, and new ones built in quite alien designs and materials.

The nineteenth century also saw the first changes to the boundaries of the county since it was established in the tenth century. In 1844 Buckinghamshire gained Lillingstone Lovell, Boycott and Coleshill, and lost Caversfield to Oxfordshire and those minute enclaves of Drayton Beauchamp to Hertfordshire. Further changes took place at the end of the century. Hudnall went to Hertfordshire in 1885. The part of Ibstone in Oxfordshire was joined to Buckinghamshire in 1895, the year in which Nettleden went to Hertfordshire.

These changes must not however be exaggerated. Towns were still very small at the end of the nineteenth century, when there were still less than 20,000 people in the largest in the county, High Wycombe. Both windmills and watermills were common sights, motor cars still very rare ones. Many parts of the county were still profoundly rural and for them the real watershed between medieval and modern falls in the August of 1914 rather than at any earlier point in time.

SELECT BIBLIOGRAPHY

Chadwick, G. F., *The Works of Sir Joseph Paxton* (1961).

Cheshire, C. T., The Growth of Aylesbury and the Development of its Urban Morphology, 1878–1957. Unpublished M.A. thesis, University of Birmingham, 1958.

Cockman, F. G., 'The Railway Era in Buckinghamshire', *Records of Buckinghamshire* XIX Part 2, (1972), pp. 156–168.

Coppock, J. T., 'The Changing Arable in the Chilterns', *Geography* 42, (1957) pp. 217–229.

Coppock, J. T., The Agricultural Geography of the Chilterns, 1870–1951. Unpublished Ph.D. thesis, University of London, 1960.

Coppock, J. T., 'Agricultural Changes in the Chilterns, 1875–1900', *Agricultural History Review* 9, (1961), pp. 1–16.

Courtman, M., Wolverton: A Study in Urban Geography. Unpublished M.Phil. thesis, University of London, 1968.

Davies, R. and Grant, M.D., *Forgotten Railways: Chilterns and Cotswolds* (1975).

Fraser, M., *The History of Slough* (1973).

Gibbs, R., *A History of Aylesbury* (1885).

Girouard, M., *The Victorian Country House* (1971).

Hitchcock, H-R., *Early Victorian Architecture in Britain* 2 vols. (1954).

Saville, J., *Rural Depopulation in England and Wales, 1851–1951* (1957).

9. The twentieth century

Population growth and change. The rural landscape. The decline of the country house. New towns — Slough — Milton Keynes. The passing of the railways. Motorways and airfields. Conservation. Boundary changes and the end of the old Buckinghamshire

THE BUCKINGHAMSHIRE LANDSCAPE has been more profoundly and more radically altered in the twentieth century than at any period since the last ice sheets disappeared from Britain over ten thousand years ago. The changes have sprung from two closely related factors: vastly increased numbers of people coupled with their quite terrifying technological power over the environment. Bronze Age roundbarrows can be bulldozed flat in a matter of minutes. A sixteenth-century cottage can be demolished in an afternoon. The ubiquitous motor car demands ever larger car parks and petrol stations, ever straighter and wider roads and bridges. The rich palimpsest which is the landscape has never been in such grave danger of total destruction as in the last part of the twentieth century. At the same time awareness of the value of what might be lost has never been greater nor more widespread. We must now look in a little more detail at some of these changes, and at some of the steps being taken to preserve what is left.

Population growth and change

At the 1921 Census the population of the administrative county of Buckinghamshire was 236,171, an increase of 7.6 per cent since 1911. However, the geographical distribution of this increase was very uneven. The demographic, social and economic trends already apparent before 1914 were becoming increasingly more marked and the drift to the south was accelerating. The development of electricity and oil as sources of power meant that industry was no longer tied to the coalfields.

Improvements in transport, and in particular the development of the motor car, gave increased mobility to more and more people. These changes taking place at a national level are reflected in the variations in population change in Buckinghamshire. In the south of the county the pull of London, an extensive house-building development backed by a sustained advertising campaign mounted by the Metropolitan Railway, and the industrial development of Slough, had dramatic and far-reaching effects. In Beaconsfield, one of the towns most affected by these changes, the population rose by forty-five per cent between 1911 and 1921. In Chalfont St Peter it rose forty-nine per cent, in Gerrards Cross it rose thirty-seven per cent. In the north of the county however rural depopulation continued. The Rural Districts of Buckingham, Long Crendon, Newport Pagnell, Wing and Winslow all showed a decline of as much as ten per cent. Even Wolverton, the success story of the nineteenth century and still entirely bound up with railway engineering, could show an increase of no more than 1.7 per cent.

The 1931 Census showed these trends continuing. The total population of the county increased by fifteen per cent in ten years, the largest increase for Buckinghamshire since the census first began in 1801, and to be set again an average increase for England and Wales of only 5.5 per cent. The pattern of rapid growth in the south of the county and of decline in the north was if anything still more clearly apparent. The outbreak of war in 1939 meant that no census could be held in 1941. By the time of the next one, in 1951, the effects of mobilisation, evacuation and the direction of labour had all but disappeared, and a large part of the shift back to a peace-time pattern appears to have been achieved.[1] The population of the county had reached 386,291, an increase since 1931 of forty-two per cent, a greater percentage for any county in England and Wales except Hertfordshire and West Sussex. It is estimated that three quarters of this increase was due to movement into the county, and only a quarter to the natural increase of births over deaths.

[1] *Census 1951. England and Wales, County Report. Buckinghamshire.* (1954), p. xiii.

But yet again the county average smooths out wide regional differences. It is the south of the county where the increases are the most marked. In Slough the population almost doubled. In Beaconsfield it rose by almost two-thirds. In Eton Rural District it went up by half. These people had to find somewhere to live and somewhere to work. The number of dwellings in the county rose fifty-five per cent between 1931 and 1951, the great majority being added before 1939. The greatest numbers were built in those areas most closely affected by the industrialisation of Slough and the inexorable growth of London. In Slough itself the numbers of houses increased by 126 per cent. In Beaconsfield they increased by three-quarters, in Eton Rural District and in Amersham Rural District by two-thirds.

In 1961 the population reached 488,233, an increase of twenty-six per cent in ten years, three-quarters again being due to inward movement. The population of Slough reached 80,000, and that of Chalfont St Peter increased by a half. The population of Amersham Rural District increased by a third and that of Wycombe Rural District by almost as much. In the north, however, growth was minimal. The Rural Districts of Newport Pagnell, Wing and Winslow all showed a slight increase, but the population of Buckingham Rural District fell by nearly a thousand.

A digression into the demographic history of the twentieth century should need no justification in a landscape history. The fifty years between 1921 and 1971 saw the population of Buckinghamshire increase from 236,171 to 587,559, an increase of 148 per cent. The impact of a population explosion of this magnitude has left no part of the landscape untouched. The houses, roads, factories, schools and airfields generated by this explosion have meant an enormously increased demand for bricks, gravel, electricity and water. Together they have erupted violently into traditional rural landscapes. Increasing and more widespread affluence has brought growing interest in and need for leisure pursuits, whether hiking, walking, sailing, bird-watching or landscape archaeology, often helping to destroy the very things they have sought to preserve. These changes and developments have had consequences which all too often have been disastrous, and occasionally catastrophic, both in town and in country.

The rural landscape

Change in the rural landscape during the twentieth century has been increasingly brought about by economic forces working upon an international scale. The long-term decline in arable farming, already clearly apparent in the last quarter of the nineteenth century, has continued, although it was halted temporarily in the periods 1914–18 and 1939–45 by wartime measures taken to increase home food production and save shipping space. By the early 1920s the fall in cereal prices was again noticeable. The extent of arable began to fall and continued to do so until 1939. On the outbreak of war in 1939 there was a much more rapid return to arable than took place during 1914–18, and the area under the plough reached a peak in 1944. In some parishes in the north it extended over forty per cent of agricultural land.

The removal of wartime pressures after 1945 saw some conversion to grass, but a policy of subsidy and support for home-produced grain has maintained a larger area of arable than has existed since the middle of the nineteenth century. Many areas, particularly in north Buckinghamshire, have been ploughed for the first time since the late fifteenth century. A view in late summer from, for example, the crest of the Great Horwood to Nash road, looking north, shows a much more even balance of golden cornfields and green pastures than could have been observed even fifty years ago. At the same time the contrasts between the Chilterns and the north have become blurred. There is now more pasture and less arable in the Chilterns, more arable and less pasture in the north, whilst sheep have been ousted from their dominant position in the agricultural pattern of the Chilterns by the dairy cow.[2]

The best agricultural land is flat and well-drained. Land of this description is also the best for building purposes. The

[2] J. T. Coppock, 'Crop and Livestock Changes in the Chilterns, 1931–1951', *Transactions of the Institute of British Geographers* 28, (1960), pp. 179–198.

phenomenal growth of the population of the county during the twentieth century has led to considerable losses of agricultural land to housing, factories, airfields, roads and schools. These losses have been particularly serious on the gravel terraces of the Thames valley, south of the Chilterns, where extensive building has turned almost the whole of the area between Colnbrook and Taplow into one vast suburban sprawl. Gravel quarrying has left huge flooded pits around Horton and Wraysbury. Rising agricultural productivity and the replacement of the horse by the tractor have compensated for these losses to a large extent, but there are limits to growth and the reserves of good farmland are not inexhaustible.

Rural depopulation has been going on in Buckinghamshire since the middle of the nineteenth century. In the south however it had already been halted before 1914 as a result of the marked improvement in transport facilities brought about by the spread of the railway network. In the years between the wars the Rural Districts of the south, particularly Amersham and Eton, really lost all pretence of being truly rural. The huge numbers of immigrants into the area had in fact no connection with the land. Instead they were attracted by the prospect of being able to live in very pleasant semi-rural surroundings, which unwittingly they were helping to destroy, and yet they were able to travel easily and quickly to London both for work and for recreation. Thus developed an entirely new society and its attendant landscape. Part-time farming became increasingly popular as politicians, businessmen and those successful in the law or entertainment sought outlets for investment that would combine attractive rural living conditions, easy communication with London and distinct tax advantages. There are now far more horses in the south of the county than in the north, but they are used for riding rather than for ploughing. Many old farm houses have been carefully restored, with lavish use of old timber and hand-made bricks and tiles; the only incongruous features are sophisticated stainless-steel kitchens and elaborate pale-blue swimming pools. The shops of old Amersham and Beaconsfield thrive on antiques, home-made pastries and hand-cut suits rather than on joinery, baking and tailoring. Private car-ownership is widespread, and Gerrards Cross has the highest proportion of two-car households in the country. Only in the western Chilterns, about Turville and Fingest, is the landscape now truly rural.

In the north of the county this kind of development was almost entirely absent until after 1945, and since then it has affected only comparatively small areas. Industrial estates have been developed at Aylesbury and at Bletchley, although this latter has now been merged into the much larger plans for the new city at Milton Keynes. Railways have all but disappeared from north Buckinghamshire and dependence upon the motor car is almost total. Some of the villages near Aylesbury are now beginning to show the effects of the coming of what has been called an adventitious population.[3] There is, for example, at least one antique shop in Whitchurch, where it is also plain that many of the sixteenth-century cottages around the Market Hill are no longer occupied by agricultural labourers or small-scale village craftsmen.

The suburbanisation of much of the countryside has been matched by the collapse of that institution which has ruled it for the past four hundred years, the country house.

The decline of the country house

The country house as a centre of political and social influence reached its zenith in the last quarter of the nineteenth century. By this time too the great gardens and parks laid out by eighteenth-century landscape gardeners had achieved their full maturity. But their downfall was imminent. The great agricultural depression beginning in 1873 undermined their economic basis, and the changes brought about by two world wars have completed the process.

As we have seen in previous chapters, country houses have been demolished before the twentieth century, but it is the extent and the rapidity with which the destruction or de-humanisation of one of the most beautiful and characteristic features of the English rural landscape has taken place since

[3] see J. Saville, *Rural Depopulation in England and Wales 1851–1951* (1957), p. 171.

1918 that gives so much cause for concern. In Buckinghamshire the story begins in that very year.

The death of Baron Alfred de Rothschild in 1918 meant that his great mansion at Halton ceased to be a private home and became instead the centre for an immense Royal Air Force establishment. The remaining contents of Stowe were sold and the buildings became a school in 1923. Great Brickhill Manor was demolished in 1935. Shortly before the outbreak of war in 1939 Bletchley Park was acquired for the Foreign Office, and here during the war years was housed the Ultra organisation that penetrated the secrets of the German military coding machine called Enigma. Aston Clinton House was demolished in 1958, and this was followed in 1962 by one of the saddest and least defensible acts of destruction, the demolition of Wilton Park.

The story is not entirely one of loss and destruction. The National Trust has come to the rescue of a number of houses in Buckinghamshire, including Cliveden, Hughenden, Princes Risborough Manor, Claydon House and West Wycombe, the latter two continuing to be lived in. The Rothschild family, which burst in upon central Buckinghamshire in the middle years of the nineteenth century, had all but disappeared again a hundred years later. They gave Ascott to the National Trust in 1949, and Waddesdon Manor in 1957, whilst the contents of the last of their great nineteenth-century palaces, Mentmore Towers, were auctioned in 1977.

Whereas a number of country houses have been demolished, for others the shell still remains but they have changed their functions. Thus Huntercombe Manor and Missenden Abbey are now adult residential educational centres. Wexham Springs is the headquarters of the Cement and Concrete Association, Dorton House and Hampden House are now schools, Shardeloes and Gayhurst have been converted into flats, and Chequers is the official country residence of the Prime Minister. Yet others have been partially demolished, sometimes to the ultimate benefit of the surviving portions, as at Hall Barn. Occasionally some of the smaller ones have been restored, usually at private expense. Iver Grove was saved from demolition by a grant from the Land Fund, and then restored by what was then the Ministry of Works. Nevertheless it is unfortunately true to state that conversion to other purposes is not always the answer to all the problems involved in preserving a country house, and grants from the public funds can help only some of them. The future of the country house in the last quarter of the twentieth century looks very insecure indeed, and there is a real danger of a disastrous loss to our national heritage unequalled in scale since the dissolution of the monasteries.

New towns

The population explosion of the twentieth century affected the countryside in that the building to accommodate the increased numbers of people swallowed up wide areas of fields, farmland and woodland. The phenomenon is however essentially an urban one. People moved into towns in search of work and of better social conditions, only to find themselves compelled to live further and further away from the centres of towns. Entirely new towns have sprung up and old ones have been transformed. These trends have been particularly noticeable in Bucking-hamshire.

Slough

In 1911 Slough had a population of nearly 15,000 and it was still essentially a residential and dormitory town, although some industrial development had begun. In June 1918 the Government bought 600 acres of land to the west of the town. Here was established a vast repair depot to service the entire mechanised transport of the British Army in France. In April 1920 the depot was sold to Slough Trading Company Ltd., which in 1926 changed its name to Slough Estates Ltd. The company began almost at once to lease factories to manu-facturers, and from 1927 it began to build them in advance of requirements. The effect on the town and its neighbourhood was immediate and permanent. By 1931 the Urban District had a population over 33,000 and by the mid 1930s there were a hundred firms on the Trading Estate, employing all together over 8,000 people. There was a rapid and almost uncontrolled residential development. Street after street was built of those three-bedroom semi-detached houses, often plastered white and with metal window-frames set in rounded bays running across both houses in a pair, so characteristic of the 1930s. Although a very pleasant Town Hall was completed in 1936 no attempt was made to design an appropriate town centre, and even today there is no real overall unity about Slough.

The 1939–45 war brought a temporary halt to this headlong expansion, but it was resumed by the early 1950s so that by 1971 there were over 87,000 people living in Slough, by which time there were 800 factories on the Trading Estate, making pharmaceuticals, confectionery, television sets and a wide range of machinery and electrical goods. Industrial development was by no means confined to the Estate, as the building of the I.C.I. Paints Division office and factory in the Wexham Road illustrates. Factories in Slough are rarely more than three storeys high. Their entrance forecourts are often planted with trees and flowers. The industrial landscape of Slough is an altogether more humanised one than that to be found over so much of northern and midland England (Plate 52). There was at the same time much rebuilding in the town's High Street, with results that are at times visually disastrous. Several tall, slab-sided office blocks of glass and concrete dominate the skyline, quite out of proportion with the nineteenth-century villas and terraced houses immediately behind them. Residential development had of necessity to keep pace with industrial, but stricter control has meant the infilling of existing estates in addition to the building of new ones such as the London County Council estate at Langley where, unfortunately, too little attention has been paid to visual variety.

The growth of Slough has taken place essentially along the east-west axis of the Bath Road. Expansion to the north has been prevented by the existence of several large parks and commons, and further encroachment into Burnham Beeches, Farnham and Stoke Commons and Black Park would not now be tolerated. Expansion to the south is now effectively barred by the building of the M4 motorway between the town and the Thames. Tuns

Lane, the A355, provides the link between the town and the motorway, and at the same time it bypasses Eton and Windsor by means of a new bridge over the Thames. Another link road now joins this bypass to the old Windsor Road. The view to the north from this road, encompassing factory and office blocks, electricity pylons and power-station cooling towers, with giant jet aircraft sailing overhead every few minutes as they make their approach to Heathrow Airport, is in stark contrast to that to the south, where Eton College chapel and the keep of Windsor Castle rise from a tree-lined horizon.

The almost break-neck pace of residential and industrial development in Slough during the inter-war years was entirely the work of private energies. Only in the years immediately before 1939 did central government and local authorities start to take any interest in the problems and the opportunities presented by such development. Since 1945 the role of public authorities in the growth of towns has become all-important, and this has culminated in the decision to build an entirely new city in north-east Buckinghamshire.

Milton Keynes

In January 1967 21,900 acres in north Buckinghamshire were designated the site for an entirely new city, to be called after one of the villages within its boundaries, Milton Keynes (Fig. 27). It was to be the largest development undertaken within the terms of the New Towns Act, and by the end of the twentieth century 250,000 people were to be housed and employed there, in a partnership of public investment and private enterprise.[4]

The Interim Report of 1969 to the Development Corporation proposed a grid pattern of main roads at kilometre intervals, although these roads were not to be rigid straight lines but would rather follow the contours of the landscape. Every effort would be made to give the areas enclosed within this lattice-work an individuality so that each would become a separate place. Residential, shopping, recreational, industrial and

[4] see 'Planning Study. Milton Keynes: New City for the South-East'. *The Architects' Journal* 149, (1969), pp. 361–376.

To Birmingham & the North
To Newport Pagnell
To Glasgow
To Towcester
GREAT LINFORD
Lake
M1
OLD WOLVERTON
NEW BRADWELL
WOLVERTON
STANTONBURY
BRADVILLE
NEATH HILL
STONY STRATFORD
LINFORD WOOD
DOWNS BARN
Willen Lake
NORTHFIELD
GREENLEYS
STACEY BUSHES
To London
FULLERS SLADE
HODGE LEA
CONNIBURROW
KILN FARM
Bradwell Abbey
SPRINGFIELD
MILTON KEYNES VILLAGE
TWO MILE ASH
R. Ouse
N
LOUGHTON
FISHERMEAD
EAGLESTONE
WOUGHTON ON THE GREEN
A 5
WALTON HALL
WAVENDON
COFFEE HALL
WOUGHTON PARK
NETHERFIELD
TINKERS BRIDGE
WALTON
BLEAK HALL
SHENLEY
BEANHILL ASHLAND SIMPSON
Lake
BLETCHLEY
To Buckingham
To Dunstable
Lakes
To London (Euston)

A 5 relief road under construction = = = = =

0   1000   2000
yards

Fig. 27. The new city of Milton Keynes

commercial centres were to be dispersed physically and ranked into a hierarchy of local and district centres. In this way it was hoped to avoid the necessity for multi-level flyovers and the worst excesses of traffic congestion. The three towns in the area, Stony Stratford, Wolverton and Bletchley, were to form the basis of district shopping centres to serve the rapidly expanding population. There is nevertheless to be an entirely new city centre. Here will be the civic buildings, one of the largest covered shopping areas in Europe, a new railway station, a sports centre, hotels, restaurants, shops, offices, houses and flats, all set in broad streets and tree-lined squares. Construction work began late in 1970. The overall strategy for the development of the new city envisaged building inwards towards the new city centre from the three existing towns, which are situated on the periphery.

If a new city planned on this scale is to achieve economic and social independence quickly then residential development and industrial and commercial expansion have to keep pretty much in step. A wide range of residential development is planned, public and private, to let and for sale. Near the new city centre it is to be distinctly urban in character, set in tree-lined squares. Elsewhere it is to be lower densities per acre, and at some sites, at Great Linford, for example, some attempt is to be made to fit new housing into a traditional village pattern. By 1976 houses were being built at the rate of 2,500 a year. Industry has been attracted by the excellent communication links, by competitive rents for factory and office accommodation and by the comparative spaciousness of the site, giving room for expansion. One of the biggest employers in the new city has proved to be the Open University, established at Walton Hall in 1969.

No attempt has been made to produce a single overall design, and there is no rigid master-plan. Instead the aim has been to provide a framework which might prove flexible enough to accommodate change, and yet firm enough to give unity beneath diversity. At the same time there is to be no wholesale obliteration of the three towns and thirteen villages within the designated area of the new city. Instead real efforts are being made at conservation, whether of isolated buildings or of the whole fabric of a town, as at Stony Stratford. A broad belt, following the line of the Grand Union Canal and the river Ousel, is set aside as a park, with another along the valley of Loughton Brook. Tongwell Lake is set aside for water-skiing, Willen Lake for sailing and fishing, and Walton Lake will eventually be reserved for wild life, with only very limited public access.

The Development Corporation has taken an enlightened attitude towards conservation. Archaeologists were appointed in 1971 to excavate sites as and when they were uncovered by building work, to record what was possible and to preserve what seemed to be the most significant. An ecologist was appointed in 1972 to study the effects on wild life of the building of the new city, and a conservationist was appointed in 1973 to list those buildings within the area of historical and architectural interest, and to renovate and restore where possible. Thus the almshouses at Great Linford have been restored and converted into craft workshops. The site there of the shrunken medieval village is being excavated and some of the house platforms will be permanently preserved. The Bradwell Abbey Field Centre was established in 1973 as the centre for the co-ordination of the work of those, both professional and amateur, concerned with the preservation of the old in the midst of the new.

A project of this kind and magnitude cannot hope to escape criticism. Much of the building that has been completed so far has been stigmatised as barren and lifeless in concept and in execution,[5] and certainly there are at present some very stark and rather forlorn-looking rows of buildings, whilst the Bletchley Sports Centre, with its huge lettering and pyramidal structure, is strongly out of keeping with its surroundings. Nevertheless a landscape takes time to mature, and trees take time to grow, as every eighteenth-century landscape gardener knew. By the end of 1975 over a million trees and shrubs had been planted within the city area, although unfortunately nearly a fifth of them died during the great drought of the

---

[5] see S. Lyall, 'Housing and Landscape at Milton Keynes', *The Architects' Journal* 163, (1976), p. 229.

summer of 1976. Perhaps in time some of the gaunt edges will begin to soften (Plate 53).

The wider impact of a city of this size upon the landscape of north Buckinghamshire as a whole remains to be seen. It is to be hoped that the lessons to be learned from the recklessly uncontrolled inter-war expansion in south Buckinghamshire will not be ignored, and that Milton Keynes will in fact be confined within its boundaries, so that when it has matured and has created its own region its magnetic attraction will not be allowed to transform large tracts of north Buckinghamshire into a featureless twilight zone of suburbia.

The passing of the railways

The railway network in Buckinghamshire reached its greatest extent with the opening in 1910 of the Great Western line from Paddington through High Wycombe to Birmingham. But even before the 1914–18 war the motor car was beginning to make itself felt as a rival. With the return of peacetime conditions in the 1920s the competition from the motor car, whether privately owned or in the form of the bus, became fierce and intense. Passenger services were withdrawn from the line between Aylesbury and Verney Junction in 1933. Two years later the Quainton Road to Brill line and that from Aylesbury to Buckingham, were closed.

After 1945 competition became yet fiercer and the rate of closure accelerated. In 1953 one of the oldest lines anywhere in the country, that between Aylesbury and Cheddington, saw its passenger services withdrawn. Ten years later the station in the High Street in Aylesbury was closed and eventually demolished and the track taken up. Passenger services were discontinued on the Buckingham to Bletchley line in 1964 and on the Bletchley to Banbury line in 1968, whilst the lines to Olney and Newport Pagnell were closed in 1962 and 1964 respectively. Since 1966 Aylesbury has been the northern terminus for trains out of Marylebone, and the remainder of the line north to Sheffield has been closed. The station at Aylesbury now looks rather forlorn, overshadowed by a giant multi-storey car-park. North of

Aylesbury the only railway station still providing a passenger service is that at Bletchley, on the main, now electrified, line out of Euston. The national decline in railway traffic has also affected the engineering workshops at Wolverton. From 1965 these have been confined to repair work and part has been sold off. Elsewhere in the north of the county long stretches of track have been taken up (Plate 54), signalling equipment has been dismantled, level-crossing gates are now permanently open. Disused railway embankments and cuttings have become *ad hoc* nature reserves, and some have been listed as such by the Buckinghamshire County Council under the terms of the Countryside Act of 1968. At least one level-crossing gate-keeper's house has been converted into a very pleasant country cottage. Only between Bletchley and Wolverton does the railway now exercise any significant influence as a means of communication over north Buckinghamshire. The passing of the railway, coupled with the decline since 1945 in rural bus services, has left many towns and villages in this part of the county more isolated than they have been for well over a hundred years.

The development of so màny of the Chiltern towns and villages during the inter-war years was to a large extent based upon the easy and convenient conveyance of commuters by rail into London, and their needs have continued to exert an influence over the pattern of railway services in the south of the county since 1945. The line from London to Amersham was electrified by 1961. The Metropolitan line out of Baker Street now terminates here, with a branch to Chesham. Two services now operate out of Marylebone, one through Amersham and Wendover to terminate at Aylesbury, the other through Beaconsfield, High Wycombe and Princes Risborough to Banbury, with a branch line from Princes Risborough to Aylesbury. The only victims of railway closure in the south of the county have been the line from Princes Risborough to Watlington, that serving the Slough Trading Estate, and that from High Wycombe to Bourne End. The branch line from Marlow to Bourne End continues in use, but trains now go through to Maidenhead, to join the main line from Paddington

Fig. 28. Communications in twentieth-century Buckinghamshire

through Slough to Bristol and the west. Brunel's splendid bridge over the Thames at Taplow (Plate 46) still continues to be used (Fig. 28).

Motorways and airfields

We have looked in previous chapters at some of the ways in which developments in transport and communications have altered the landscape by introducing new elements into it, but each new development in transport seems to be more intrusive into the landscape than the last, to take more and to give less, to leave greater scars and to arouse greater and more passionate opposition. It will be a long time before a disused railway (Plate 54) is as unobtrusive as a disused canal (Plate 37). The demands made by twentieth-century transport on the landscape have increased geometrically rather than arithmetically over those of the nineteenth century. The motor car placed flexible, convenient and, until quite recently, cheap transport at the disposal of very large numbers of people, including, it must be said, landscape archaeologists. After 1945 the motor car became so popular and traffic congestion so bad that eventually an entirely new network of motorways, planned at a national level and designed specifically for motor transport, had to be built (Fig. 28). The first of these, the M1 from London to Leeds, cut through the north-east corner of Buckinghamshire, underlining yet again the consequences of the county's lying across some of the most important communications routes in the country. In Buckinghamshire at any rate the M1 is comparatively unobtrusive. Cuttings are more frequent than embankments, and nowhere are there multi-level approach roads. Its coming has certainly brought some relief to towns along the A5 such as Stony Stratford, once in real danger of being choked by lorries and cars.

In the south of the county the building of the M4 and the M40 (Plate 55) and their link roads has caused much greater disruption to the landscape. The Chiltern terrain, with its steep-sided valleys and hills, has been slashed through with a series of cuttings and embankments that visually are little short of disastrous. The approach road from High Wycombe to the M40 cuts through the hillside like a knife and joins the motorway at an enormous intersection. Near Loudwater the motorway strides across the valley on giant concrete legs. To say that they intrude into the landscape is an understatement of Gargantuan proportions. In the far south of the county the very flat, level nature of the countryside of the Thames valley serves only to accentuate the embankments which carry the M4, particularly the link road to Windsor. What sort of landscape they can be expected to blend into is a matter for only the gloomiest speculation.

The influence of motorways in the last part of the twentieth century has been as pervasive as that of railways in the nineteenth. Just as railway stations drew to themselves dozens of country carriers from surrounding villages so do motorway intersections draw traffic. The quiet country road from Winslow to Stony Stratford has to endure far too many heavy lorries squeezing over the narrow bridge at Great Horwood or trying to negotiate the sharp right-angle bends in Nash without doing too much damage as they make their way to and from the M1 intersection to the north of Stony Stratford. Ominously, some short stretches have already been straightened and widened.

Motorways have dealt the landscape sledgehammer blows from which it is difficult to see how it can recover. Fortunately, however, the impact of the second great transport innovation of the twentieth century, the aeroplane, shows some signs of being blunted, at least as far as Buckinghamshire is concerned. By the end of the 1939–45 war no less than fifteen airfields had been built in Buckinghamshire (Fig. 28). Their construction had to be quick, with no time for the niceties of archaeological rescue excavation. We can only guess at what was lost, although it must be added that without their contribution something very much more valuable might have been lost.

The impact of the construction of an airfield upon the landscape is immense.[6] Field boundaries are erased, earthworks of

[6] R. N. E. Blake, 'The Impact of Airfields on the British Landscape', *Geographical Journal* 135, (1969), pp. 508–528.

every kind are flattened or filled in, long concrete runways are constructed, together with hangars, control towers and a range of support buildings. The perimeter is marked off by a high barbed-wire and chain-link fence. Since 1945 these airfields have been progressively abandoned, becoming over-grown, gaunt and rusty. Occasionally they have been returned, at least partially, to agriculture, as at Great Horwood. Silverstone, partly in Northamptonshire, has become a motor-racing circuit. Those at Haddenham and Denham continue in use as small civil airfields, capable of taking light aircraft, and Booker is used for private weekend flying. The rest remain, particularly sterile contributions of the twentieth century to the making of the Buckinghamshire landscape.

Conservation

It was apparent even before 1914 that unrestricted building could not be allowed to go unchecked. The first steps at town and country planning were tentative and lacked any real power of control. It first began in Buckinghamshire under the Town and Country Planning Act of 1925, supplemented by the Local Government Act of 1929, as a result of which a County Planning Advisory Committee was formed. It published some outline proposals in 1936, emphasising even then that "the actual landscape should be treasured as a highly valuable heritage", although it lacked any real powers to protect this heritage. It was the idealism bred out of the destruction and bloodshed of the second world war that acted as the catalyst in this, as in so many other spheres of social and economic activity. The recommendations of the Scott Report of 1942 on land utilisation in rural areas led eventually to the Town and Country Planning Act of 1947 and the National Parks and Access to the Countryside Act of 1949. The Outline Development Plan for the county prepared under the first of these Acts proposed that development in areas of scenic beauty should be controlled, and it specifically listed the Vale Hills, the Brickhills, Stowe and the Ouse valley as well as the Chilterns and the Thames valley under this head. The National Parks Act also provided for the creation of Areas of Outstanding Natural Beauty in addition to the formal National Parks, and 309 square miles of the Chilterns, in Oxfordshire and Hertfordshire as well as in Buckinghamshire, were designated in this way in 1965 (Fig. 29).

The Chilterns Standing Conference was formed in 1967. Three years later it published a detailed study of the problems and pressures facing the Chilterns.[7] The resident population within the area as a whole it found to be about 80,000, but no less than 8.6 million people lived within twenty-five miles of its boundaries. The demands made on some well-known beauty spots had become intolerable. Some footpaths on Ivinghoe Beacon, for example, had become so worn that they had to be closed, returfed and new ones laid out. Quarrying and mineral extraction were considered not to be serious threats within the Area as a whole, save that the quarrying of chalk at two points along the scarp would need to be carefully controlled. The cement works at Pitstone have a capacity of about a million tons a year, but there are sufficient permitted reserves for about thirty years, and some land has already been restored to agriculture. What these rather arid phrases mean in visual terms can be seen in Plate 15.

By 1974 almost the whole of Buckinghamshire south of the Chiltern scarp was either within the designated Area of Outstanding Natural Beauty or else within the Metropolitan Green Belt, which had been established in 1959. Only the principal urban areas, High Wycombe, Slough, Amersham, Chesham, Beaconsfield, Marlow, the Chalfonts and Gerrards Cross were excluded, and several of these have had at least part designated as conservation areas under the Civic Amenities Act of 1967. Development within the Green Belt itself has been rigorously controlled, and almost the whole of postwar residential building has been confined either to the infilling of existing settlements or else to those towns not actually within the Green Belt. Thus, almost at the eleventh hour, the landscape of south Buckinghamshire is at last protected from destruction. In some places it has been seriously disfigured. The expansion of High Wycombe in the years immediately after 1945 saw both

[7] The Chilterns Standing Conference, *A Plan for the Chilterns* (1970).

housing and industrial estates swarm up the steep hillsides which overlook the valley of the Wye, particularly on the south, to culminate in a Sports Centre, the contribution of which to the landscape so far lies beyond the language of conventional aesthetics. At Amersham the nurses' hostel to the hospital (Plate 49) continues the tradition begun when the gas works was built next to the parish church. On the other hand even the busiest road can suddenly, in a gap through the traffic, give a glimpse along a valley whose curving slopes, whether of grass or in late summer the dusty gold of ripening corn, are everywhere edged with the cool green shade of trees. It is still possible to get well and truly lost in the deep narrow lanes winding through thick hedgerows between Wheelerend and Fingest, and to remain lost because there is no-one else about of whom to ask the way, only

> The grass, the thicket, and the fruit-tree wild;
> White hawthorn, and the pastoral eglantine.

The landscape of the north of the county has not been subjected to the pressures endured by that in the south, and those which it has had to face are of quite recent making. It lies too far north of London to be attractive to the majority of commuters, and it lacks any very large centres of population. It lacks too those areas of really outstanding natural beauty which almost proved to be the ruin of the south. Nineteenth-century industrialisation left it almost untouched, save for the building of the new town at Wolverton and this was on a very small scale. It is only in the years since 1945 that it has come under attack, and this from three directions.

The first was the designation in 1967 of a vast area of north-east Buckinghamshire as the site for an entirely new city, conceived and planned from the first on an altogether larger scale than any previous urban development in the country. Fortunately both consultant planners and Development Corporation have been aware of the environmental threat, and both have refused to attempt to plan for the future without thought for the past. The Development Corporation has appointed archaeologists whose rescue work has already proved so fruitful. Several archaeological sites are to be permanently preserved as focal points within the overall city plan. A valuable photographic survey of buildings in the area which are of historical and architectural interest has been published. A conservation officer was appointed in 1973 and there are now over 400 buildings listed as being worth preserving. Bradwell Mill and its machinery, the Rectory Cottages at Bletchley with their fine hammerbeam roof have both been restored. Almost the whole of Linford Wood is to be preserved. Much of the Ousel valley and the Grand Union Canal are to be incorporated into parks. There is a very good prospect of a restrained and reasonably sensitive development of Milton Keynes. The urge to go for high-rise blocks of flats and skyscraper office blocks has been largely resisted. In a comparatively flat landscape their impact would have been disastrous.

The second, much graver, attack, and one that would have involved almost the whole of the north of the county, has been forestalled – once. It was proposed in 1969 that the third airport for London should be sited in the area from Whitchurch to Soulbury, from Drayton Parslow to Wing. Late in 1970 the Roskill Commission recommended that development should go ahead, although to his credit Sir Colin Buchanan in his note of dissent to the Report of the Commission described the proposal as an environmental disaster. The scheme would have involved the demolition of the village of Stewkley and its splendid Norman church (Plate 16), the bulldozing of a subtlely varied landscape and the uprooting of communities remarkable for the depth and tenacity of their links with their past. Resistance to the proposals came from every quarter and in every form that imagination and ingenuity could devise. Communities long practised in organising church bazaars and fêtes turned in grim earnest to raising money to pay for legal representation and advertising campaigns. National newspapers and periodicals lost no opportunity to report every twist and turn in the campaign and to caricature those involved. When in April 1971 it was announced that the Government had rejected the Commission's recommendations there was a torch-light procession and a service of thanksgiving in the church of

Stewkley.[8] But thanksgiving may prove to have been premature. The Government Study Group's 1979 report recommends Hoggeston (within miles of both Stewkley and Cublington), as well as Yardley Chase on the Buckinghamshire-Northampton border, among a short list of six possible sites for the new airport.

The third attack upon the landscape of north Buckinghamshire began only in the 1970s, has proved much more insidious than the other two, just as destructive, and impossible to stop. Dutch Elm disease has killed thousands of trees all over north Buckinghamshire (Plate 56). Gaunt leafless skeletons stand in rows in every hedgerow, not yet sufficiently dangerous for them to have to be felled, their timber now so cheap that its sale will not repay the cost. Only with their passing does the extent of their contribution to the texture of the north Buckinghamshire landscape become apparent. Trees other than elm have slipped away more quietly, in ones and twos, under the pressures of building and industrial agriculture, but their going is likely to be no less catastrophic. It is estimated[9] that there are growing now less than a tenth of the young trees necessary to ensure that existing mature ones are replaced. Within a generation the landscape could be almost empty of trees. Chiltern woodland is now mature, but the lack of proper felling and restocking, combined with the effects of disease and fungi, means that the beech woods now so characteristic of the hills are failing to regenerate themselves adequately. By the end of the twentieth century they may well have degenerated into scrub. The loss of so many trees is an ecological disaster, and it will take a long-term programme of felling and replanting to put it right. Some few chosen areas in Buckinghamshire where the wild life and vegetation are particularly interesting are now protected and managed as Sites of Special Scientific Interest by the Nature Conservancy, and other nature reserves are in the care of the Berkshire, Buckinghamshire and Oxfordshire Naturalists' Trust (Fig. 29). It is to be hoped that they do not become oases

---

[8] see D. Perman, *Cublington: A Blueprint for Resistance* (1973).

[9] Buckinghamshire County Council, *Buckinghamshire County Structure Plan. Report of Survey. Draft for Consultation* (1976), p. 246.

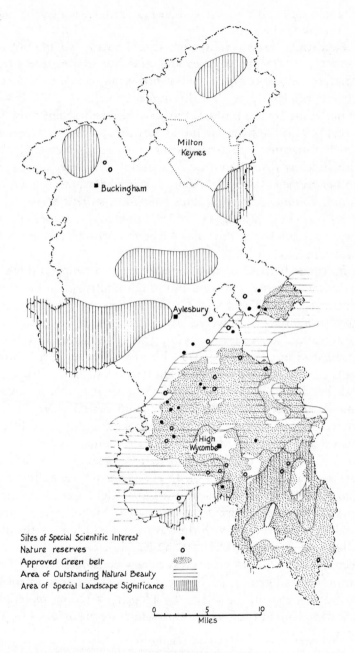

Sites of Special Scientific Interest •
Nature reserves ○
Approved Green belt
Area of Outstanding Natural Beauty
Area of Special Landscape Significance

0   5   10
        Miles

Fig. 29. Conservation in Buckinghamshire

of green quiet in a desert of housing estates, motorways and prairie-like fields.

Landscape, however, is more than scenery. No amount of cosmetic replanting of trees and grass can restore the rich, intricate texture of the human contribution which transforms scenery into landscape. It is this human contribution which was so badly hit by the building boom of the 1960s, not only by actual physical destruction but also by the spiritual destruction which comes from the juxtaposition of glass and concrete blocks into hideous discord with neighbouring Georgian houses or timber-framed cottages. The Buckinghamshire landscape cannot accommodate buildings over three storeys high (Plate 57). Concrete in vast slabs is cold and alien in an environment of warm red bricks, of flint and wichert, of thatch and timber-framing.

Fortunately there are now some signs of a growing awareness of the value of tradition, continuity and stability in the fabric of human society. The Civic Amenities Act of 1967 and later legislation has empowered local authorities to designate conservation areas. By 1975 sixty of these areas had been established in the county. The objectives of conservation were declared to be the prevention of the destruction of the character and the 'wholeness' of an area, either from stagnation and decay due to neglect or indifference, or from despoliation due to redevelopment. At the same time the surroundings, both the inward and the outward views, were to be protected. For some areas it is openly acknowledged that designation as a conservation area has come too late. In Haddenham for example it is recognised that much new residential development is unsatisfactory on both visual and functional grounds, often being totally out of keeping with the streets and buildings of the old village. In Townside, Dollicot and Rudds Lane much harm has been done in order to give access to new housing estates.[10] On the other hand great pains have been taken over the design of at least one school in the village by adopting building materials that complement the wichert walls which are the unique feature

[10] Buckinghamshire County Council, Departments of Architecture and Planning, *Haddenham Village Plan* (1970), pp. 4, 5, 9.

of Haddenham and by keeping almost entirely to one storey so that neighbouring buildings are not overwhelmed.

Of all the generations which have contributed to the making of the Buckinghamshire landscape that of the 1960s was probably the most selfish, the most conceited and the most short-sighted. The signs that exploitation may be giving way to stewardship as the spirit of the age may offer some hope that our grandchildren may yet enjoy something of that richly diverse landscape which we received from our grandparents.

Boundary changes and the end of the old Buckinghamshire

The Buckinghamshire of this book came into existence as a separate legal and political entity early in the tenth century. Its boundaries were an artificial creation reflecting the needs of that time. Its landscape was already ancient, and much of the first two chapters of this book have been concerned with the factors at work in the moulding of this landscape before Buckinghamshire itself emerged. Within the terms of landscape chronology Buckinghamshire is not very old, and its boundaries have themselves changed, slowly at first, in response to at least some of those same factors at work on its landscape. Thus Towersey and Caversfield have been lost to Oxfordshire, Boycott, Lillingstone Lovell and Stokenchurch have been gained from that county. Coleshill has been gained from, Ashridge has been lost to, Hertfordshire. The county boundaries taken for the purpose of this book were those of the 1961 Census. But these in their turn have proved no more stable than any other. Linslade was lost to Bedfordshire in 1965, and from 1 April 1974 Eton and Slough were transferred to Berkshire. At the same time the pattern of urban and rural districts, itself the creation of the last years of the nineteenth century and of changes made in 1934, was swept away. Five new districts were created – Aylesbury Vale, Beaconsfield, Chilterns, Milton Keynes and Wycombe. Of these Milton Keynes was granted the status of a borough. From the same date the Thames Conservancy was dissolved and replaced by a much larger authority with wider powers and greater responsibilities. These changes are sufficiently substantial and far-reaching to form a convenient terminal point for this account of the making of the Buckinghamshire landscape.

SELECT BIBLIOGRAPHY

Best, R. H. and Coppock, J. T., *The Changing Use of Land in Britain* (1962).

Best, R. H. and Rogers, A. W., *The Urban Countryside* (1973).

Buckinghamshire County Council, *Outline Development Plan for Buckinghamshire* (1950).

Coppock, J. T., *The Chilterns* The Geographical Association Landscapes Through Maps No. 4 (1968).

County Planning Advisory Committee of Buckinghamshire County Council, *Town and Country Planning in Buckinghamshire* (1936).

Jones, K. M., A Short History of Slough. Unpublished typescript in the Buckinghamshire Collection, County Library, Aylesbury (1973).

Milton Keynes Development Corporation, *Building Conservation in Milton Keynes: a photographic index* (1971).

Ministry of Housing and Local Government, *The Green Belts* (1962).

Ministry of Housing and Local Government, *The South-East Study 1961–1981* (1964).

Seeley, I. H., *Planned Expansion of Country Towns* (1968).

Index

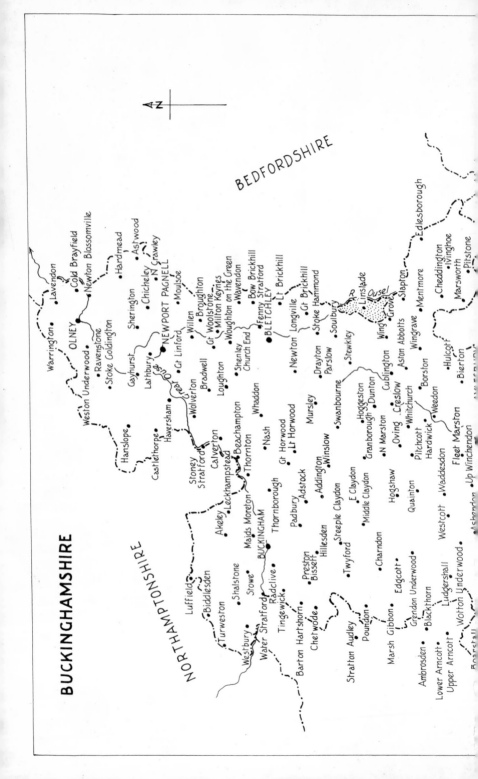

BUCKINGHAMSHIRE